D0629671
MICHAEL McCOY

# REVIVALS
## THEIR LAWS AND LEADERS

by
James Burns

TWO ADDITIONAL CHAPTERS
by
Andrew W. Blackwood, Sr.

BAKER BOOK HOUSE
Grand Rapids 6, Michigan
1960

Reprinted, 1960, by
Baker Book House

Originally printed
in 1909 by Hodder
and Stoughton, London.

Printed in the United States of America

## CONTENTS

# A PREVIEW OF THIS VOLUME

Among the many books about revival and evangelism, this one seems to me the best, except the Bible. So do I feel after a lifetime of study and teaching in the field. Several years ago the friends at the Baker Book House asked me to recommend for reprinting a first-class religious book from yesterday. In response I told them about *Revivals, Their Laws and Leaders* (1909), by James Burns. Now I rejoice in their decision to republish the volume as it stands, even though some few parts seem to be outdated. I also welcome the opportunity to write this Preview, and later to add a chapter about "Lessons for Today."

First let me tell certain facts about the author. James Burns was born (1865) in East Lothian, Scotland. After a thorough schooling he served as pastor of four congregations, the last of them in London. Once he served as Moderator of the Presbyterian Church in England. In later years he devoted himself to Church Extension and to lecturing on Christian art. The publications of Burns include these bound volumes: *The Christ Face in Art, Sermons on Art, Illustrations from Art, Laws of Life and Destiny,* and the *New Pulpit Manual.* In its time the first of these books became well known. In our day the last of them is still in use, occasionally. From any point of view no one of them compares in importance with *Revivals, Their Laws and Leaders.*

James Burns sent out this volume five years before the outbreak of World War I. During the intervening half century and more, conditions on the surface of life have vastly changed, not always for the better. Even so, his account of the Laws that undergird Revival, and of Leaders in Revival, will repay a careful reading, and reward a diligent study. Only when Burns tries to look round the next few bends in the road does he seriously fall short. However, there is one prominent slip. Owing to some quirk in the brain of a man who knew and loved Christian biography, our author persisted in spelling the name of Whitefield the way it is pronounced, Whĭtfield. Otherwise, I commend the volume from beginning to end. My reasons appear below.

This entire book relates to revival, with some emphasis on evangelism. In my parts of this volume the term revival points to a sort of activity common in Old Testament times. After a period of declension, as in the days of the Judges, there would come a season of religious awakening, or quickening, as in the time of Samuel. Among the six leaders whom Burns holds up as examples, the first five had to do mainly with revival among persons and communities professedly Christian. The sixth exemplar, John Wesley, had more to do with evangelism, or the winning of the unsaved. In this sense of the term evangelism flourished throughout New Testament times.

Really these terms belong together. At times they are as closely related as identical twins. Hence Burns did no violence to the facts when he used the term revival as the main heading of a work that also dealt in part with evangelism. In our day the latter word has to do with what scholars term the *kerygma,* which means "preaching the gospel." With Burns let us think about revival and evangelism in their praiseworthy aspects. As for a present-day term, "revivalism," let it serve as a stigma, non-Biblical and reprehensible. As a foil to make clear what he does not mean by revival and evangelism, a writer in this field needs some such term, as unworthy as the name of Judas Iscariot or Benedict Arnold. Unlike American Revivalism, the activities now in view conform with certain laws, which come from God.

### A Statement of Certain Laws

The volume before us presents five laws that operate in all worthy movements of revival. To these five I have added two others, both of which the author sets forth, but not under that title. With the resulting seven laws the reader may wish to include still other guiding principles. To me the statement of these laws seems better than anything of the kind that I have seen. I only wish that Burns had developed some of his laws more fully. Without exception he drew these principles not from his own philosophical rationacinations, but from long, careful study of the Scriptures and of church history, especially in the form of Christian biography. What a sound working method!

1. *The Law of Progress.* First of all the writer sets forth as an ideal for the Christian Church "The Law of Progress." Everywhere in the world about us, especially among the pursuits of men, he calls attention to "progress through revival." He says that in every local church, as in much wider circles, "Revivals are necessary for the spurring of man to high endeavor, and for the vitalizing of his [spiritual] life." Ideally, in every congregation, there ought to be a sort of continuous revival. Here and there in church history there seem to have been such churches; for instance, the London Tabernacle under the leadership of Charles H. Spurgeon. More recently, and on a smaller scale, some of us have taken part, locally, in what have seemed to us continuous revivals.

Thus far all of us ought to agree with Burns in dealing with "The Law of Progress." But in view of two World Wars, laden with catastrophe, and the coming of our "atomic age," which may issue in a Third

World War, and the destruction of our so-called "civilization," many of us would throw more stress on what Burns presents later: the fact that progress can seldom be uniform. Surely he does not wish us to feel that "every day and in every way the world has been growing better and better." Meanwhile we all thank God that whenever He has His way in the Church its life and work show what Burns means by his "Law of Progress."

During the past fifty years and more, this law seems at times to have been in abeyance. Here and there certain movements and leaders have shown that the basic principle still operates. On the other hand, a distinguished leader in the Church of Scotland has rightly declared that no person born since the outbreak of World War I has witnessed a widespread revival with Pentecostal power. For many such reasons we all ought to pray: "O Lord, revive thy work in the midst of the years, in the midst of the years make known; in wrath remember mercy" (Hab. 3:2bc). If during the coming year, or decade, the Lord grants our desire, we shall praise Him for all the quickening and other blessed tokens of "Progress through Revival."

2. *The Law of Spiritual Growth.* Under this heading the author deals with revivals as recurrent, not continuous. Both in the hearts of believers and in the life of a congregation there come times that correspond somewhat with the ebb and the flow of the tides. Also in the growth of an oak tree there comes a season of waiting for growth again to begin. But all such analogies fall short of the truth about revivals. A man who knows the ways of the waves, or of an orchard, can judge fairly well what will follow after the present stage. On the contrary, nobody but God can begin to tell when a long-awaited revival will begin, what form it will assume, or how long it will continue at the crest. Among "the secret things [that] belong

unto the Lord our God" (Deut. 29:29a), we ought to include "the times and the seasons" for the blessings we know as revival.

3. *The Law of Periodicity.* To a certain degree the second law and this third one overlap. They both serve to modify the first one, with its emphasis on progress. As for "periodicity," at no time in the past has anyone but God ever known when the next spiritual awakening and quickening would occur. With reference to something of the kind our Lord told His disciples before Pentecost: "It is not for you to know the times or the seasons, which the Father hath put in his own power" (Acts 1:7). This much we know, both from the Scriptures and from the later history of the Church: times of declension are sure to come — it may be, as with us today, in the form of widespread secularism. All of us have had experiences of such declension. It may be that some of the younger readers have never known anything else.

According to the law now in view, however, we ought not to feel downcast. The prospects for revival are still as bright as the promises of God. Both to believers, one by one, and to many a local church, there comes a "profound sense of dissatisfaction" with things as they are. Not at all disconsolately many of us love to sing with Isaac Watts, "Come, Holy Spirit, heavenly Dove":

Dear Lord, and shall we ever live
At this poor dying rate?
Our love so faint, so cold to Thee,
And Thine to us so great!

4. *The Law of Leadership.* In the opening chapter from Burns the facts about leadership do not appear under the heading of a "law." The reason may be that the author is preparing the way for the main portion of his volume, which will deal with leaders of revival. Even so, these facts about human leadership (pp. 16-

31) show the operation of a law like this: In the Providence of God revival comes through the leadership of a man whom He has called and equipped for this work of grace. In the entire history of our subject it would be hard to find any revival worthy of note where some person has not stood out as the leader sent from God. For instance, look at "Billy Graham," and his city crusades, with their vitalizing effect on countless congregations and ministers.

For examples of God's blessings on human leadership, turn to the narrative parts of Holy Writ. "The law was given by Moses, but grace and truth came by Jesus Christ" (Jn. 1:17). In the time of Samuel or of Nehemiah, of Peter or of Paul, the rise and the progress of a movement corresponding to revival seems to have depended mainly on the personality and the leadership of one man, chosen and blessed of God. In the volume before us, six personalities emerge as heaven-sent leaders of revival. In forms and ways far different, the same "law of leadership" applies to every movement of the sort, both in the Church at large and on any local field.

In the central part of his introductory chapter the author sets forth certain characteristics of a revival that comes under a leader sent from God for this specific work. As a rule the movement bursts out all at once, sweeps across its field like a prairie fire, and everywhere leads to a deepened sense of sin. Then comes an outburst of joy through assurance of pardon and cleansing, with peace of heart and eagerness to serve. As a consequence of such a revival believers begin again to "possess their possessions" in the form of doctrines dear to the heart of God. There also comes a transformation in the morals of persons and congregations whose hearts have been touched with cleansing fire from above.

Unlike other men who write in our field, Burns

never loses sight of Bible ethics. Almost without exception he looks on moral improvement as a consequence of revival under the right sort of leadership, and as a proof that the movement has come from God. All the while the persons who have received "showers of blessing" rejoice in the public worship of the Most High. In the house of prayer, as on the Mount of Transfiguration, they long to see and hear no man, but Jesus only. In His presence they love to feel "lost in wonder, love, and praise." Out from His transforming presence they come to win the unsaved and the unchurched. What an ideal for any local church today!

5. *The Law of Variety.* This part of the introductory chapter from Burns deals with variety in the history of Great Britain. If necessary he could also have pointed to his six chosen personalities as living proofs that God works through all sorts of strong leaders, and in all sorts of unexpected ways. For example, think about Francis of Assisi as the most saintly leader in the Church during more than a thousand years, between Augustine of Hippo (d. 430) and Martin Luther (b. 1483); of Savonarola (d. 1498) as a mighty reformer with the spirit of Elijah or John the Baptist; of Martin Luther (d. 1546) with a personality that excelled in love of truth, of people, and of beauty; of John Calvin (d. 1564) with a tremendous intellect; of John Knox (d. 1572) as the maker of a new nation; and of John Wesley (d. 1791) as an evangelist who led in the transformation of his native land, and became the founder of the vast Methodist Church. What a galaxy of stars in the firmament of church history!

In the modern history of revival, the leaders have been equally worthy of note for their dependence on God and their unlikeness to each other. In our own American history think of the difference between Jonathan Edwards (d. 1758) and Charles G. Finney (d. 1875), or between Dwight L. Moody (d. 1899) and

Billy Graham (b. 1918). These men have shown endless variety of working methods. And yet our Lord has blessed them every one. So is He waiting to bless the worthy leader of any congregation, whatever his personality, all of which (except the sinful infirmities) has come from God. Nowhere in all his book does Burns suggest that any future leader of revival ought to pattern after any one of his six departed heroes. Let no young David go out to fight for God while clad in the armor of some older King Saul.

6. *The Law of Recoil.* In times past every revival has proved to be temporary. This is what Burns means by his word recoil. Some of us would prefer to substitute a milder term, such as recession. After the Protestant Reformation had begun to lose part of its transforming power there came the Roman Counter Reformation. Still the Protestant movement never sank back to the low level of the days before Martin Luther. And so with each of the other five leaders whom Burns studies, there came a period when the new movement no longer proceeded apace. From time to time students of history have tried to estimate the average length of a revival. Burns wisely refrains from trying to trace any fairly uniform cycle. The course of a prairie fire depends on the direction of the wind and on the nature of the terrain. So does God cause every revival to be unique in its length, as well as in other characteristics. In thinking about the revival for which we pray, let us leave to God the length of its work in our midst. While it lasts, let us prepare for a backwash.

7. *The Law of Doctrine.*Once again I am counting as a law what Burns presents under another heading. Let us think of the law this way: In the Providence of God a revival comes through stress on doctrines known as evangelical, especially the saving power of Christ's death. In the history of revival every leader worthy of note has held to the revealed truths of Holy Writ, and

has relied on these truths of God as the super-atomic power of the Almighty in setting men free from sin, and in making them strong to serve. About certain matters of belief Calvin differed from Luther, and Wesley differed from both. But each of the three held tenaciously to the doctrines known as evangelical. On the other hand, in the history of the Church, men and groups that have not held this "faith of the fathers," or else have held it lightly, have not excelled in promotion of revivals. Many of them would not resent such a statement, for they seem not to believe that a revival like that under Billy Graham in Australia has come from God.

## The Coming of Revival

In the latter part of his introductory chapter (pp. 43-56) Burns attempts to serve as a reverent forecaster. His description of unseemly conditions, religiously, before the outbreak of World War I sounds strangely like what many of us feel about the Church at large today. In our time, however, these black facts seem far more ominous. During the past decade or so we in the States have witnessed a widespread (if not deepseated) "return to religion." We have welcomed the increase of attendance at church, the sale of Bibles by the million, and the growth of giving, though in a depreciated currency. But often we wonder about the character of the "religion" to which throngs of men have "returned," and about the degree to which they have responded to New Testament ideals about holy living and fervent prayer. In vain we have looked for any "return to religion" that would cause a decline in adultery, in drunkenness, and in juvenile delinquency; or, on another level, in the prevalence of greed, the depth of race prejudice, and ungodly passions that lead men to war.

So it seems that in our time the "religion" to which hosts of men have returned part way must have sadly depreciated from the "gold standard" of Holy Writ. But even if the recent upsurge of church going and Bible buying had led to all the moral betterment for which we once hoped, the movement seems now to have passed its crest. No longer does the book review section of the *New York Times* devote much space to books about religion, or list them high among current best-sellers. No longer does television do more than pay occasional lip service to the sort of Christianity embodied in the New Testament and in the volume from Burns.

Other observers look on these facts with more of promise. No one, however, dares to predict that present religious conditions, if continued, will lead to a revival like that of 1858 and thereabouts, a revival that swept across our land, and left in its wake nothing of a sort that men could deplore. So it seems that we can all echo what Burns says in an opening paragraph about the need for revival in the Church of 1909: "No one pretends that it is well with the Church today." For more evidences in the way of diagnosis read with care the next few pages from Burns (pp. 44-47). Except for an item here or there, the entire picture holds true today, and in colors much darker. "Deeper, deeper grow the shadows."

Over against this black background the author presents a beautiful picture. "The Church of Christ . . . is on the eve of revival" (p. 47, line 14). In the light of church history, and on the basis of revealed truth in Holy Writ, Burns confidently expects to see a widespread revival soon. Evidently he feels "The morning is breaking; the darkness disappears." On our side of the water many of us ordained before World War I shared his rosy dreams. But after that earth-shaking explosion of demonic forces, we changed our sanguine predictions about the sure coming of a revival. In fact, some of us began to fear that God would soon bring our world into judgment, and pronounce doom on our "sensate civilization."

In the revival that Burns anticipated before many moons, the greed of commercialism was to give way before the Spirit of Christ; there would be a lessening of theological unrest, and of bowing down abjectly before the deliverances of secular science. Among his other glorious anticipations two stand out in special contrast with the state of things religious today: the coming revival would sweep out among masses of unsaved and unchurched folk, especially those who labor with their hands. Also, the movement would cause deepseated and lasting ethical reforms, both in the lives of men, one by one, and in the larger concerns of nations.

After the lapse of fifty years and more, some of us can not see that the Church and the world have begun to enjoy any such revival. Like Burns, however, we rejoice to believe that such a movement will come when God's professed children begin again to pray, as they did before Pentecost. Meanwhile we thank Him for every token of city-wide revival under the leadership of Billy Graham, and elsewhere in more than a few local churches, each of them under the leadership of a pastor sent from God. We likewise thank Him for the laws that still operate, laws that come to us anew from the pen of James Burns.

## The Ability to Write

A preview of this book ought to include something about the literary form. With some exceptions, we who believe heartily in revivals often seem careless about our ways of public speech and writing. Without going much into detail let us notice how this man has planned and written a book that calls for a reprint after the conditions that produced the book have passed away. At a time when other writers, especially in the States, were dealing with revival and evangelism as matters of man-made method, this author dared to treat the subject historically. He would have us look at revival in the light of laws that come from God, and as embodied in varied leaders whom Burns has portrayed.

In pursuance of his project, as difficult as it was fascinating, Burns dealt with only six leaders. In writing about each of them he practiced "the fine art of omission." In a chapter about Wesley, for instance, any of us would likely have made an excursus into the revival under Jonathan Edwards, who was born in the same year as John Wesley (1703). Then there would have been more or less about Charles Wesley and his hymns praising Jesus, with still more about George Whitefield and his differences from John Wesley. As a consequence, like many of our sermons, the resulting chapter would have seemed heavy, and would have lacked the sort of constructive clarity that comes from doing only one thing at a time, the one thing promised in the heading of the chapter, or sermon.

Even to a reader not versed in the history of the Church, or in Christian biography, each of the six biographical studies will prove easy to read, and to remember. After decades of work in this field I have come back to this volume with more relish than when I saw it first. As with any other piece of first-class prose, the style calls no attention to itself, and away from the subject in hand. There are relatively few quotations, and these few are brief, but almost every one of them "helps to advance the ball." There is more than a little dialogue, or "indirect discourse," which adds much to the human interest. The sentences often have a pleasing balance, with stress falling on the word or phrase at the end. The style tends to flow with a prose rhythm that tells of a man who has a heart as well as a head. A man, also, who loves fine art and from it has learned how to write for the glory of God. A man who rightly feels that only his best prose can begin to be good enough for the service of his King.

If only because of the literary form, many a pastor would do well to live for a while with this book. From it any of us can learn how to make our holy faith seem clear and luminous by showing how God has revealed His holy will through living characters, one by one. "Truth through personality," for the sake of life, here and hereafter! More directly, any minister can learn much that he needs to know as God's leader in a church that needs to be revived.

Through prayerful reading of this book from James Burns any pastor or layman can become a more intelligent and zealous promoter of a local revival. All of these laws still apply, and in spirit every one of these leaders ought still to live. If the home pastor and his most active laymen accept the counsels of this book, and enter into its spirit, before long the home church will have a revival worthy of the name. So let every reader continue to pray: "O Lord, revive Thy work here in the home church, and let the revival begin with me."

# THE LAWS OF REVIVAL

In the history of religion no phenomenon is more apparent than the recurrence of revivals.

At certain intervals there sweeps over certain districts a passion of repentance. Large numbers of persons who have been dead or indifferent to spiritual realities then become intensely awakened to them. They are arrested in the midst of their worldly occupations ; they are suddenly seized by a terror of wrong-doing, and fear as of an impending doom haunts their minds. Flinging all else aside they earnestly seek a way of escape, and cry out for salvation.

These movements, when once begun, are found to spread with amazing rapidity. They pervade the atmosphere like a contagion, and burst out in unexpected places as if carried by unseen hands. They often produce phenomena of the strangest character, and awaken forces at other times quiescent, or too faint to be recognised.

Frequently these movements are local and limited in their area, but sometimes they sweep over whole peoples, and produce the most momentous results. Nor is to be assumed that they are limited to Christianity. They may, on the contrary, be traced in all historic religions. Judaism had its revivals under Samuel, David, Solomon, Asa, Jehoshaphat, Hezekiah,

Josiah, and Ezra. The religious history of India and China shows a recurrence of such movements, and there is no reason to doubt that they have played their part in the evolution of those religions whose history remains unwritten.

While not limited to Christianity, however, they are supremely characteristic of it. Certainly no history of the growth of the Christian Church, and no examination of the reasons of its survival, would be of any value, which ignored their constant recurrence, and their momentous influence.

In the face of these facts it is clearly impossible to deal with revivals as mere isolated phenomena or sporadic movements tossed up by chance in the convulsions of society, admitting no law, and each isolated in cause and effect from the other. We have to deal instead with permanent elements in the nature of man, with deep, underlying laws which everywhere confront us in human history, and which are worthy of our most earnest study, since it is only by such means that we can interpret the mind and will of God in His dealings with humanity. Such movements are witness to us on the one hand of the supremacy in this world of spiritual realities. They reveal the permanent, spiritual instincts which lie in the nature of man, and which, however obscured and threatened by lower ambitions, ever burst forth afresh to vindicate their supremacy. They are a witness also, on the other hand, to the divine working in human history, and are thus an encouragement to faith. They reveal the operation of God's laws in the realm of spiritual experience, and in the guidance of His Church. They declare that God does not sit unmindful of His Creation, but that through His laws He is ceaselessly operating for the world's good, and for the salvation of His people.

I

## Revivals a Law of Progress

This recognition of revivals as part of the divine method of operation in human history is encouraged when we take a wider view, and when we see them appear in spheres outside the Church. All progress we perceive is a progress through revival. In no sphere whatever is progress uniform, and unbrokenly continuous. Progress in the world is effected, we perceive, not by a steady, onward movement, like the march of an army, but by an oscillating movement like that of an incoming tide. Each wave is a revival; it rushes forward with impetuous haste and with exultant joy; it carries everything before it, and then, having spent its strength, recedes, only to be succeeded by another wave, and yet another. To the careless onlooker it seems as if nothing were gained, but behind the ebb and flow of wave is the unconquerable power of the tide.

It is so in that vast drama enacted by the nations of the earth. First one nation appears, gains wide and undisputed power, and carries forward human progress to the highest point then reached. But having done its work it falls back, and another takes its place, and so, by successive revivals of fresh life when exhaustion has overtaken the old, the progress of humanity is maintained.

It is so in all the different realms of human thought and activity. In one epoch Science revives; new discoveries are made, new realms of investigation opened out, the scientific outlook dominates the minds of men, and other spheres of activity are depressed. But nothing holds an unbroken empire over the human mind; having spent its initial force, having added to the wealth of human knowledge, and enriched life by its discoveries, it gives way; another revival takes its place; some different sphere of human thought or activity occupies the field, and progress is effected in another realm. Each epoch has its own characteristic; it is marked by an outburst in some particular direction —in poetry, or in art, in material progress, in intellectual interests, in scientific discovery, or in some other realm of human activity—but each outburst is in the nature of a revival. There is a quickening of life in one particular sphere, a gathering up of its energies, a leap forward, and then, when its strength is spent, a 'melancholy, long, withdrawing roar.' Even commerce, we perceive, is not exempt from this law. Trade depressions are succeeded by trade revivals, and in the world's markets there are constant fluctuations, and a ceaseless ebb and flow.

In all this we can see marks of the divine wisdom. Revivals are necessary for the spurring of man to high endeavour, and for the vitalising of his life. Were progress to be uniform—no part of man's nature moving until all the other parts could move also—advance would be so slow that life would stagnate. There could then be no high hopes, no springtide of exulting life, no eager and impetuous rush forward. Progress would be so slow as to be imperceptible, and man, robbed of high inspirations, would cease to hope, and cease to struggle. By the breath of revived life, however, God keeps the world in eager activity, and keeps the human heart ever fresh with hope. In His divine purposes no part of man's nature is left unrevived; His dealings with men reveal a continuous Pentecost, and each revival is needed for the perfecting of man's nature. The world, then, may be said never to be left without a revival; if in one part of human activity the wave recedes, in another it flows; but the order is the secret of the Most High, the equipoise is in His Hands. Behind all the ebb and flow is the inexorable tide of His redemptive purposes.

II

## Revivals the Law of Spiritual Growth

When, now, we discover revivals to be the invariable method by which progress is effected in all other realms of human thought and activity, we are prepared to approach their recurrence in the realm of religion freed from that bias, and emptied of that suspicion, and even scorn, which have been thought by many to be the right attitude to adopt toward them. And it is in this realm that the word 'revival' begins to vibrate with a new intensity. For religion has to do with things august and illimitable, with the deep things of man's spiritual consciousness, and with his destiny. Interesting, therefore, as revivals may be in other spheres, these become mere phantoms when compared with the absorbing interest and importance of revivals in the history of the Church, and in the spiritual life of man. Yet, though they occur in this mysterious realm, it is not necessary to suppose that there is in them something capricious or arbitrary which should hinder us from examining them, or from trying to bring them under the domain of law. The supreme discovery that there is nothing capricious in God's universe, which is the dominant conviction of modern thought, encourages us to believe that even here, dimly perhaps, yet not without helpful suggestion, characteristics common to all may be found, sufficient to lay a foundation to build upon, and suggestive enough to prove a buttress for faith.

When now we turn to examine revivals as phenomena

appearing in the realm of the spiritual life, we are confronted with a mass of interesting material. Revivals, we perceive, are used of God for the quickening of man's spiritual life, and for the effecting of his spiritual education and progress. They are characterised in this realm, as in others, with the same frequency, and with the same fluctuations of feeling and activity.

First of all we discover such fluctuations in the common experience of men and women before definite decisions in the realm of religion have been made. 'If we were able to recall,' says Canon Hay Aitken, 'the action of the Holy Spirit upon our hearts during the years in which our decision for Christ was not yet made, should we not find that this has never been uniform? There have been times in which we have been conscious of definite, spiritual influences moving us more or less powerfully to yield ourselves to Him, and then, again, there have come long periods in which we seemed to have no consciousness of any such spiritual pressure; then, once more, after months, or even years of spiritual lethargy and spiritual insensibility, the influence has made itself felt.'

This ebb and flow of spiritual experience is no less characteristic of the life of the individual even when he has passed into the realm of definite conviction and decision. No life is maintained at the same level. The Psalms, which are so marvellous a chart of spiritual experience, reveal on every page the varying nature of the divine life in the heart of the believer. Now, caught by the inflowing wave, the writer exults in his strength, his heart rejoices in God, though an host should encamp against him he shall not be afraid. But this jubilant note does not last; soon, caught in the trough of the wave, his voice cries out for help, his heart is in despair, light and hope alike seem to have forsaken him.

From this he is rescued by the hand of the Lord, and carried forward in a new tide of joyful, spiritual experience.

This same experience characterises, we find, all corporate, Christian life. The spiritual life within any given congregation is never maintained in equipoise. Each organism is conscious of times of slackness and lifelessness, times when there is a dryness in the spiritual life, and only a feeble response to spiritual appeals, followed by times of awakening and revival.

In all these different realms of spiritual life and experience there is thus going on, we perceive, a continuous ebb and flow; progress is never effected along the whole line in unbroken sequence; the pressure of the Holy Spirit upon the life of the individual and upon the Church is never uniform. And the reason of this it is not difficult to discover. The divine method is justified by human experience. 'A pressure which is uniform and continuous,' says the writer we have already quoted, 'becomes a mere condition of our existence, and we accommodate ourselves to it, without its attracting any attention; whereas a pressure that is occasional and variable at once claims our attention. Hence the Holy Spirit shows His interest in us as truly by the withdrawal or diminution of His influence at certain seasons, as by His manifestation of it at other times; for it is by adopting this method that the conscience is reached and aroused, and the heart won for Christ.'

In the inflow of the tide, however, there are not only tiny ripples which feel with their baby fingers along the inland creeks, there are also the tumultuous waves and mighty breakers which come rolling in with majestic movement and mighty avalanche of waters. And in the inflowing tide of man's spiritual progress there is the same infinite variety of wave. There are revivals which affect, in an endless variety of degrees, the individual; there are those larger movements which affect separate congregations, and there are movements larger still, which affect, not single churches, but geographical areas, and spread themselves over a wide district. Such, for instance, was the recent revival in Wales; such the revivals in Ireland and in Scotland in 1859.

But the history of revivals discloses larger movements still, infrequent in their appearance, but epoch-making in their character. Movements which change life's conditions, and deeply affect the history of the world. With some of these great movements we deal in the following pages, with the object of discovering, if possible, the laws which call them into being, and which govern their activity. For that which is found common to all great movements is likely to be present in the most minute ones. The law which moves the mighty tides of the ocean is the same which ruffles the surface of the little pool made by the rain of a summer afternoon. But the law is best studied in the greater rather than in the less, in the large letters, rather than in the small. Its workings then become more apparent, its accumulated effect more convincing and overpowering.

## III

## The Law of Periodicity

That revivals are one of the supreme methods used of God for the fulfilling of His purposes in the world we may now assume. These revivals, we perceive, are part of the divine plan; they move to a divine law; that there is an orderly sequence in their movements we may believe. But can we discover this sequence? Do revivals recur at definite intervals? Can we forecast their appearance with the same precision as astronomers forecast the appearance of a comet or a star? Obviously this is impossible. The movements of human beings cannot be treated as an exact science. Human life does not move in its orbit with unvarying precision. Man's will enters with all its inconstancy; unexpected incidents arise which retard or deflect the course of events; and while these cannot annihilate the divine purpose, they may retard it, and certainly they make prophesying the most hazardous of experiments.

While, then, it is impossible for us to map out with mathematical precision the recurrence of revivals in human history, this does not close us down to the conviction that all that pertains to them is hidden away in the inscrutable purposes of God, that no facts can be elicited as to their appearance in history, or as to the conditions which call them into being. It is clear, for instance, that their appearance at certain times in our experience, and in history, owes nothing to hap-hazard. It is not found that through long periods man's spiritual nature is allowed to stagnate through the absence of any quickening breath, while at other times a series of revivals rushes in upon him at random, without preparation or fixed purpose. This does not happen in the spiritual experience of the individual, it does not happen in the experiences of individual congregations, and it does not happen in the larger movements detailed in history. In all of these a certain law of periodicity is discernible. Thus we have the Reform movement in the sixteenth century; the Puritan movement in the seventeenth; the Wesleyan movement in the eighteenth; and the Oxford movement in the nineteenth. These facts indicate that though we cannot mark the recurrence of revivals with figures on a dial, or prophesy with unerring accuracy their arrival, we can at least declare that their appearance is subject to no caprice, but that behind them there is divine law and order. They suggest that what is variable in the recurrence of revivals owes itself to the inconstant nature of man, but that beneath this there are the unchanging purposes of an all-wise and beneficent God, whose constant care is the spiritual education and quickening of His people.

When now we turn to those great movements in history, some of which are dealt with in the following pages, it is not difficult to discover certain facts common to them all.

## IV

### The Ebbing Tide

First of all we find preceding each revival a time of spiritual deadness, when faith has waxed dim, when no great hopes cheer men's hearts, and when a dull and heavy lethargy has settled upon the spiritual life of man. At such times there is a breaking away from the Church of all those alienated from her in heart, and of those who are sceptical of her authority. In these dark days unbelief in some of its forms holds the field, and proudly boasts of its power; while the enfeebled Church, without the strength to resist, sits in humiliating impotence, suffering the blows of her assailants, and groaning under their insolent scorn.

Nor is it found that in such times the Church is blameless. Her loss of hope is seen to have followed on her loss of spiritual power, and her loss of spiritual power has followed the opening of her heart to the world. That happens on a large scale which happens in our individual experience when the doors of our hearts are thus left open. Immediately we are conscious of chill;

the inner fires cease to glow; the warmth departs. The outward duties of religion may still be performed with the old regularity, nay, with even an increased vehemence to make up for the decreased sincerity; but the Spirit is not there, our praises are of the lip, our sacrifices are without the incense of a broken and contrite heart. The extent of this relapse will depend upon the character of the individual; in some, because of their intense spirituality, the ebb and flow will be faint; in others, whose natures contain violently discordant elements, it will be most pronounced.

In those large movements thrown upon the pages of human history we see these facts enlarged so that all may read them. The defection of the individual spreads until it reaches the Church. In the lowered spiritual tone abuses begin to creep in, at first furtively, but with ever-increasing effrontery until the whole body is permeated with worldliness. How far this may grow will be seen in those pages which follow, which describe the corruption of the Church in the days which preceded each revival. These descriptions vary in darkness according to the century and the condition of civilisation. It would be impossible now, we hold, for the Church of Christ ever to sink so low as it did in Italy in the twelfth century, in Scotland in the sixteenth, or in England in the eighteenth. In the growth of the Christian consciousness and the gradual uplift of society, things in one century permissible, become in the next impossible. It is not necessary, before we eagerly examine the signs of the times for the advent of a revival, to wait until the old excesses have been repeated, or until the Church has sunk to the low level of these other days. Each generation has its own level. There is ebb and flow, but it is the ebb and flow of an ever-advancing tide. Yet, for all this, the extent of the defection may be as great, for the fall has to be measured from the fresh advance which has been reached.

In the application of this to the present day, for instance, it is not valid to point out that the gross abuses which characterised the Church in these earlier days are absent in ours, and that therefore there is no real defection, or, if defection, no signs of revival; that before a revival can come, these abuses must be repeated. The Church to-day stands at a different altitude. It is possessed of a clearer spiritual vision, and is surrounded by a more enlightened public opinion. The Church to-day could not fall so low as in past days, for it falls from a loftier height. It may reveal, in its defection, none of the old abuses, and in this respect may compare favourably with even the best periods in other and earlier epochs; but this standard of judgment is false. Each age has its own standard of judgment, and by that standard the Church may be condemned of pitiful defection, even while in comparison with other ages full of good works. When the light that is in the Church is darkness, then how great is that darkness!

## V

## The Fulness of the Times

The next fact which the study of revivals discloses is the profoundly heartening one that this time of spiritual deadness has its definite limits. The wave of spiritual progress recedes, but even in receding it is gathering in power and volume to return, and to rush further in. Evil thus can claim no final empire over the soul of man. God has set a limit even to the defection of His Church; when the night is at its darkest the dawn is on the way.

This next period in the inner history of revivals is characterised by a profound sense of dissatisfaction awaking in many hearts. A period of gloom sets in, a weariness and exhaustion invade the heart, the pleasures of the world no longer satisfy, they set up a deep distaste and satiety. Sick in soul, men turn with a sigh to God; dimly they wake to the consciousness that, in bartering heavenly for earthly joys, they have encountered irremediable loss; that in the decay of spiritual vision the world has lost its soul of loveliness. Slowly this aching grows, the heart of man begins to cry out for God, for spiritual certainties, for fresh visions. From a faint desire this multiplies as it widens, until it becomes a vast human need; until in its urgency it seems to beat with violence at the very gates of Heaven.

Within the Church itself, also, through all its days of defection, there have been many who have not bowed the knee to Baal, who have mourned its loss of spiritual power, and who have never ceased to pray earnestly for a revival of its spiritual life. For long their prayers seemed to be unanswered; it appeared as if God had forgotten to be gracious. Gradually, however, the numbers are found to increase; prayer becomes more urgent and more confident; the condition of the Church, its want of spiritual life, the weakness of its spiritual witness, the need of a fresh baptism of spiritual power become apparent. This need weighs more and more upon the hearts of the devout. Longing for better things becomes an intense pain; men begin to gather in companies to pray; they cease not to importune God day and night, often with tears, beseeching Him to visit with His divine power the souls of men, and to pour into the empty cisterns a mighty flood of divine life. In many different parts, quite unconnected with each other, this spirit of intercession awakes, and with it an expectation that will not be denied, a premonition that there is at hand the dawn of better days.

In those recent publications which deal with times of awakening in the individual, it has been pointed out that these occur mostly at times of transition, especially when the individual is passing from one stage of development into another. In these vaster, spiritual awakenings it will also be found that they synchronise with some profound change coming over the social or political life of the people. The spiritual awakening accompanies the new stage of growth in the life of humanity. And the value of this is immediately apparent, since the new energies are conserved, and directed into channels which will safeguard the race, and lead to true progress.

Thus the twelfth century saw Europe passing out of the darkness of the Middle Ages; the feudal system was breaking up; men were gathering in cities; a new sense of corporate life was beginning to emerge, and men were re-arranging themselves in wider combinations as they felt the inspiration of fresh loyalties and worthier ambitions. Papal absolutism, also, which had held men's minds so long under subjection, was beginning to relax its hold, being assailed on the one hand by the growing independence of the secular authorities, and on the other hand by the irritation under restraint of the newly-awakened intelligence. At this time universities began to spring up; there was a widening of sympathies which the Crusades did something to foster; and over the whole of Europe there was passing the ferment of new ideas. The period thus marked the close of one stage of human development, and the beginning of another.

When we come to the next great movement, we stand

again at a crisis in human affairs. Europe, which, in the period noted above, was passing from childhood into early youth, was now, in the sixteenth century, passing from youth to the first dawn of conscious manhood. From gathering around the Baron's castle for protection, men, in the thirteenth century, began to gather in cities; now, in the sixteenth century, men were forming themselves under larger combinations; loyalty to the city was giving way to loyalty to the state. It was the time when peoples were arising conscious of a vigorous, national life; when kings were creating courts, and forcing the nobility to acknowledge their supremacy; when Europe was re-arranging itself under modern geographical and national divisions. It was the time, also, of the awakening of learning and of art; a time of extraordinary intellectual interests; when a new-born sense of freedom thrilled men's hearts, and made the old constraints intolerable. Here, again, we see then one stage of growth completed, and a fresh stage begun.

After the sixteenth century, revivals disappear from the European plane, and have to be considered under narrower fields of operation. For this there are two reasons. First, the breaking up of Europe into nationalities destroyed the old unity, and tended to create a separate national life. The nation then became a kosmos in itself. But second, and more particularly, this unity was destroyed by the Reformation, which broke up the universal control of Rome, and split Europe into hostile camps. Revivals, therefore, after the sixteenth century, have to be considered within the compass of national movements, since each nation became a world of its own, and each differed in the stage of development which it had reached.

Even in those more limited movements, however, which are confined to a separate nation, revivals are

found to synchronise with crises of her development. As an illustration of this, the revival under Wesley has been chosen, since it was limited in extent, and almost entirely confined to this country. When we consider the conditions of England at the time of the revival, however, we see that she was passing through just such a period of transition as those we have been considering on a wider scale. 'The old order was changing, giving place to new.' And this new was the birth of the great manufacturing class, the birth of industrialism which was to revolutionise society, and produce the most momentous changes in its political and commercial conditions. 'The chief feature of English history from the middle of the eighteenth century,' says Fitchett, 'is the rise of the great manufacturing towns. In the last fifty years of the eighteenth century the population of England increased fifty per cent.' It was the period marked by the awakening of the people, by the dawn of a new consciousness in English political and social life.

Thus we see how at such times all things seem to unite and cry out for a revival; the waters are far withdrawn, and heaped up, are foaming and fretting behind the barricade. The times are ripe; the soul of man, weary of wandering, cries out for God; a spirit of intense expectation is abroad, of dissatisfaction with the past, of earnest longing regarding the future. Once more the long and bitter night has ended; the dawn is at hand, for 'the fulness of the time' has come.

## VI

### The Advent of the Prophet

The next event common to the history of all great revival movements is the appearance of the man destined

of God to be its leader. The man is the incarnation of the idea; he sums up in himself, in its most intense form, the longings of the times, and interprets to his day and generation their inmost needs. To all those intangible and mysterious longings and ideas dimly felt and comprehended by others, he gives startling visibility, so that the moment he appears he is recognised as leader, and the moment he speaks his hearers recognise his authority.

In this sense, then, the leader is recognised not as the creator of the movement, but its interpreter. Made in a more intense mould, his ear catches the faint whisper which to duller ears is lost in the confused noises of the world. The burden of the times, which others only dimly realise, becomes to him an intolerable load; he feels the Hand of the Lord upon him; voices speak to him which he cannot disobey, and at length he goes forth possessed by the Spirit of God to be the Spirit's agent in leading men into newness of life. The call has come to him, and he is conscious of the call.

But though only the agent and the interpreter, the leader of the revival is not a machine. He brings into the movement his own individuality, and within certain limits defines its characteristics. Thus when we survey the leaders in the world's regenerative movements, we see how wide is the selection, how varied are the characters of God's chosen servants. Isaiah is separated from Paul by more than the separation of centuries; Francis of Assisi seems to have little in common with Luther; Savonarola differs from Wesley as far as the east differs from the west. The same wide difference may be detected in the movements themselves, and the characteristics of the movements bear so strong a mark of the individuality of the leader that the casual student might incline to the conclusion that the leader was the creator as well. The truth, however, seems to be, that these characteristics were essential for the success of the movement. Luther was not the type of man needed in the thirteenth century, nor was Francis the type most needed in the sixteenth, and this is true of the others. What was required in the thirteenth, was just that return to evangelical poverty which so startled the age of Francis, and brought men back to the eternal simplicities; while in the age of the Reformation, instinct with new ideas, what was wanted was a reconstruction of its faith, and a re-interpretation of Christianity in terms of its new intellectual outlook, and its new-born sense of freedom. In the eighteenth century, again, it is clear that what was needed was not a reconstruction of dogma, or the rebuke of a Church given over to the worship of material things by a return to evangelical poverty, but an inspiration, which, by appealing to the emotions of a vast class just awakening to life, would lift them up into contact with the unseen, and give them a new dynamic of life. The strange influence of each of these men, therefore, arose from their representing in themselves, from their incarnating in their message and lives, as it were, the very inmost need of the times.

Here, however, the differences end. Each of these great leaders has in common with all the others an unshakable faith in God, an overwhelming sense of a call to great service, a mysterious equipment of spiritual power which moves mountains, and a determination to do the work he is called of God to do even at the expense of life itself. In the Picture Gallery of the good and great, such men occupy the noblest place.

## VII

### The Awakening

When, now, preparation has been made, when the forerunner has appeared, when the fulness of the time has come, and the leader has awaked into consciousness of his mission, up above the horizon there suddenly appears the light and glory of a new day. The people that walked in darkness now see a great light, and, seeing it, they fling off the garments of despair, and exult in newness of life.

In each movement of this kind there is something incalculable; vast energies, hitherto slumbering, are awakened, and new forces—for long preparing under the surface—burst into being. Its tide rolls in from an unseen continent, and moves with a gathering momentum which nothing can resist. Yet, while there is in each something characteristic and individual, there is in each also something which is uniform.

I. Each revival, for instance, is characterised by the *extraordinary swiftness with which it spreads.* When once the first words of the new message vibrate upon the air, mysterious forces seem to arise and carry them from place to place with the swiftness of the wind. The revival spreads like a contagion; it bursts out in places where there seems to have been no evident contact with other places infected, and men are moved by it not in twos and threes, but in multitudes.

Thus, in four years, in the Franciscan movement, the twelve brothers had changed to many thousands, and in a few years more the whole of Italy seemed to have been swept by its radiant joy. The nailing of the Theses by Luther on the church door at Wittenberg seemed to suggest little of importance, but it was as a tiny flame set to a vast combustible material, and the fire begun that day has never been put out. Knox, as he went up and down Scotland, was amazed at the changes he saw wrought; in a few years the Lowlands of Scotland were so altered as almost to become unrecognisable. And it was so in England under Wesley. Nothing seemed to indicate any startling change in the life of the country as Wesley stood up in the open air, in the month of February 1739, to address a crowd of illiterate miners near Bristol. No one could have dreamed that this was one of the most momentous acts of the eighteenth century; and yet it was the beginning of a movement which spread like wildfire, and which laid the foundations of a Church destined to become one of the largest Protestant Churches in the world.

This swiftness of growth is no less a characteristic of those movements which occupy a smaller area, and it is an indication of the silent preparation which goes on beneath the surface long before the revival itself takes place. It shows how the Spirit of God is ever active, and how, even in the dark winter-tide of man's religious experience, there is the promise and potency of the spring.

II. No one can study, even superficially, the phenomena of revivals without being struck by the similarity of the effects produced upon those who come under their sway. Two of these stand out with startling vividness, and are common to all.

(*a*) Every revival movement sees an awakening in the individual and in the Church of a deep sense of sin. In the intense spiritual light, the sin and guilt of the awakened soul stand out in terrifying blackness. Not only are the cardinal sins laid bare in all their hideousness, but the convicted see themselves as in a mirror; they see themselves as God sees them; every fault, every meanness, every deviation from the truth, every act of self-interest, of betrayal, of hypocrisy, confronts them ; their sins drag them to judgment ; they cry out in their despair ; an awful terror seizes them ; under the pressure of the Spirit they often fall to the ground with loud cries and tears, the conviction of sin burns them like fire. Yet this 'terror of the Lord,' remarkable though it may seem, is not the terror of punishment; it is inspired by a sense of having rebelled against the divine love, of having failed to give glory to God, of having crucified Christ afresh. This is the sin which, above all others, gives to the awakened soul at such times its most poignant bitterness.

Under the pressure of this agony of conviction men openly confess their sins. They go through the long and terrible catalogue, hiding nothing ; their one intense longing is to cast their sins for ever from them, and to be brought into reconciliation and be at peace with God. 'I simply cannot describe the scene,' says one who recently passed through such an experience in Manchuria. 'It made one think of the Judgment Day. God had come among us. All knew it, and every heart was open before Him. For myself, I had the most intense realisation of the holiness of God, and of my uncleanness in His sight.'

The curious thing is, that even in China, where the sense of sin is so difficult to arouse, the same terrible agony of conviction has been awakened wherever the revival movement appeared. And even the heathen, who never had heard the name of Christ, but who were attracted to the building by curiosity, hearing of the strange things happening, felt the irresistible power dragging them to confession. 'Whenever I entered,' said one, 'I felt some mysterious power seize me, impelling me to confess my sins, and it was only with the utmost difficulty I could drag myself away.' Others, however, remained, and though entirely ignorant of spiritual things, yet to use the words of the missionary, 'were brought under conviction, and converted.'

At such times a like conviction of sin falls upon the Church. In lax epochs the dulled conscience of the Church permits many things to creep within her doors which, if they be not wrong in themselves, at least tend to dull the fine edge of her spiritual life. When, also, the inner fires cease to glow with intense love for Christ, there is nothing left to defend the Church from the world spirit, which enters with its acrimonies, and its hatred of all spiritual earnestness and enthusiasm. In many cases divisions arise, harmony between minister and people is rent; or there is a lowering of the spiritual tone, which reduces worship to coldness and formality. Practices are permitted in order to maintain interest which are an exact copy of the world without, and although these are by many condemned, they have not the power to eject them. The Church becomes at such a time, worldly, selfish, almost Christless.

With a revival, however, all this is changed. The Church's long defection then ends. A new consciousness of sin is awakened in the Church as well as in the individual. She realises how far she has wandered, how untrue she has been to her divine Head, how little glory she has given Him. There passes over her a wave of deep conviction and of shame. She humbles herself in the dust, and in deep humility confesses her false witness, her worldly practices, her indifference to the spiritual wants of those around her. Then there follows a time of reformation, when the evil practices which in a time of low ideals she has permitted are dragged out and condemned; when turning with joyful heart to spiritual things, she seeks by united prayer, by intense zeal, by sublime sacrifice, to bring into the Kingdom of Jesus Christ those who remain without.

This reformation of the Church is not attained with the dramatic suddenness of the individual; it follows the admission into the Church of those large masses affected by the revival, and the fresh life poured into the hearts of its members.

(*b*) The second characteristic effect produced by a revival movement is its wonderful outburst of joy. When the night is past, the agony of conviction, the awful sense of abandonment, the grief and terror of sin, there breaks upon the agonised heart the blessed peace of forgiveness. No joy that earth has to offer can compare with this mysterious and ineffable gladness which awakens in the heart forgiven and restored. Men have exhausted language trying to find for it a worthy expression. At such a time the splendid imagery of Isaiah—that the mountain and hills break forth into singing, and all the trees of the field clap their hands—does not appear excessive. To those caught in its flood, all the world seems changed; their hearts are light, and their faces glow; like those of the early Church, 'they eat their meat with gladness and singleness of heart.'

Nor is this joy limited to those who, outside the Churches, have been won by the evangel; it fills the hearts of those who are already avowed followers of Christ; it sweeps with its radiant life into the Church, and makes all its worship pulse and glow with spiritual fervour. Dr. Dale, describing the effect produced by Moody and Sankey at the close of their first mission in Birmingham, which produced the deepest impression on the life of the city, and its churches, says: 'I hardly know how to describe the change which has passed over them [*i.e.* the members of his church]. It is like the change which comes upon a landscape where clouds which have been hanging over it for hours suddenly vanish, and the sunlight seems to fill both heaven and earth. There is a joyousness and elasticity of spirit, and a hopefulness, which have completely transformed them.'

This is the effect of a revival wherever it appears. It irradiates the atmosphere; it leaves in its track numberless happy men and women whose faces are aglow with a new light, and whose hearts throb with an intense and pure joy.

This new-born gladness finds among other outlets its most characteristic one in an outburst of song. Song is the natural expression of the jubilant heart; it is human nature's way of escape for feelings which are too rapturous to remain silent. Most of the great leaders of revival have been poets as well, and the revival is borne along on the wings of exulting praise. The Franciscans sang the 'Canticle of the Sun'; the Reformers in Germany sang the mighty strophes of Luther; Scotland found in the Psalms that which answered to her triumphant mood; while Wesley's hymns remain to-day long after the revival has spent itself. In recent times we have seen the same fact expressed in a most striking way in the revival in Wales. And even in China, in the revival which has lately taken place amongst some of the most degraded tribes in the South-west, singing has been a prominent feature.

Whether the new-born gladness of heart find its outlet in song or no, however, the gladness itself is never absent. In many it becomes so extreme that where the mind is ill-balanced it leads to dangerous excesses. Almost every revival is accompanied by outbursts of excitement, and by startling physical phenomena.

Outbreaks of physical anguish are followed by outbursts of uncontrollable joy, and the effect of these extreme emotions on ill-balanced natures is often disastrous. The spiritual value of a revival, however, is not to be negatived because of the disastrous effect produced upon a certain number of excitable natures. Many who are on the outlook to cast opprobrium on all such movements select these excesses to prove the justice of their condemnations. They only prove the narrowness of their judgments, and show how, by prejudice, movements which carry with them untold blessings to the race may be belittled by minds that fix upon the trivial, and by hearts that are bankrupt of lofty, spiritual emotions. No true revival of spiritual religion ever failed to lift men up to higher altitudes, or failed to enrich the spiritual experiences of mankind by giving new sanctions for faith and love.

III. The next fact common to all revivals is that they profoundly affect large masses of the community; that they leave a permanent influence behind them for good, and create a new era in the progress of the race.

All revivals, it may be said, begin from below; their leaders are almost entirely of the people; and their greatest influence is exerted upon the poor, and upon those whom the Churches have neglected. For, in an age of declining faith, the Church becomes depleted of its spirit of sacrifice; it becomes self-seeking and worldly; it uses its enormous influence over its members to obtain ease and worldly comforts. As a consequence, the heroic spirit departs from it, and those masses of the community who are unattractive because of their ignorance and poverty are neglected, and become more and more degraded.

When, however, the glad news of redeeming love is proclaimed with that passionate exultation and conviction which are the authentic notes of every revival, then it is to the poor that the Gospel is preached; it is the common people who hear it gladly. Living in their mean streets and wretched hovels, neglected and uncared for by those who ought to give their lives for them, they listen with awe-struck ears and beating heart to that announcement which declares that the very hairs of their head are numbered, and that they are of more value than many sparrows. Having found little of love, yet full of hunger for it, their hearts are drawn to the message of that divine compassion which, in love for them and pity of their need, did not shrink from the uttermost sacrifice; while, poor in this world's wealth, their eyes are filled with the glory of those spiritual riches which the Gospel so lovingly and freely offers them.

Brought thus within the sphere of religion, their hearts uplifted by pure emotions, their whole lives are changed, and they become a new asset in the wealth of a nation. Thus a revival means the uplifting and re-creation of large masses of the community, and usually of that part of the community whose lives, because of their poverty and degradation, are a menace to the state. There is no doubt, for instance, that the revival under Wesley saved England from the peril of a revolutionary movement such as broke out in France, and it did so by setting the affection of those masses—awakening to a consciousness of their strength in the industrial revolution—on things above, and not on things beneath.

In the light of this fact, it is the merest platitude to assert, as it seems popular to assert at present, that the next revival will be an ethical revival. All revivals are ethical revivals. They move—if they are authentic revivals sent from above, and not merely stimulated from below—not merely in the realm of the emotions, but in the sphere of the conscience and the will. They leave behind them not merely joyful, but changed lives. They make drunkards sober; they break the chains of evil habits, and implant a new set of emotions within the heart; they arouse dormant faculties, and inspire men to develop their natures, and by education, by self-discipline, and especially by prayer and spiritual exercises, to enrich their lives. 'It seems to me,' says Dean Church in *The Gifts of Civilisation,* 'that the exultation apparent in early Christian literature, beginning with the Apostolic Epistles, at the prospect, now at length disclosed within the bounds of a sober hope, of a great moral revolution in human life—that the rapturous confidence which pervades these Christian ages, that at last the routine of vice and sin has met its match, that a new and astonishing possibility has come within view, that men, not here and there, but on a large scale, might attain to that hitherto hopeless thing to the multitudes, goodness—is one of the most singular and solemn things in history.' This 'singular and solemn thing' is seen in the effect of every revival. In the history of each it is still possible to use the wonderful words used by Paul in reference to the Corinthians: 'Fornicators, idolaters, adulterers, thieves, covetous, drunkards, revilers, extortioners—and such were some of you; but ye were washed, but ye were sanctified, but ye were justified in the name of the Lord Jesus Christ, and in the Spirit of our God.'

The effect of a revival upon the Church is no less profound and far reaching. For while the word 'revive,' strictly speaking, means 'to bring to life again,' the word, in its religious application, has been widened to include the awakening of those who were dead, and the quickening of those already awakened.

Every revival, when it appears, discovers to the Church its spiritual decay, its worldliness, and the insincerity of its witness. This spiritual decay seems to move along two distinct lines.

(*a*) The first tendency is for the doctrine of the Church to lose its power of convicting the conscience, convincing the mind, or moving the heart. After a time of immense theological interest, that interest begins to wane; men's minds are attracted in other directions, and by fresh discoveries made in other fields. Thus theology drops out of the running; it fails to keep pace with the fresh thought of the age. It is out-distanced, and then treated with contempt by other departments of human thought which are in the vanguard of progress.

In addition to this, each age requires a restatement of truth. The truth may not alter, but our comprehension of it does. We are taught to see it from new angles, and with the fresh perspective and light of the new age. Hence the necessity for a new statement, for a re-interpretation of the old in terms of the new. For words are like coins—of full value when fresh from the mint, but capable of being rubbed and defaced, and robbed of their original worth. In dead and unspiritual times preachers continue to use the old words once so full of convincing and converting power, but now devitalised, partly because the age has drifted from them, partly because to those who use them they have become the mere jargon of the pulpit. They mumble out their shibboleths, but they fail to strike home to the conscience, or to gain response from the heart, for they themselves have ceased to be moved by them.

Thus the Church passes through a dreary period of scepticism. Unbelief chills its vital fires, and the consciousness of insincerity makes its message halting and unredeeming.

With the first pronouncement of the inspired leader, however, all this hesitation and sense of insincerity which come from the absence of a living message pass away. Some new aspect of divine truth is declared, or some old and forgotten truth is restated, and suddenly men's hunger is appeased; they are fed once more with the Bread of Life.

(*b*) The second tendency in the history of spiritual decay within the Church is for worship to become formal; for the priesthood to exalt the ritual until the spirit is crushed, and to represent religion, not as the response of the soul to God, but as a rigid performance of outward observances and ceremonies.

Ritual, and forms of worship, even when they are elaborate, are not evil in themselves; many crave for them as satisfying some demand in their nature, and find their spiritual life enriched by them. Nor are they dangerous to the general worshipper as long as the spiritual life within the Church is intense, and the form is made the expression of the spirit. It is when the spiritual glow departs that their danger appears. For then the forms become ends in themselves; strict obedience to them becomes religion, and is coldly offered to God in lieu of spiritual worship. At such times forms and outward observances increase rather than diminish; they give opportunity for the self-righteous to display his zeal, while upon the hearts of the humble and the ignorant they impose burdens grievous to be borne. This altering of the focus, too, from the inner life to outward observance, lowers the moral sense; it throws open the door for the practice of grave abuses, and divorces religion from morality.

At such a time the priesthood degenerates; those who minister in holy things become worldly; the love of wealth, of ease, and of power—the three deadly sins of those who occupy this high vocation—appear; they give the sanction of an evil example to the worldly, and become the object of scorn to the sceptical and indifferent.

Of the fatal power of the form to crush out the spirit no more startling illustration is to be found in history than in the condition of Israel at the opening of the Christian era. On the return of the Israelites from the Captivity, the rulers of the people—their hearts chastened by their long exile—turned to the Law with passionate devotion, and sought by their obedience to its minutest precepts to honour the name of Jehovah. While this devotion remained, the spiritual life of Israel was maintained at a high level, but no sooner did it diminish than the minute observance of the Law became an intolerable bondage. Religion, emptied of its spiritual contents, became a worship of externals; and so bankrupt of spiritual discernment did the people become, that the arch-hypocrite became the popular ideal of the religious man. 'Woe unto you, Scribes and Pharisees, hypocrites,' said Christ, with withering scorn, 'for ye tithe mint, and anise, and cummin, and have left undone the weightier matters of the law, judgment, and mercy and faith. . . . Woe unto you, Scribes and Pharisees, hypocrites! for ye are like unto whited sepulchres, which outwardly appear beautiful, but inwardly are full of dead men's bones, and of all uncleanness. Even so ye also outwardly appear righteous unto men, but inwardly ye are full of hypocrisy and iniquity.'

Not only had they sunk thus low, but even when Christ appeared, and by His perfect life revealed what the religious life was, they did not recognise it as such, but put Him to death as an irreligious man.

This dispiritualising of religion, this worship of the

form rather than of the spirit, is a constant menace to the Church, and its presence will be found to have existed in each of the periods considered in the following pages.

The moment, however, the first breath of revival touches the heart of the Church, then instantly, as if awakening from a long stupor, men start up; they break the chains which bind them, and with a new-found joy return to simplicity of worship, and intense sincerity of life.

## VIII

## The Law of Variety

The cumulative effect of what has already been stated will, we trust, have convinced the reader of the fact that revivals, in their appearance, owe nothing to chance, but that they are a supreme witness to the spiritual governance of the world. They are used of God, we perceive, for the progress of the world, and for the quickening of man's life. They appear at certain intervals, and at definite crises in men's lives, and although these cannot be marked out with mathematical precision, we are able to discern a certain regularity in their appearance, and within certain limits, to anticipate their coming. Next we perceive that though much in these movements is mysterious and incalculable, there are sufficient data common to all for us to work upon, and from which to conclude that the laws which create and sustain them are as invariable as any of the other laws by which God operates in His universe. First of all we perceive that they come 'in the fulness of the times,' that is when preparation has been made for them, when the times are ripe, and when the heart of man is ready for them. Next their appearance is heralded by certain infallible signs; by a growing discontent in men's hearts at prevailing corruption or backsliding; by an intense craving in many for better things, and by a growing spirit of expectation in many that such changes are at hand. At last, when all the contributing streams which have been converging toward a definite point meet, in answer to an intense and imperious demand, there suddenly appears the prophet, the messenger who, with authentic voice, speaks for God, and whose accent men instantly recognise and obey.

No less striking in their similitude are the phenomena which appear when the revival movement is set in motion. Immediately the voice of the leader is heard, vast forces, which seem hitherto to have been lying dormant, are awakened; the revival spreads with wings of fire, and huge numbers of men, women, and children are affected by it. Wherever it moves, and into whatever heart it enters, it creates an overwhelming sense of sin, and with sin's forgiveness an intense joy, a joy which expresses itself in jubilant song, and often in strange outbursts of feeling. The chief effect, however, of the revival is felt in the sphere of the inner life. It awakens new spiritual emotions; it quickens the conscience; it brings thousands of lawless lives into subjection to the will of God, while it brings the Church back to simplicity, to sincerity, and to a quickened spiritual vitality.

Striking as are these points of identity, they must not be allowed to carry us too far. In other spheres each law is found to admit of variety in operation, and it is so in the spiritual realm which we are considering. This variety has distinct limits, but nevertheless it exists, and, as in all God's dealings with His creation, there enter the elements of the mysterious and unaccountable. No revival, for instance, is identical with any other in every particular. While each contains elements common to all, each contains characteristics also singular to itself. Each is adapted to the need of the times, and is modified first by the conditions of the age in which it appears, secondly by nationality, and thirdly by the individual characteristics of its leader. This outward variety, which in no way destroys the inner unity, is a necessity, we can easily perceive, for its success. Were all revivals to be moulded upon a cast-iron system, large masses of the people would remain unaffected. Variety, therefore, is a source of life.

Frequently it is found that a revival which affects one nation or people exerts but little influence upon another. Thus, though the preaching of Fox and Wesley affected great masses of the population of England, both had to confess that their influence upon the people of Scotland was unaccountably insignificant. Nor was this because of greater spiritual indifference, since both acknowledged that they found the spiritual life of Scotland intense and sincere. This same fact is borne out by the recent revival in Wales, which, though it spread with amazing swiftness over the Principality, seemed to be immediately arrested when it came into contact with another race, notwithstanding all the attempts made to promote it. Indeed, in many cases where the attempt was made to repeat elsewhere its characteristics, the attempt was not only attended by failure, but also by the stirring up of irritation and of strife.

A larger illustration of this same fact may be discovered in the history of the Reform movement of the sixteenth century. That movement, which so profoundly affected the Teutonic races, left the Latin races almost totally unaffected. Its geographical area was so pronounced that it remains still, and the chasm which it created is still that which separates the Roman from the Protestant community.

Another striking fact about revival movements is the variety in the character of their appeal. Sometimes that appeal moves in the realm of the affections, as in the revival under Francis of Assisi; sometimes its chief characteristic is theological, emerging in the discovery of some new truths, as with the Reformers; or again its chief centre is in the submission of the will, as in the movement under Wesley. Each revival, we see, has its own characteristic note, and each adapts itself to the clamant need of the age, and thus produces the most permanent results. The appeal of Calvin, for instance, would have been received with deaf ears by those whom the tears of Francis melted into joyous acceptance of Christ; but it does not follow that Calvin's influence was less deep or permanent in character because it worked less in the sphere of the emotions than in that of the conscience and intellect. Indeed emotional revivals are found to be of all revivals the most immediately effective and the least enduring. Each, however, wins its way because of its adaptation to the needs of the times, and to the temperament of the people, and what is effective for one cannot be made effective for all.

One other significant fact regarding this variety in revivals is that one pronounced movement in one direction is often followed by a movement in a contrary one. In religion, as in politics, there are two distinct camps, the one liberal in its outlook and aspirations, the other conservative. The watchword of the one is Freedom, that of the other is Authority. The one side is represented by Protestantism, the other by the Roman Catholic Church. The conflict between the two is constant, but each represents too deep a factor of human life to destroy the other. Thus, while the one is visited by a revival which carries everything before it, the very extreme to which it carries its demand for freedom provokes a counter movement which once more reverses the position.

A striking illustration of this is found in the counter-reformation of the sixteenth century. At first, when Luther sprang his thesis on the world, it seemed as if the whole Church were to be swept into a new channel, and as if the demand for freedom which was one of its main characteristics were to completely revolutionise it. The spread of the movement, however, was arrested, as we have seen, and kept within a distinct geographical area; then when the movement had run its course in the affected district, a counter-movement arose in that part which had remained unaffected, this movement being of a diametrically opposite character. For whatever we may think of Loyola, or however far the Jesuits may have wandered in the paths of intrigue in after days, there can be no doubt that they not only saved the Roman Church, but infused new life into it.

Or, if we care to come nearer home for an illustration of this same fact, we may find one of the most interesting character in the Oxford movement at the beginning of the nineteenth century. That movement was a conservative reaction brought about by the extremes to which the evangelical revival had been carried in the Church of England. For one of the direct consequences of the preaching of Wesley was to change the whole character of the life of the Church to which he had belonged, and which was so dead that it could not tolerate him. This was succeeded by an evangelical wave of the most pronounced type, which for a considerable period swept everything before it. When this had run its course the leaders of what is known as the 'Oxford Movement' arose. The movement was a revival of spiritual life which has left a deep mark upon the century, but it was also a return to 'authority,' a re-adjustment of the balance between two conflicting forces. Now this movement also, after a long and triumphant course, gives signs of decay, and of losing itself in externalism.

Striking, then, as are the points of identity in revivals, moving as they do to certain fixed laws, there are also, we can see, no less striking illustrations of variety. The same laws are in each, but as with all the laws of God, there is adaptation and re-adjustment.

We pass on now to consider another characteristic of all revival movements.

## IX

## The Law of Recoil

To every revival there is a time limit. It has its day, then it ceases to be. Luther set the limit to a revival at thirty years; Isaac Taylor at fifty years. Fitchett, in his *Wesley and his Century*, restricts it to a generation. 'Time,' he says, 'is a remorseless critic of religious movements. Its arresting force is visible in the spiritual realm. A great revival is usually linked to a single commanding figure . . . and the revival ends with the individual life; sometimes, indeed before it. It is a wave that spends itself within some little definite area of time. Barely does it outrun the span of a generation. A great revivalist, like a great statesman, easily becomes a spent force.'

This attempt to set a definite limit to the duration of revivals, however, breaks down in the very movement with which he is dealing, namely that of Wesley, and a superficial knowledge of the subject is sufficient to prove that any such attempt is extremely hazardous. In the respect of their duration hardly two revivals are alike. For that duration is determined by the initial impulse, by the intensity of the need, by the preparation made for them, by the nature of their appeal, and by the condition of the times. All these are variable, and, as a consequence, their character, extent, and duration are variable also.

That which is invariable, however, is, that large or small as the wave may be, it has its limits marked out for it, it spends its strength and then recedes.

The first reaction sets in when it receives its first temporary check. Then many, swept into its current by a yielding to emotion while their natures remained unchanged, cool down, are unable to withstand the recoil, and so are swept back into the world again. The Churches in Wales, for instance, are suffering from this recoil to-day. The number of those who have fallen away seems to be considerable, although, when full allowance has been made for these, a large majority is found to have remained constant, and the increase in the membership of the Churches is very large.

As to the percentage of those who, after the first wave of emotion, fall away, nothing final can be said. Revival movements differ in this particular also, though it may be said that in those revivals where emotion is most held in check, and where the appeal is made in a large degree to the conscience, the permanent effect, though not the immediate effect, is greatest.

Although the good effect of a revival runs on long after the surprise and emotion which it first awoke is spent, and although its spirit and message enter widely into the life of a people, there comes a time when this, too, seems to end, and when the movement falls into decay. The life goes out of it, or it becomes in itself not an influence for good, but for evil; instead of liberating it becomes an agent of oppression. Few things in life are more pathetic than the swiftness with which the good gets tarnished or corrupted. Take, for instance, the Franciscan movement. Never since the birth of Christianity has anything appeared on earth more pure or fair than that movement as first conceived by its originator, or practised by his early followers. Yet in a hundred years 'their poverty was converted into riches; their humility had become a tyranny; they forced themselves into houses and carried away the food they found there; since they gained the privilege of hearing confessions, they have built everywhere monasteries and princely palaces, while they will do nothing for the repair of a bridge, or a Parish Church.' So says Wycliffe, the Father of the Reformation in England, the great struggle of whose life was directed against the greed and rapacity of those very mendicant orders.

No less remarkable was the recoil which set in after the heroic days of Luther, its bitterness and rivalries, its war of sect and party. And even that noble doctrine, which was the watchword of its spiritual side, has not escaped this same law. 'Justification by faith,' says Froude, 'as originally proclaimed by Luther the deepest of moral truths, bandied about as a watchword of party, has by this time hardened into a formula, and has become barren as the soil of a trodden footpath.'

The same thing is true of the evangelicalism of the past century. In its early days its message was radiant with life, the words it used rang with meaning and conviction; gradually, however, as the life went out of it, its gracious words hardened into dogmas, imposed the dead burden of their beliefs upon men's hearts, and ended in narrowness and an embittered intolerance.

In all revival movements this law of recoil must be recognised, and wisely and prayerfully anticipated. A wider knowledge of such movements will prepare the

Church for this, and so its dangers will be minimised. For this inevitable recoil, we see, is a part of the law of progress. It is the ebb of the wave which falls back only to gain strength to push further on. When each revival has made its contribution to the wealth of human experience, it falls back to give place to something else. There is, therefore, no need to lament. No words ever written by Tennyson contain a truer or more healthy philosophy of life than those which he wrote over the decay of the Round Table :

> 'The old order changeth, yielding place to new,
> And God fulfils himself in many ways,
> Lest one good custom should corrupt the world.'

## X

## The Theology of Revivals

It is of supreme importance for us now to know what the great doctrines have been which have awakened men in all those different centuries to newness of life, which have brought back life to the Church, and filled the heart of the believer with radiant joy.

First of all we see that revivals in every case fall back upon simplicity. They cut through the accumulated doctrines and subtle complexities of the schools until they arrive at some living message, some aspect of truth which has become forgotten, or has been so overlaid by tradition as to become lifeless.

Every revival goes back more or less to apostolic times, to apostolic simplicity, to primitive conditions, and to the spirit of the early Church. It attempts to rid the Church and the individual soul of the heavy encumbrances imposed in a time of lifelessness and decay ; times when men are more intent in proving the doctrines of the Church than in living them. Its central effort thus is to get back to the fountain sources of inspiration and of life.

When we analyse those profound messages which have sprung from the lips of God's messengers in those great days of revival, we perceive one message which is never absent, one message which is at the heart of every such movement, and the vital fire of all its noblest emotion,—this is the message of the Cross. The reader may safely be challenged to name any revival which has taken place in the Christian Church of which this is not true.

In every case also in which the life of the Church has become feeble, and its witness ineffective, and its worldliness pronounced, it will be found that the message of the Cross has fallen into decay; it is either denied or lost sight of.

If this be true, and it is true, then its evidential value is of the most tremendous importance. It shows that whenever the heart of man is profoundly moved, it turns for satisfaction to the Cross of Christ, with the same instinct with which a child in need turns to its mother. Redeeming Love! this was the message underlying every pronouncement made by those who have led the great spiritual movements of the Church. Never once has there been a spiritual movement in which Christ has not been realised as the source of its life, and the subject of its joy. Every revival, therefore, is a return to Christ; it arises from a fresh recognition of His power to save the sinner awakened to a new consciousness of his sin, and to lead him into a new life of blessedness and peace with God. Even in those movements which have made for authority rather than freedom this is still true. The followers of the Oxford movement were not less evangelical although they emphasised the authority of the Church, and the High Churchman of to-day still retains much of the passion for the Cross with which the movement began.

This fact, which is so apparent in all historic revivals, is true also of those revivals which have lately broken out in China and Manchuria. 'Those who philosophise sceptically regarding the reality and efficacy of the Atonement,' says J. R. Mott, 'will find little to support their views in the fact that the refrain epitomising the central message of this revival, as sung by these men from the lowest classes socially, was this !—

"There is a fountain filled with Blood,
Drawn from Immanuel's veins;
And sinners plunged beneath that flood
Lose all their guilty stains."'

It is a significant fact also, and we point this out without disparagement of those who do not hold this doctrine, that neither Unitarianism, nor Deism, nor any other system which rejects the Cross, knows anything of revivals. Their ranks are recruited from those who become sceptical in the days of depression; they are never flooded with enthusiastic life, or charged with messages which move great masses of men, and bring them into the knowledge of things divine. The Spirit of God, when He breathes upon the Church, seems ever to take the things of Christ, and show them unto us.

With Christ, and the message of the Cross as its central fire, each revival also is characterised either by the revivifying of some doctrine coldly held, or by the discovery of some new aspect of divine truth, revealed in Scripture, but lost sight of.

The Reformation is the supreme example of the latter. Justification by faith is one of the clearest of Pauline doctrines, but it was a doctrine so utterly lost sight of that it had ceased to exist for the Christian Church. Ecclesiasticism so dominated men's minds that for centuries men had read Paul's Epistles without discovering that the words they read were diametrically opposed to the beliefs they held. And this is one of the most curious facts connected with the human mind —its power to see only that which corresponds with current opinion, and of failing to see, not by conscious rejection, but by a strange incapacity, all that opposes it. Every age is imprisoned in its own conceptions, and has to be set free by the master minds which refuse to be enslaved.

When Luther took up the Epistles of Paul, then, he brought to their perusal that rarest type of mind, which is able to survey truth as it is, and wholly apart from the current and conventional way of looking at it. Instantly he discovered this supreme Pauline doctrine which removed, as with a stroke, the vast and insufferable incubus which the Church had imposed upon the shoulders of men. Not only did it offer an escape from a load which had become insufferable, but it was the one doctrine which above all others accorded with the new spirit of the age, crying out, as it was, for freedom, and entering from every side into new realms of conquest. For the sixteenth century saw the beginning of the struggle of the individual to rid himself of the dominance of the community, and the doctrine of justification by faith, which offered all men unreserved access to God, represents the same effort from the spiritual side.

No sooner was this message proclaimed than it instantly met with acceptance. It was the supreme message for the age, and though it rent the Church in pieces, that rending was necessary before that higher unity, which is so increasingly dominant a note in modern thought, could be effected.

Of the other type of revival—which revivifies doctrines but coldly held—the Wesleyan revival is a supreme example. Wesley claimed that there was nothing in his teaching which was not already written in the articles of the Church of England; and that was true.

Only there is a vast difference in the way men hold the same doctrines, whether they are held as supreme or as of secondary importance, whether they are alive or dead. It makes all the difference, also, in the life of the Church, when prominence is given to the doctrines which are essential. The blighting characteristic of the Church in Wesley's day was that the doctrines most insisted upon were trivial, and those most essential for man's spiritual well-being were sneered at. With Wesley, however, all this was changed. The Church recovered its sense of proportion when it recovered its earnestness, and when there came from its pulpits those large and ennobling messages which make its power unequalled. The change was so great that it amounted to a new birth. And this is the supreme fact about revivals. They are conversions of the Church as well as of those masses who have drifted from it. And the Church is converted when it is brought back to Christ, when, casting out the world, it takes up again the Cross, and when, with the message of salvation burning in its heart, it goes out once again as its Master did 'to seek and to save them that are lost.'

## XI

## The Coming Revival

It may be permitted us to close this introduction with a glance into the future, and, with the help which those facts which we have stated gives, ask what the future has in store for us.

Before we can do this, however, we must first examine the present condition of the Church, and read, if possible, the signs of the times.

First of all, no one pretends that it is well with the Church to-day. When every allowance is made for exaggeration there is enough left to arouse deep searching of heart. On every side there is complaint of the Church's loss of spiritual power, of the increasing indifference of the people toward her services, and of a startling decrease of her membership. Where there is not decline there is at least a conscious arrest of her influence, and in the world a wide-spread hostility to her claims. It is not that the Church herself is inert. Never, perhaps, was there more activity, and less result. There is abundant energy, but it is not conquering energy conscious of its power, but feverish energy conscious of its impotence. Nor is it that the pulpit is asleep. Never was learning more wide-spread, and never has the pulpit reached a higher average of ability and culture. Nevertheless, the message of the pulpit has largely lost its power to convince, and the preacher his power to convert.

When we look beneath the surface we see much to account for this. We have been passing through an age of commercialism. Never in the history of the world have the hearts of men been set with such a passion of avarice upon material things, and this has deadened men's hearts, as it must always do, to the gospel of renunciation.

But this is not the sole reason. It is more than a fear that the Church herself has not escaped from its corrupting spirit; that the love of wealth, of ease, the palliation of commercial immorality, the pampering of the wealthy and the neglect of the poor, the judging of things according to material standards, have been allowed to creep in, and to devitalise her spiritual witness.

A new conscience, too, is arising, which is judging the Church by new standards of judgment. Men are growing increasingly conscious of a contradiction between Christ's attitude to the masses of the poor, to the lapsed and the social outcasts, and the attitude of many of those who profess and call themselves Christians. There is growing around us a burdened sense of social injustice, of mal-administration, and with this an indignation that in the presence of these things the Church has remained silent, smiling upon the well-to-do, and closing her places of worship in the poverty-stricken areas because unable to maintain ordinances.

Much of this accusation no doubt, is undeserved, and can be repudiated by individual congregations; but it is impossible to deny that of the general tone and conscience of the Church to-day, it is true. So true is it that many are making feverish efforts to rectify their attitude, though with a consciousness that they have not the awakened and passionate enthusiasm of the Church behind them.

Another reason for the present state of impotence which characterises the Church to-day, arises from the fact that we have been passing through an age of theological unrest, of the shifting of our foundations, and of prolonged theological conflict. It is an age of transition, and all transition periods are periods of suffering.

This unrest in the sphere of belief has arisen through the scientific revival which has characterised the second half of last century. Amazing, indeed, have been the results. Science 'has broken through the barrier of the skies; it has bound the lightning to its chariot, has wrested from nature a thousand secrets, and, with impatient curiosity, has forced every door of knowledge.'[1] In no department of human thought has its effect been more disturbing than in the realm of theology. The discovery of evolution challenged the whole Christian creed, and has demanded a reconstruction and re-editing of its most essential beliefs; while historic research, dealing both with the gospel narratives, and the prophetic and historical writings, has left nothing unexamined of that which was once considered too holy even to touch.

The result of these changes has been for many the unsettlement of belief, for many others the loss of faith, and for all a certain hesitation regarding even the most central doctrines. It has introduced into the pulpit, also, a certain conscious insincerity, as of men who were not quite sure of their ground. A disposition has grown up to leave many of the disputed doctrines alone, and fall back upon moral precepts, and the inculcation of good living.

The result is that much, if not all that is most distinctive and life-giving in the message of Christianity, has been lost; passion is simulated, earnestness is often directed toward useless things, and men in the pew, even though they do not consciously realise it, are yet unconsciously affected by the absence of the note of certainty and of intense conviction.

So pulpit and pew are united in a common misgiving; men find it easy in the midst of declining ideals to drift from the Church; their conscience is unaffected by their relapse, because there is little of that atmosphere of reality which makes in spiritual times the neglect of God's house an awful thing.

[1] *Sermons in Art*, p. 10.

If this be true, if it be even partly true, then it is a fact which should awake the dullest heart concerned about the progress of Christ's kingdom, the welfare of the world, and his own spiritual life. For a weakened Church means the strengthening of every influence which works for man's undoing, and no heart escapes its sorrow. It makes us turn, then, with intense earnestness, to the future to ask, 'What is before us? Is the day of the Church indeed over, as many would have us believe? Must we live on to see it declining until it passes away for ever?'

From such prophecies we can turn away with a smile. The Church of Christ is not on the eve of perishing. It is on the eve of revival. For sure as day cometh when the long night is ended, so revival comes after every such time of tribulation. Nothing in the world is more certain than this. The question is not, 'Will the Church be revived?' One may as well ask, 'Will the sun rise to-morrow?' The question for us is, 'When will the Church be revived? Is the dawn near? Is God even now commissioning His prophet, saying, as in the long ago, "Comfort ye! Comfort ye my people! Speak home to the heart of Jerusalem, and say unto her that her warfare is accomplished!" Or is the night but partly over? Have we still long to wait?'

On a question of this kind it would be impious to speak with authority, for it is not for us to know the times and the seasons which the Father hath hidden in His own hand. At the same time there is much to encourage us to hope.

(1) In the first place we have seen that great religious movements usually synchronise with some crisis of national development, or with some profound change coming over the social or political life of the people. The reason of this is not far to seek. It is that the heart

of every question which concerns man's well-being is essentially religious. 'The religious element,' said Mazzini, 'is universal, immortal. . . . Every great revolution has borne its stamp and revealed in it its origin or its aim. . . . The instinctive philosophy of the people is faith in God.' Were this not so, every great movement would be a menace to the progress of the world; but because this is so, then every great movement aims at reformation, and behind all reformation is God.

When, now, we turn to the present social and political conditions, it is not difficult to see that a great, silent revolution is taking place. Up from the depths there is emerging a multitude of the neglected, demanding recognition, justice, and human rights. A new cry is heard to-day, and the cry not only pierces into the Houses of Legislature, it echoes like a wail in our Temples and our Churches, and refuses to be drowned by our chants and solemn litanies; it is the cry of unrequited labour; of the underfed and overworked; of those who are awakening to a sense of bitter wrong, and of social discontent. Misdirected, incoherent, unintelligent this cry for social righteousness, for economical readjustment may be, but behind it is that dull sense of wrong, that sense of injustice which the teaching of Christianity itself has created and encouraged.

We seem, then, to be approaching a great crisis. New forces are arising; who is to guide them? A vast multitude around us is awakening to a new sense of their rights; to a recognition that they are not 'dumb, driven cattle,' but men and women, made in the image of God, and having a right to the tree of life. All such awakenings are full of menace if unattended by spiritual illumination, and allowed to grow in hostility to religion. Who their leaders are to-day, we know; but they are not, as a rule, of those who are found within the Churches, but of those who stand without, accusing the Church of betraying the spirit of its Founder.

Whether this is true or not we need not discuss, only this pathetic and humiliating fact of history has to be recalled—that nearly every great revival has originated outside the Church, and has awakened her active and embittered hostility. This may not happen to-day, but it shows that in times of degeneracy the spirit of Christ is often found in larger degree outside the Church than within ; and again, that when that spirit is freshly poured out, it is not the Church, but those without it who make the first response, and are most deeply affected by it. Only afterwards, and from without, the Church is awakened.

(2) Another fact, which has to be noted, is that in face of her growing responsibilities there is a consciousness in the Church to-day of helplessness to cope with them. The problem of distress, of social mal-administration, of social injustice ; the complexities of the issues, and the difficulties attending their solution are so great that the Church seems to sink under the weight of them. It does not seem to have occurred to the Church to-day, however, that her duty is not so much to find a solution as to give an inspiration. It is a flood of new spiritual life, a re-awakening within the Church of the glowing love of her Master, that is needed. When the heart is aglow, then the hardest problem becomes soluble ; love awakens and finds her own gracious channels ; it is only when the Church suffers from cold and chill that any problem which deals with human needs becomes insoluble.

The solution, then, is a revival of spiritual religion : a new breath which will pass over the valley of dry bones, and make them live. And with that coming of life, a Prophet, whose word shall be like fire, and like a hammer that breaketh the rock in pieces. For this revival the Church herself may not be ready, but the world is ready. For to the Church a revival means humiliation, a bitter knowledge of unworthiness, and an open and humiliating confession of sin on the part of her ministers and people. It is not the easy and glowing thing many think it to be, who imagine that it fills the empty pews, and re-instates the Church in power and authority. It comes to scorch before it heals; it comes to condemn ministers and people for their unfaithful witness, for their selfish living, for their neglect of the Cross, and to call them to daily renunciation, to an evangelical poverty, and to a deep and daily consecration.

This is why a revival has ever been unpopular with large numbers within the Church. Because it says nothing to them of power such as they have learned to love, or of ease, or of success; it accuses them of sin, it tells them that they are dead, it calls them to awake, to renounce the world, and to follow Christ.

Is the Church to-day ready to hear that voice? Is she bowed down before God in prostration of need? in conscious dejection of unworthiness? in passionate self-abasement and desire for that renewal which comes through renunciation? It may well be doubted. It is upon the hearts of the few that the agony falls. Revivals are not usually preceded by the awakening of the Church to a sense of need, but by the awakening of devout souls here and there, who, feeling the need, begin to entreat God in prayer for a revival. Gradually this deepens and spreads until the sense of need becomes a burden, until the cry, 'How long, O God! how long!' becomes an agony. This is the cry which God cannot deny. It is for that cry that we must intently listen.

For until the need becomes vehement the answer is not given. Not until the Kingdom of Heaven suffereth violence comes there the divine response.

How then can we hasten this ? No revival, we know, can come from below. All attempts to 'get up' a revival fail. Nor can we bring a revival down, since prayer is not so much the cause of a revival as the human preparation for one. Must we remain inert, therefore, waiting patiently until it is the will of God to revive His Church ? Surely not. Prayer illumines us to a sense of our own and the world's needs. By prayer we can prepare the soil, and so hasten the advent of the new day of grace. 'The surest sign of the approach of a season of revival,' says Canon Hay Aitken, 'is the disposition to pray for it, which, while it is itself the product of the divine influence, may be regarded as the human response to God's call, which is the condition of the further extension of that spiritual influence.'

Is there, then, to-day a disposition to pray for a revival? Are devout men everywhere becoming alarmed, not for the success of the Church, but for the glory of Christ, lest it be lost altogether ? Is there a sense of a burden lying upon men's hearts which will not give them rest, but which makes them agonise in prayer ? If not, then the night is not far spent, a deeper darkness still awaits us. For what use would a revival be if we are not prepared for it ? It would pass over us without doing its work.

Happily, however, there are signs that this burden is being laid upon the souls of men ; many are beginning passionately to long for better things, many to agonise in prayer ; and if we would seek to hasten the coming of that great day of the Lord, then we must seek with that 'shameless importunity,' which Christ commended, until the burden is laid upon us. To fail in this is to be a traitor to Christ, and to the deepest need of the world around us. To this we are called by every impulse we call Christian.

(3) Encouragement that the dawn is not far distant comes from another side. It has been pointed out that we have been passing through an age of criticism, when much that was accepted as truth has not been able to stand the test, and when apprehension has been aroused lest the very foundation of the faith be found to crumble.

Most careful onlookers are convinced that the worst has now been said, that the movement has spent itself, that the destructive era has ended, and the constructive era has begun. A great change has come over the leaders of science, and those who occupy to-day the front rank as leaders of thought, compared with what existed a few years ago. There is a new reverence for the things of the spiritual life, and thought has drifted far from the old agnostic position.

One of the most significant facts connected with this new constructive movement is its return to the orthodox position. It is not that nothing is changed. Much is changed, but it is beginning to be seen that nothing vital in Christian belief has been lost; that the old lives still in the new.

With this reaction against the negative attitude of past days, and the positive recognition of the reality of spiritual phenomena, it is possible to return to that sense of security of belief which makes a revival of religion possible. As long as belief was in a fluid state, and those responsible for a defence of the Church's faith were panic-stricken lest all should be lost, this was impossible. With the new confidence which is dawning in even timid hearts, however, there is arising also a longing for victory, and for a revived Church. This longing must surely grow, and it is in itself a prophecy and portent of better things.

(4) There is one remaining fact to be registered which is of immense encouragement to those who are depressed by the spiritual stagnation around us. It is the fact that it is only local. The wave that is ebbing here is flowing with majestic power elsewhere. Especially is this so in missionary work. Never was there such a wide outlook, or a more enthusiastic response. In China, in Japan, in Manchuria, in Korea, Christianity is making its way with marvellous swiftness. In the awakening of the East that has followed the uprise of Japan, there is taking place a spiritual awakening of immense importance. No one can tell what the future contains. Power may once more swing back to the East; a rejuvenated Asia may sooner than we imagine snatch the sceptre from the hands of an enfeebled Europe; and the centre of organised Christianity pass away from Rome to Pekin. The swift growth of Christianity in the East to-day is a heartening assurance that with the recovery of power there will be a discovery of faith.

But not only in the far East is Christianity 'marching on'; in America also the growth of the Christian Churches, and especially of the Evangelical Church, is remarkable. 'There never was a time, says an American writer in the *Times* of April 8, 1909, 'notwithstanding what pessimistic and unbelieving critics may say to the contrary, when the religious forces of the United States were more fully organised for religious and philanthropic work, or more devotedly or enthusiastically engaged in prosecuting it.' This statement is fully borne out by statistics. Since 1890 the increase of communicants in the various Protestant communities has been at the rate of sixty-six per cent., which is far beyond the increase of the population in the same period. Of this increase, it is significant, the Evangelical Churches claim fifty-five per cent.

In face of these facts, there is surely little justification of the despairing cry so often heard to-day, as if the Church of Christ were on the eve of perishing, and all hope regarding her further usefulness had to be abandoned. Far otherwise is it.

> 'For while the tired waves, vainly breaking,
> Seem here no painful inch to gain,
> Far back, through creeks and inlets making,
> Comes silent,—flooding in,—the main.
> And not by eastern windows only,
> When daylight comes, comes in the light;
> In front, the sun climbs slow,—how slowly!
> But westward,—look! the land is bright.'

(5) If now we may take it for granted that the signs of the times proclaim that a time of refreshing is near —and every devout Christian earnestly prays that this may be true—then what will its character be? No one can foretell; but there are certain things for which we may with confidence hope, and others we may regard with certainty.

First of all, to many who represent the best instincts of the times, no revival of religion would be worth the name which left the large masses without the Church to-day still alienated and unmoved. Whatever be the supreme message which will awaken the Church to fresh loyalties and fresh life, it must contain, it is felt, a message that will bring the masses of the people back to their heritage within the Church of Jesus Christ. It must contain, also, a message to the Church herself, which will bring her back to associate herself, in a closer and more intimate way, with the needs of the poor and down-trodden. Such a message will demand from her a sacrifice greater, perhaps, than any she has been called upon to make since Apostolic times. For it was not her pomp, her worldly power, her culture, or her education, which won for her her empire over the hearts of the poor and outcast in those early days, but her evangelical poverty, allied with her immense pity and love; and it is not to be supposed that by any other gifts than these can she ever win the masses to-day.

In the next place a revival of spiritual life could not fail to immensely quicken that movement toward union which accords with the best spirit of the age. Denominationalism is breaking down around us; the old controversies have ceased to awaken interest; the bitterness and sectarian animosities are now things of which men are ashamed. In face of the complexities of modern life the cry for union is persistently heard; it has taken place with happy results in the Mission field, it is taking place slowly in our Colonies, and in America. All that is needed is that quickening of the heart, that increase of love which a time of spiritual awakening gives, to cement those unions already formed, and bring together into mutual sympathy those parts still sundered.

Whatever form the coming awakening may take, we may be certain, at least, that it will bring us back to essentials, to concentration on the vital issues of the spiritual life, for every true revival does this. It cuts through all the trappings until it gets at the centre of life. It leads men back to glowing certainties, and to simplicity, for simplicity is one of the great characteristics of a revived spiritual life. When the heart earnestly seeks God, it goes to Him by the shortest route. Above all, it will bring us back to Christ, back to discipleship that will be something more than name, back to the Cross, and to bearing it.

The day may be near ; even now He may be preparing His messenger. ' But who may abide the day of His coming ? and who shall stand when He appeareth ? for He is like a refiner's fire, and like fuller's soap : And He shall sit as a refiner and purifier of silver : and He shall purify the sons of Levi, and purge them as gold and silver, that they may offer unto the Lord an offering in righteousness. Then shall the offering of Judah and Jerusalem be pleasant unto the Lord, as in the days of old, and as in former years. And I will come near to you to judgment : and I will be a swift witness against the sorcerers, and against the adulterers, and against false swearers, and against those that oppress the hireling in his wages, the widow, and the fatherless, and that turn aside the stranger from his right, and fear not me, saith the Lord of Hosts.'

' BUT UNTO YOU THAT FEAR MY NAME SHALL THE SUN OF RIGHTEOUSNESS ARISE WITH HEALING IN HIS WINGS.'

## THE REVIVAL

### UNDER

## FRANCIS OF ASSISI

No great man can be rightly understood outside of his own day and generation. To estimate his influence and character aright he must be set in the surroundings in which he did his work, and judged from the standpoint in which he lived. Something must be known of the impulse of the times, of the new hopes struggling for expression, of those changed needs which prepared the way for him, and which finally made him the architect of the age's fortunes, and the leader of its progress. For, while it is true that the great man is the leader of great movements, it is not true that he is the creator of them. His hand lifts the sluice to let the pent-up waters free, but through long years the waters have been slowly gathering, trickling in from many hidden streams, until at length, fretting and chafing, the hour and the man arrive. Thus it is ever in the fulness of time that the elect of God appears, when the world has been prepared for him, when eager hearts expect him, when anxious eyes scan the far horizon and wait for his appearing. And when at length he comes, those who have waited for the consolation spring to his side, he interprets for them their needs, he gives shape and life to those dim aspirations in them for which they cannot find expression, a new day dawns for humanity, and another step forward is taken in the toilsome march of the ages. It is with such a man that we deal, one who summed up in his own wonderful personality all the best emotions and pent-up aspirations of his times, who gave living embodiment to movements that had long been preparing, and who, in one of the darkest periods of the world's history, brought men back to the evangelical faith, and to a revived sense of the joy and power of a spiritual life. And if it be an ennobling thing to live, even for a little, in the companionship of the great and good, then no one can fail to breathe a purer atmosphere who dwells, if but for an hour, in the presence of St. Francis, who was one of the purest saints who ever trod this earth of ours, and who, perhaps, beyond all who have ever lived, best reflected the spirit, and walked in the footsteps, of his Master.

St. Francis was born in Assisi in the year 1182. The town of Assisi, which remains now much as it was then, is built on a hill, and overlooks that lovely vale of Umbria, whose still rivers, and whose silent glades, Pietro Perugino delighted to paint. To this distant century then, and to the hill of Assisi, it will be well to transport ourselves, in order that we may look around and see what is happening in the world.

### Europe in the Twelfth Century

The Europe which presents itself to our eyes as we view it from this year of grace, 1182, is hardly recognisable. On all sides there is unrest and insecurity, with war as the only serious occupation. To the North, Russia, which accepted Christianity at the mandate of a Czar in the eighth century, is engaged in her long struggle against the savage hordes of Mongols and Tartars, which sweep across her borders, ravage her cities and her plains, and by delaying her civilisation beyond the rest of Europe, is laying up for herself a heavy burden of future woes. The ancient Roman Empire, with its capital at Byzantium or Constantinople, is staggering under repeated attacks of Turks and Arabs from the East, and Bulgarians from the West, its long and somewhat inglorious resistance now nearing its end. To the West, the Moors, having crossed the narrow strait which divides fertile Europe from barren Africa, have swept over the sunny plains of Spain, and for centuries still are to maintain their sway. The Germanic tribes have seated on the throne the impressive figure of Frederic Barbarossa, that doer of doughty deeds, and ancient foe of papal absolutism; while England, too, is torn by unrest and civil war. For Henry II., having conquered Ireland, had made his way to France, but is hastily recalled to defend his kingdom against an invasion of the Scots, and a rebellion instigated by his wife, and headed by his three sons.

It is to Italy, however, we must turn, if we would realise the heaviest vicissitudes of fortune. The fall of the Empire, which Charlemagne had sought so strenuously to consolidate, menaced Europe with a return of barbarism. Its dismemberment, by destroying the central authority, opened its several parts to attack. One after another, the Normans, the Huns, the Wends, and the Czechs burst from their enclosures, and rushing over the plains of Europe, pillaged its cities, and devastated its civilisation. In these misfortunes Italy was the greatest sufferer. The fruitfulness of her soil, and the age and wealth of her cities, made her at once an object of envy and cupidity. So appalling was the ruin which followed these incursions that her population began seriously to decline; fear took possession of the hearts of the people; a settled gloom and apathy sank down upon them; in the anarchy which followed it seemed as if all the progress gained through toilsome centuries were to be lost, and Europe were to reel back into the jungle and the beast. It was during this period that the feudal system sprang up, and spread over Europe. For mutual protection the peasant population clustered around the castle of the baron, and became his vassals. Thus military centres were enormously increased, private wars were constant, all sense of patriotism disappeared in a condition of affairs in which the State had practically no existence. 'Each castle,' says Voltaire, with his usual pungency, 'became the capital of a small number of brigands, in the midst of desolate towns, and depopulated fields.'

At the close of the twelfth century, however, a change for the better was taking place; a higher sense of patriotism was slowly awakening, and although the State had not yet arrived, men were now gathered in cities with a higher sense of corporate life. These cities, however, were also military centres, strongly walled, and jealously guarded, each at enmity with the other. Thus Assisi, perched up on the hillside, watched with unfriendly eye Perugia in the distance, and her citizens, with the youthful Francis amongst them, were all too willing, at the first note of the bell, to rush out to avenge a wrong, or to inflict one.

Such, then, were the political conditions in Italy in those distant days, slowly recovering from her wounds, issuing out of the dark centuries, weakened and dismembered, but beginning to breathe with renewed hope, and with desire for better things.

### The Mediæval Church

It is time for us now to turn from surveying the political conditions to survey the state of the Church, and to inquire how Christianity is faring in these distant days.

Evil as were the political conditions throughout

Europe at this time, the state of the Church was even worse. The Church in the twelfth century was divided into East and West, and over the whole of Western Europe the Pope reigned with undisputed sway. The period with which we are dealing marks the very zenith of papal absolutism. Through the dark days of the Middle Ages that power had been stealthily and securely built up. Holding the minds and consciences of men fettered by superstitions ; possessing, as they declared, not only rights to the lordship of the present world, but almost absolute authority in the world to come ; threatening the disobedient by the terrible power of interdict, and menacing even the mightiest who dared to defy their authority, those popes of olden times exerted an influence over the human mind which has never been equalled perhaps since the world began. But a hundred years previous to the time with which we are dealing, Henry IV. of Germany, having dared to defy Pope Gregory the Great, was forced to stand as a penitent outside that haughty prelate's gate at Canossa, barefoot and almost naked, and in the dead of winter, humbly begging for forgiveness. It was at this very time, too, that our own Henry II. was seeking for mercy at the hands of Pope Alexander, owing to the murder of Becket, gaining absolution only after years of anxiety and self-abasement. To such dizzy heights of power had the papacy climbed.

Not less unqualified, within their appointed spheres, was the power of the priests. Separated from the rest of mankind by their vows, representing to the dull and uninformed minds of their worshippers the awful things of the unseen, claiming to possess power in virtue of their office to change the bread and wine into the actual body and blood of the Redeemer, holding in their keeping the rights of entrance to the kingdom of heaven, and threatening the disobedient with eternal woes in the world to come, these priests appeared to the people as little less than gods, in whose presence, when fulfilling their mysterious office, they could only tremble and adore.

Vast as was this power, it cannot be admitted that it was used in the spiritual interests of the people. It is too much to expect from human nature the possession of such unlimited power over human lives and consciences without that power being abused, and the priestly class has ever been the most human in this respect. In the days of terror the ecclesiastical power, wielded by spiritual men, stood as the only buttress between the weak and the savagery of the strong; but soon ecclesiastics, intoxicated by that very power, not only forgot to use it in defence of the down-trodden, but became themselves the incarnation of the worst form of tyranny the world has ever seen. The lust of power soon sapped the spiritual motive, leaving only the vast machinery to be used in a despotism which weakened the minds, as well as drugged the consciousness of men. The effect upon the papacy and priesthood was of the most appalling description; indeed, it is impossible to do more than hint at the depths of ignorance and depravity into which the priesthood sank. In the tenth and eleventh centuries there followed a succession of popes, the details of whose lives are a long catalogue of murder and the worst depravities. The 'Pornocracy,' or reign of Harlots, is the awful name by which part of this period is known in history. The vilest vices of Paganism reappeared, and infested the chambers of the highest official representatives of the Christian religion. Most of the popes of the tenth century, declared Mabillon, a fair-minded and scrupulous historian, 'lived rather like monsters, or like wild beasts, than like bishops.'

With this example before them of their superiors, it is not to be expected that the lower clergy showed a greater regard for the spiritual character of their office. Most of them lived in open profligacy, benefices were publicly sold to the highest bidder, bribery and corruption were shamefully practised, and the whole atmosphere of the Church was tainted and corrupt. Nor were the monasteries much better. While cities were depopulated by war, while poverty and wretchedness abounded in the homes of the people, the monks at their well-laden tables fared sumptuously every day. The monastic walls offered a safe retreat to the timid and devout, but they also offered a place of security to the easy and indulgent, and to a worse class still, to whom religious exercises offered no attraction, and who carried within the cloistered walls the worst vices of the world.

Meanwhile the hungry sheep looked up and were not fed. The people were sunk in superstition, were ignorant of even the rudiments of the Gospel, and both in mind and body were the serfs of their ecclesiastical superiors. Christ to them was a dim and mysterious Figure, bound upon the Cross, looking down upon them from an awful height, with eyes that held but little knowledge of their needs, or sympathy with their sorrows. He sat enthroned in their churches and basilicas, surrounded by angels, impassive, remote, unbending, and as the worshippers lifted their eyes to Him a solemn awe filled their minds, and terror their hearts. To reach that strangely impassive Being they had need of intermediaries to come between them and Him, and so they called in the help of His mother and the saints, who again could only be successfully invoked through the medium of the priests. Haunted thus by gloomy terrors, frightened and excited by sham miracles worked by the relics of the saints, crushed to the ground by the tyranny of their masters and by the rapacity of the clergy, their lives at the mercy of the one, their consciences at the mercy of the other, and their possessions at the mercy of both, they present a spectacle to the historian which might well move his heart to pity.

Evil as the condition of affairs was, we must not imagine that all was corrupt within the bosom of the Church. The leaven of righteousness was there, though it was working in secret. God is never left without a witness in even the most corrupt society, and the most convincing testimony to the divine life in the Church is, that it survived in such a time as this, that neither the corruptions within it, nor the prevailing worldliness without it, could accomplish its destruction or decay. Although the forces of evil seemed to hold the field, there were doubtless many whose names are unknown to history, who were waiting for the consolation of Israel, who in humble homes and quiet retreats were praying for a revived Church, for some spiritual awakening which would cleanse it from its worldliness as Christ had cleansed the Temple of Jerusalem. 'When things are at their worst they begin to mend,' is an axiom well authenticated by the historian, and evil can only work within certain prescribed boundaries. Iniquity never holds entire possession of the field. When it has reached its limits, there arises in the heart of men a revolt. There comes over the human heart a sickness of sin, a nausea of evil; unsatisfied and empty, men turn from seeking after vanities to seek the living God; they turn from the empty cisterns which can hold no water to the deep wells of divine mercy. A spirit of restlessness and profound dissatisfaction is discoverable at such a time; men grope for the light as the blind sea wave gropes for an opening along the long sea wall, and, finding it, the whole tide of human hope and longing bursts tumultuously in. This is what happened at the beginning of the thirteenth century. The darkness was of the hour which precedes the dawn. Men were not sunk in heavy slumber, but were beginning to toss and moan as when sleep is ending. The world was waking to new hopes; a spirit of expectation was abroad; the very excesses of the times were the outcome, not so much of an inner depravity, as of a craving for something to still the restlessness of the heart. Throughout Italy and in Europe strange sects were springing up, which, however lawless or however erroneous, still aimed at bringing back to the life of the Church something of its primitive simplicity and evangelical fervour. Within the Church itself a new spirit was awakening; the leaven of righteousness was appearing, and the rulers of the Church set themselves to cleanse it from its most intolerable abuses. The movement, though wide-spread, was still vague; a leader was needed, some great personality to sum up in himself the vital needs of the hour, to give them visibility to others, to lead men back to Christ, to evangelical Christianity, to the simplicity and beauty of the Gospel. The times were ripe, the hour had come, the world waited for the Man. It did not wait in vain.

### The Youthful Francis

The story of Francis's early days, as related in his various biographies, is full of interest and charm. It does not come within the scope of the present work, however, to do more than trace the leading events which brought him to that momentous decision to forsake all for Christ, and those characteristics of the revival which he initiated which proved one of the most remarkable movements in history.

Of his parents, little of value is known. His father, who was a merchant, a dealer in cloth, and of considerable means, does not appear as an attractive personality. He travelled widely in pursuit of business, as was customary in those days, and was absent in France when Francis was born. Merchants of his class occupied a considerable social position, and were regarded as a second nobility; their travelling brought them into contact with many types of men, and they were welcomed as the purveyors of news at a time when there was little inter-communication. Though intensely proud of his son, and willing to humour him as long as he did him credit, Pietro, the father, appears in the light of a man somewhat vain and miserly. Nor of Pica, the mother, do we know much that helps us in the elucidation of Francis's strange personality, except that she firmly believed that her son was destined to be a great man, and to do great things in the world, a conviction shared by most mothers who have but an only son.

From earliest youth, Francis showed a disposition to enjoy life to the full. Having plenty of money at his disposal he soon collected around him a band of youths as pleasure-loving as himself, and together they made the town of Assisi ring with their merry-makings and youthful escapades. Dressed always in the gayest attire, Francis attracted notice wherever he went, by his lordly manners, and irrepressible gaiety. 'He is like the son of a prince, not like our son,' Pietro and his wife said to each other, the father basking in the reflected glory, the mother's heart swelling in pride at the honour her son received. Even when the more malicious neighbours related to her the wild exploits of her son, and the excesses of both Francis and his companions, she was in no way discouraged in her belief. 'What are you thinking about ?' she is reported as saying; 'I am very sure, if it please God, he will become a good Christian.' The conduct of her son at this time gave little indication of the fulfilment of this pious prediction. Gay, impressionable, debonair, he seemed to be without a serious thought, and to be given wholly over to pleasure and frivolity. Yet, even in these early days, the biographer is able to detect a certain whimsical sense of life's contrasts springing up in him, as when he had his fine clothes lined with the coarsest fabric. Something unaccountable, which separated him from others, which gave to his conversation and habits the element of the unexpected, seems always to have been present in him. It is related of him, for instance, that standing on the piazza, attending to his father's customers—for this was his early employment—a beggar besought him for alms. Too busy to attend to his needs, Francis sharply ordered him to depart, but, soon reproaching himself, he ran after him, and gave him lavish help. 'I am no better than a clown,' he said. 'Had the man been a prince or baron, how obsequiously would I have assisted him.' He then made a solemn vow that from that day forth he would never refuse alms to any one who should ask for it in the name of God.

About this time one of the many contests for supremacy, which took place between Perugia and Assisi, was being waged. Francis, now in his twentieth year, eagerly joined the other combatants, and marched out of Assisi like a young knight, clad in the gayest garments. His side, however, was defeated, and he himself, with others of the leaders, was captured and thrown into prison. Here, though their captivity lasted for a year, his gaiety of spirits never failed him. So unquenchable was his cheerfulness that his companions accused him of indifference to their misfortunes. 'What do you say?' Francis is reported to have replied; 'you will see that one day I shall be adored by the whole world.' At length he and his fellow-prisoners were released, and, returning to Assisi, he was welcomed back with great joy by his companions, and was soon plunged into the gaiety of his old life. So zealously did he pursue the paths of pleasure that he fell ill, and for weeks lay hovering between life and death. And now, the tide which ran so madly in pursuit of earthly pleasure is arrested, and begins to flow hesitatingly at first, and with painful effort, in a new direction. This sickness seems to have brought to Francis painful reflections on the character of his own life, and a certain world-weariness, not uncommon to those of ardent temperament. On one of the early days of his convalescence he ventured as far as the Porta Nuova. Here, stretching away beneath, is the lovely vale of Umbria with its vines and olives—a scene of incomparable beauty—and Francis, as he toilsomely made his way, hoped, no doubt, to revive the delightful sensations of other days. But, as he sat and looked abroad upon Nature, no helpful balm came to heal him; instead, a great darkness rose up within—he felt that life was wretchedly empty, his heart was sick within; and so he staggered back to his couch again, weak and ill, tormented by an anguish he could not explain, and the origin of which he did not understand. The impression which this made upon his mind was not definitely religious; he heard no voice of God speak within the silent chamber of the soul, but the effect was to make his past life impossible. A deep self-disdain, a restlessness and great unhappiness of mind, a deepened sense of the seriousness of life, a craving for some inner satisfaction which he could not name, these seem to be the feelings uppermost in the mind of Francis at this time, now five-and-twenty years of age.

On his recovery, his friends once more enticed him to return to his old life, and seeking to get rid of the oppression and restlessness of spirit which were hanging over him, he once more plunged into his old excesses. Hearing of a war being carried on in South Italy by Walter of Brienne—'a certain count of great magnificence and liberality'—the ardour of Francis was immediately kindled. He determined to join him, and this project seemed to bring back to him something of his old gaiety and assurance. He went about making the most elaborate preparations, publicly boasting that he would return a great prince. He was absent from Assisi only for a single night, and he returned bereft of his gay armour and flashing sword. What happened is not known; by some it is suggested that with his wonted liberality he gave his gay attire away, by others that his enemies took the first opportunity to avenge themselves upon him for his boastfulness, and so, despoiling him of all that he had, left him to return in disgrace. As a result of this disappointment sickness once more closed down upon him; he took long and solitary walks in the country, but he could not rid himself of the dispeace within. Again his old companions surrounded him, trying to entice him into a midnight revel. Seeing his dolorous looks, one of them inquired if he were about to take a wife. 'Yes,' answered he, 'I am thinking of taking a wife more beautiful, more rich, more pure than you could ever imagine.' This marks a crisis in his life. The tide now turns, leaving the old course for ever. From this time a new and deeper life begins.

### The Changed Life

For some time longer Francis remained in darkness and anguish of soul. Finding no joy in anything, he wandered about the fields by himself, often spending hours by wayside shrines, beseeching God, with tears and supplications, to remove the darkness from his mind, and the anguish from his heart. A story told of him at this time reveals the startling change that had taken place in the life of this once gay youth. Walking along the road one day he met a leper—of whom, unhappily, there were numbers then in Italy. At first he shrank from him in horror of contact, and hurried past; but a voice seemed to arrest him, commanding him to go back. In obedience he returned, and kissed the leper, all loathsome with his sores, giving him all the money he possessed. This act shows the extraordinary tension of his mind, the breaking down within him of self-will, his willingness to obey, at whatever cost, the promptings of the Spirit. Care of the leper became afterwards one of the chief concerns of the Franciscan Order.

This strange experience of pain and uncertainty could not last for ever. Light was bound to come at last, but in Francis's case it was long delayed. His entrance into the kingdom was with bitter and long travail of heart, but it was so complete that it left little afterwards to struggle for. So light came at last; light which, after the prolonged darkness, seemed to Francis blinding and terrible in its intensity. In one of the wayside chapels—dedicated to St. Damian—where Francis spent many hours in prayer, he was kneeling one day in profound agony of heart. 'Great and glorious God,' he cried, 'and Thou, Lord Jesus, I pray ye shed abroad your light in the darkness of my mind.'

As he looked up, he seemed to see the eyes of Christ fixed upon him in tender love. Immediately his spirit leaped to embrace the Saviour. From that hour his heart was transfixed by the love of Christ.

The first resolve of Francis, after this radiant experience, was the practical one of restoring the little chapel where peace had been bestowed upon him. The churches and chapels of Italy at that time were many of them in woful disrepair, and that of St. Damian was almost falling to pieces. This church restoration became another care of the Order of St. Francis; it marks how an increased sense of the value of spiritual benefits naturally expresses itself in the desire to make God's House worthy of His worship.

A new set of trials now began for Francis. His friends, finding him no longer of their way of thinking, denounced him as mad; but the most embittered of all was his own father. As long as his son spent his time rioting and feasting with the young nobility of the town Bernardone was satisfied. It gratified his vanity and ambition to see his son the leader of such company, even if the cost gave him many twinges. But when he found his son spending his money upon the poor, and in renovating God's sanctuaries, his wrath knew no bounds. Finding his floggings, his threats, his entreaties unavailing, Bernardone at length disinherited him, and appealed to the civil magistrates to have him punished for appropriating his goods. But Francis, renouncing all his possessions, putting his money and his clothes upon the ground, thus made, before a huge crowd gathered in the market-place, his public confession :

'Listen, all of you, and understand it well : Until this time I have called Peter Bernardone my father; but now I wish to obey God. I return him the money about which he is so anxious, and my garments, and all that he has ever given me.

From this moment I will say nothing but "Our Father in Heaven."'

Taking an old cloak, which the Bishop's gardener had given him, he turned his back upon his father's home, never to return. The effect of this action, so dramatic and unexpected, was enormous. Some said that he was mad, but others, wondering, held their peace, remembering, perhaps, that there is a higher wisdom which is always madness to the complacent and the worldly.

Leaving Assisi, Francis returned to St. Damian, and continued the repairing of the ruined sanctuary. Having no money, he begged bread from door to door. Thus another link in the chain was forged. Francis became wedded to 'my lady Poverty,' and no lover was ever more faithful to his bride than he.

In the spring of the year 1208—Francis was now twenty-six—having finished the repairing of St. Damian, he resolved to continue his work amongst the other ruined sanctuaries around Assisi, and so turned his attention next to what was to become the birthplace of the Franciscan Order—the Portiuncula—the Church of St. Mary of the Angels. This church still stands, and is one of the sacred churches of Christendom.

One day—it was the 24th of February 1209, the festival of St. Matthias—Francis was kneeling in prayer before the altar; still with head bent, he remained listening to the words of Scripture, when suddenly he felt himself seized and overpowered with a profound emotion. The Gospel for the day was the Tenth Chapter of St. Matthew, and as the words were spoken, 'As ye go, preach, saying, The kingdom of heaven is at hand. Heal the sick, raise the dead, cleanse the lepers, cast out devils: freely ye have received, freely give. Get you no gold, nor silver, nor brass in your purses;

no wallet for your journey, neither two coats, nor shoes, nor staff: for the labourer is worthy of his food.' These words burst upon Francis as if spoken in his ear by God Himself. Immediately his spirit leaped forth to embrace them in all their entirety of sacrifice. 'This is what I want, what I have been waiting for; this shall be from henceforth my daily, hourly practice.' Immediately throwing aside everything he possessed, he went forth, leaping for joy, and shouting and praising God. To him the apostolic call had come. Amongst the millions who had listened to these words with deaf ears, here was one who heard and obeyed, whose heart leaped forth to embrace them as though they were priceless pearls, whose whole nature they irradiated as though with heavenly light. Like Matthew, whom Jesus called, this other disciple rose up, left all, and followed Him.

Here, then, we have been tracing the making of a messenger of God. Out of the midst of the world He called this gayest and most worldly life, and at last, after long agony and tears, the soul had separated itself from its sinful past, had bent itself to the divine will, and by self-abnegation and implicit obedience, had made itself a worthy instrument to be used of God for the salvation of men, and for the purifying of the world.

### The Founding of the Order

It was characteristic of Francis that he should allow of no delay when once a clear certainty of the call reached him. The very next day he was in Assisi preaching in the streets, accepting, without a moment's hesitation, the hardest task that could have been set him. And a strange portent, indeed, he appeared, for on that day a new era was ushered in. No longer was the Gospel of Jesus Christ to be imprisoned within stone walls. From that day the Reformation began, a reformation wider than that even which Francis longed to see, a reformation which was to give back to men the open Bible, and to free them from every vestige of ecclesiastical tyranny. The sermons which Francis preached were simple and direct. He spoke to his listeners of the need of repentance, of the joy of obedience to the will of God, of the shortness of human life, and the certainty of judgment to come; but behind the words was the personality of the speaker, of one whose heart was flaming with love to God, who had relinquished every earthly ambition to gain it, who was passionately convinced of a divine mission to his hearers, and whose one consuming ambition was to awake in men's hearts the joy and rapture which burned in his own. 'His words were like fire, piercing the heart,' says one who heard him—Thomas of Celano, who also gives us a sketch of his personal appearance. 'He was of middle stature,' he says, 'rather under than over, with an oval face, and full but low forehead; his eyes dark and clear, his hair thick, his eyebrows straight; a straight and delicate nose, a voice soft, yet keen and fiery; close, equal, and white teeth; lips modest yet subtle; a black beard not thickly grown; a thin neck, square shoulders, short arms, thin hands with long fingers, small feet, delicate skin, and little flesh; roughly clothed, sleeping little; his hand ever open to charity.' Such was the appearance of the man who startled the inhabitants of Assisi by the tenderness and the passion of his appeal to them to forsake evil, and seek the love of Jesus Christ. At this time, too, he was clad in a brown woollen gown, bound with a rope, his head uncovered, and this, with wide sleeves and a large hood, which Francis afterwards chose, became the habit of the Order.

It was not long before men began to feel the strange fascination of his character. They could not fail to see the intense joy of heart which was his ; instead of depression on account of his poverty and privations, they beheld one whose being seemed to thrill with an intense and unaccountable gladness. Even the most indifferent, too, felt moved by his intense sincerity, by the thrill of love and pity in his voice. From being laughed at as a madman, Francis began to be talked about with wonder and awe. There was something about him unaccountable, something which did not belong to their world or to the region of their daily thoughts, yet something which they could not but feel was inexpressibly beautiful, something which their hearts longed for, even though they refused to seek it.

Soon, attracted by his personality, disciples began to gather around him. The first of any importance was Bernardo di Quintavalle—'one of the most noble, rich, and learned of the city.' Bernardo had watched Francis carefully, and had concluded that such sacrifice as he exhibited could only spring from a heart captured by the love of God. He earnestly desired to follow him, but before finally deciding, he resolved to put Francis to the test. Inviting him to his house to spend the night he lay down in the chamber in which Francis also lay, pretending to be asleep. When he saw Francis, however, arise and spend most of the night in prayers, constantly repeating the words as if in a holy transport, 'My God! My God!' his last doubts disappeared. In the morning he intimated to Francis his determination to distribute all his possessions, and to become one with him. Together, then, they went out into the streets, Bernardo carrying with him all his wealth; nor did they cease distributing it to the poor until nothing was left. This public act of renunciation produced the most extraordinary impression upon the inhabitants of Assisi, and deepened the awe with which Francis was now being regarded by the common people. Amongst the others who were in these early days attracted to him, the most famous were Brother Egidio, a 'carissimo fratello,' as Francis declared when he saw him, to whom God had given 'much grace'; Brother Ruffino, a richly-endowed and contemplative nature, belonging to one of the noblest families of Assisi; Brother Ginepro, who could not keep his own tunic when any one asked him for it, and, most loved of all, Brother Leo, the 'pecorello,' the little sheep of Francis's tender care, who followed him everywhere, and loved him with the purest devotion.

When the followers of Francis had reached the number of seven, recalling the action of the Lord, he sent them out, two by two, telling them to preach the Gospel in every place. 'Go,' said our sweet father to his children, 'proclaim peace to men; preach repentance for the remission of sins. Be patient in tribulation, watchful in prayer, strong in labour, moderate in speech, grave in conversation, thankful for benefits.' The reception these early missioners met with was varied. Some thought them madmen; women and children fled from them at the sight of their strange dress; in some places they were received with kindest welcome; but everywhere they aroused the public mind, whetted curiosity, and evoked discussion. Their intense seriousness, their freedom from every worldly ambition, their gaiety of heart amid the most trying experiences, the strange unworldliness of their whole life and discipline, were things so new that men did not know what to make of them; they could hardly believe such things to be possible, and yet they could not detect the slightest evidence of fraud.

Small as their numbers were at this time, they were

buoyed up by the most sanguine hopes. Francis, in the midst of his devotions, began to have dim, prophetic visions of future greatness. Spending whole days and nights in prayer, with that clarified vision which enables the intensely spiritual to project themselves into the future, and forecast events, Francis saw the movement begun at Portiuncula widen into a great world movement. 'Be comforted, Carissimi,' he said, 'and rejoice in God, and let us not be sad because we are few; for it has been shown to me by God that you shall increase to a great multitude, and shall go on increasing to the end of the world. I see a multitude of men coming from every quarter—French, Spaniards, Germans, and English, each in their different tongues, encouraging the others.'

## The Rule

So far the little company had lived together without any definite rule to guide them; their hearts had been captured by lofty ideals; they had renounced all to follow Christ, and they were held together by intense love to their great leader; but as their little community grew, it became evident to Francis that something more was required than this free and unattached life, that some rule was required for their future guidance, which would enshrine the longings which burned in their hearts. The name which he selected was characteristic of him. He did not choose that they should be called Franciscans, as now is the case, but 'Frati Minores,' Brothers Minor, or, as Francis meant the title to express—the Least of all Saints. The rule itself covered the three great monastic vows of poverty, chastity, and obedience, but the poverty was to be real, not feigned. They were not to be mere mendicants, though, arriving at some town or village, and breaking to the people the Bread of Life, they were not to be ashamed to beg for their immediate necessities; at all times, however, they were to be ready to repay in actual labour. No provision for these necessities was to be made; they were to go out as Christ enjoined His disciples, 'without gold or silver,' without even the scrip to collect the fragments in. No wonder that many, like the Bishop of Assisi, stumbled as they heard of such a rule. 'Your life, without a single possession in the world, seems to me most terrible,' said the Bishop. 'My lord,' answered Francis, 'had we possessions of any kind, arms and force would be necessary for our protection,' a reply too obviously true to be gainsaid. Unlike other monastic orders, they were to be confined in no monastic walls, but were to go out into all the world. And their object in going was to preach, to win men to repentance, to capture human hearts for Jesus Christ. For this they were to sacrifice all things earthly which men set prize by; for this they were to be homeless, and hungry, the vagrants of the earth, if so be that they might gain the world for Him who died for it. 'Because they possessed nothing earthly,' says Bonaventura, 'loved nothing earthly, they were secure in all places; troubled by no fears, distracted by no cares, they lived without trouble of mind, waiting, without solicitude, for the coming day, or the night's lodgings.' Nor did this renunciation produce in them depression of spirits, or rob them of joy; on the contrary none were so gay as the little band from whom no man could steal, for they had nothing of which they could be dispossessed. Having nothing, they yet possessed all things; radiant gladness was in their hearts; they went along the road singing their songs in sheer happiness, unable to keep silence. Although attached to the Church, Francis laid down no rules for the observance of canonical hours; if that were possible they were to hear Mass once a day, as the Church of Rome enjoins, but the elaborate services of the Church made no appeal to the mind of Francis. Nor did he enjoin that certain hours of the day should be specially set apart for prayer, or that his followers should engage in any elaborate ritual. Being asked to prescribe a form of prayer, he replied by advising them to repeat the Pater Noster, and added this simple prayer: 'We adore Thee, O Christ, in all Thy Churches which are in all the world, and we bless Thee because by Thy holy Cross Thou hast redeemed the world.'

The rule having been made out, Francis and his companions, now numbering twelve, set out for Rome to gain for it the sanction of the Pope. Many accounts are given of the famous interview which followed, when this great, yet humblest follower of Christ stood before him who claimed to be Christ's earthly representative. It has been represented in art by Giotto, and it stands as one of the most interesting events in ecclesiastical history. Fortunately for the world, Pope Innocent granted them an Order. 'Go, in the name of the Lord,' said he, 'and in His strength preach repentance to all. And when God has multiplied you in numbers and grace, come back to me, and I will grant you greater gifts, and commit to you better privileges.'

With great joy the little band left his presence, and returning home, filled the way with their songs, Francis, as ever, the most gay and jubilant of them all. From this time forward he is to be regarded no longer in his individual character, but as the leader and inspirer of a great movement which is to assume world-wide dimensions, to draw within its community a great multitude of men, and to bring to their hearts the glad message of Christ's Gospel, and the joy of salvation.

### Growth of the Order

The fame of Francis and his strange Order began now to spread throughout Italy, arousing curiosity in some, suspicion in others, but also in the hearts of many an earnest hope. Penitents began to stream in from every quarter to Portiuncula, which had now become the headquarters of the movement. Only four years had passed since Francis had left his father's house, renouncing the world, and already crowds were seeking him, and finding in his words the fulfilment of their hearts' desires. It was at this time that he was visited by Clara Sciffi, a daughter of one of the noblest houses of Assisi, known to fame as Santa Clara, who, taking up her residence at St. Damian, founded the Order of the Clarisses, or Poor Clares. A character of rare sweetness and unsullied purity, she appears in the history of the movement like some angelic figure; in the rare moments when they meet, she strengthens Francis with her wisdom and sympathy, and while others are shaken, remains true till death to the inner spirit of the movement.

Sent out as before, two by two, the brothers returned with great joy, relating their experiences, holding fast their profession, and regarding their leader with profoundest affection. Nor through all the subsequent years could any change be detected in him. He remained through all the success of his Order the same simple, humble, loving soul, thinking nothing of himself, rejoicing in tribulation, counting himself the least of all saints, ever seeking to the last some more effectual way of serving his master Christ. 'Sweetest Lord,' he would cry, 'I would love Thee! Lord, my God, I give to Thee all my heart and body, and vehemently desire, if I might know how, to do more for Thy love.'

Though ever the first in service, the first to rise, the last to rest, he fervently desired to begin to serve God. 'My brethren,' he would say, 'let us now begin to serve God. Up to this time we have done nothing.'

Fired by a burning enthusiasm to carry the message of the Gospel to the heathen, Francis set out on a series of missionary journeys. At different times he traversed Italy, extending his journeys to Egypt, where he actually preached before the Sultan, and to Spain, intending to preach the Gospel to the Moors. This purpose, however, he was unable to accomplish through enfeebled health, and so with great reluctance he returned to Portiuncula. Hither at Pentecost all the brethren gathered who had been scattered abroad, and as the years passed, the numbers swelled until they were assembled in thousands. They gathered together, not to talk on secular matters, but for mutual encouragement, to relate to each other their joys, and the sufferings they had borne. It was as if a large family had gathered its members from all the parts whither they had been scattered, so much pure gladness of heart was there, so much inward rejoicing, so little envy. In and out amongst them Francis walked, speaking words of loving counsel, and of cheerful encouragement, the gentlest and humblest of them all, the most loving, and the best loved. To these meetings there gathered, in vast numbers, the inhabitants of the districts round about, pilgrims from all parts, and even the nobles of the land, and high-placed cardinals of the Church. The whole heart of Italy began to be stirred with a new enthusiasm for spiritual things, with an awakened, spiritual life. And with this awakening there came a new joy, a spirit of expectation, a longing for better things. Multitudes, who, because of their domestic ties, their age, or because of the dependence of others upon them, could not join the brotherhood, yet longed to be enrolled amongst its members, or at least to have some part in its organisation. So profoundly moving, too, was the preaching of Francis that, sometimes, the whole audience rose, carried away by emotion, ready to follow the rule and forsake their homes and duties. But Francis was too wise to permit of such extravagances. 'Remain in your homes,' he said, 'and I shall find you a way of serving God.' So there came into being what is known as the third order, the object of which was to help to a holier life those who were compelled to live in the world, who had others dependent on them, and yet who were eager to live for God, and to obey His will. All were admitted to this third order who were willing to keep God's commandments, and who were prepared, if they had done a wrong, to make full restitution. Multitudes hastened to obey. Into that age of lawlessness, when might was right, when every man's hand was against his neighbours, there arose a new enthusiasm. Cruelty and selfishness were held in check by this new enthusiasm after God, and this new obligation of restitution to the weak and the wronged. Thus another step was taken which brought the movement within the scope of the common people, and which made the poorest feel that he had a place in it.

So vast a movement could not exist without entailing upon its founder heavy burdens, burdens too heavy for Francis's overwrought frame. So unworldly a passion, too, could not long continue without being abused, and even in Francis's life-time the strictness of the Order was found by many too heavy to bear. In 1223 the rules of the Order were confirmed by Pope Honorius III., and Francis was made the first general, but his work on earth was done, and in the following year he died. He met his sufferings with that cheerful acceptance which makes his life so wonderful, and his sufferings were great. 'He began to suffer from so many infirmities,' says Bonaventura, 'that there was scarcely one of his members but was tormented by increased pain and suffering. At last, by reason of these various heavy and continual sufferings, his flesh was consumed, and there remained nothing more but the skin attached to the bones.' But these sufferings of his Francis called 'his sisters,' and even in the midst of the bitterest pangs bravely jested with those around him. One day, we are told, a 'certain simple brother,' seeing the agony he was enduring, cried out to Francis, 'Brother, pray to God that He would deal more gently with thee, for His hand, methinks, is more heavy upon thee than is meet.' 'If I did not know thy purity and simplicity,' answered Francis, 'I should from henceforth abhor thy company, because thou hast dared to blame the divine judgments which are executed upon me,' and then rising from his couch in a transport of love and joy, he knelt, kissing the ground, and crying, 'I thank Thee, O Lord my God, for these my sufferings, and I beseech Thee to add to them an hundredfold; for this shall be most acceptable to me that Thou spare not to afflict me, for the fulfilment of Thy holy will is to me an overflowing consolation.'

The last days of Francis are inexpressibly beautiful. He met death, as he met all other things, with a song. 'He went to meet death singing,' says Thomas of Celano.

'Be praised, Lord, for our Sister the Death of the body,
whom no man may escape;
Alas for them who die in a state of mortal sin;
Happy they are who conform to Thy most holy will,
For the second death will harm them not.'

This other verse did he add to the song he was always

singing—the Canticle of the Sun—which he had himself composed. Gathering the brethren then at Portiuncula around him, he gave them his last message and benediction : 'Adieu, my children,' he said ; 'remain, all of you, in the fear of God, abide always united to Christ ; great trials are in store for you, and tribulation draws nigh. Happy are they who persevere as they have begun ; for there will be scandals and divisions among you. As for me, I am going to the Lord and my God. Yes, I have the assurance that I am going to Him whom I have served.' At eventide on Saturday, October 3, 1225, amid the silence of the dying day, in peace with all the world, humble and patient to the end, he breathed his last sigh. Even as he did so an innumerable company of larks alighted on the thatch of his cell, and as his pure soul winged its way to God, sang their song of jubilation. Nothing could have been more fit, nothing would have delighted his heart more ; the requiem, which he would himself have coveted most, was sung by his 'little sisters, the birds.' So passed away from this earth one of the purest souls that ever lived.

### Character of the Revival

We are able to understand now more clearly the character of the great religious revival which he initiated.

In the first place we see the preparation for its coming in the unrest of the age, the growing consciousness that the Church was proving false to its mission, the increased desire within the Church of a return to evangelical simplicity. Towards the close of the twelfth century innumerable sects were springing up, many of these fanatical and extreme, but all goaded into activity by a sense of outrage, and by the longing for better things. The nobler spirits of the age cried out for reform, and over the whole of Europe, where the Church held sway, there was a growing nausea at existing conditions. The Cathari, the Poor Men of Lyons, the Waldenses, and other less known sects, all swelled the chorus of condemnation, and threatened the existence of the organised Church itself. For the first time that vast edifice, built up through successive centuries, claiming divine powers, and unlimited sanctions over the consciences of men, defying at once the secular arm and popular criticism, began to feel its foundations tremble. Men began to suspect that an organisation so corrupt, so infused with worldliness, so passionately desirous of material wealth, could not be the holy society it claimed to be ; that it was either false in its claims, or false to its mission. So there appeared first a yearning, then a demand for reform, which we perceive as the first evidence of a new movement in the world, a movement which was to widen out until it reached its climax three centuries later in what is known in history as the Reformation.

But a contributing stream was entering into the world through another channel. The end of the tenth, and the first half of the eleventh centuries may justly be regarded as the darkest period in the whole history of the Christian Church. Relying upon the statement in the Apocalypse, in which Satan is represented as bound for a thousand years, the belief gained universal dimensions that the end of the world was near, and that at the close of the tenth century the dread day of Judgment would break upon the startled earth, bringing fire and destruction in its train. As the time drew near, a paralysing terror seized hold of the hearts of men. Doomed, as they believed, to end their days at an appointed hour inexorably advancing toward them, living their lives as condemned criminals marked out for sudden death, and for an eternity of woe beyond, all joy in life, all provision for the future, all interest in human affairs were abandoned. Nature herself seemed to lend her aid to deepen the gloom. The seasons were bad, the grain rotted in the fields, catastrophe followed catastrophe, men with minds unhinged began to see portents in the sky, strange voices were heard in the air, apparitions and ghostly visitants were of daily occurrence. To add to the horrors of the time a famine broke out; the numbers of the dead were so great that wolves feasted upon their bodies, and into the rude trenches into which the bodies were thrown many who were alive threw themselves in sheer terror of living.

When the day fixed came and went without disaster, instead of finding relief, men were plunged into new anxieties. Since the date had been calculated from the birth of Christ, and the prophecy had not been fulfilled, it was next believed that the date should have been fixed from His death. There is no doubt that the Christian world was suffering at this time from a form of dementia. There must have been some light amid the darkness, some men whose health of mind made them shake off the gloomy terrors of the times and walk God's earth with confidence, but these were few. The art of the period bears only the evidences of sadness, of gloom, or of terror.

When at length the year of dread had come and gone, when there arose each morning the smiling day, when Nature clothed herself in her old garb of loveliness and ministered lavishly to man's needs, a new hope like the first faint breath of dawn began to tremble in men's hearts. They began, as we have seen, to chafe at the fetters which the Church had riveted upon their supine limbs in the hopeless days through which they had passed, but with this a new sense of the beauty of the world, of the joy of living, of man's wide heritage, began to possess them. A fresh energy began to appear; the natural buoyancy of man's spirit to assert itself; over all the departments of human thought and activity a vivifying breath was passing. This activity expressed itself, as we have seen, in a demand both within the Church and without for reform, for a revival of spiritual religion, for a return to evangelical simplicity; but it affected the whole domain of man's life. In every realm of human activity bonds were breaking, the prison doors were being flung open, and emerging from them men began to look with new wonder and delight upon the world, holding out their hands to earth and sky, and seeking for new avenues of expression for the thoughts kindling within them.

These two forces, converging at the close of the twelfth century, only waited for the man to appear, for the hand which would open the gates and let the pent-up waters free. And in Francis the world found what it needed.

First of all we see how he voiced in himself the longing after simplicity, for the casting aside of forms, for the reaching behind the letter to the spirit. When he appeared before men in the garment of poverty, when he preached repentance and the love of God, when outside the Church he proclaimed the willingness of God to forgive independent of all forms and ceremonies, he announced good tidings which the world through long years had waited to hear, and his voice broke on ears not dull or indifferent, but eagerly expectant. Over the face of the earth the Spirit of God had been passing; a new Pentecost was being prepared, and when at length the fire descended, it passed from city to province with joyous leap and rush. A new joy dawned in the world, men were brought back to simplicity, they heard the sweet evangel proclaimed by lips full of evangelic fervour, and saw it wrought in deeds of unselfishness and love. They saw men in an age of rapine and cruelty, when might was right, and when the most rapacious were the princes of the Church, voluntarily turn from these things, refuse them as useless, turn from them with contempt. They saw that instead of depressing them this voluntary relinquishing of the world's gifts filled them with the utmost joy, gave them a freedom of movement and a power of appeal which none others possessed; and when once they were convinced of the genuineness of these marvels they flocked in thousands to be enrolled in this new army of Jesus Christ; they listened to the message of these men with tears of thankful love. 'Our clock strikes,' says Carlyle, 'when there is a change from hour to hour, but no hammer in the horologe of time peals through the Universe when there is a change from era to era.' Yet if there was ever a voice heard which rung out the old and ushered in the new, it was that voice which Francis heard in the Portiuncula which commanded him to go out, to forsake all, to take neither purse nor scrip, but to follow Christ.

But the influence which Francis initiated was wider even than this. It broke the fetters imposed upon the mind as well as those of the spirit. Francis was the real precursor of the Renaissance. From that first day when he preached liberty to the captives, and recovering of sight to the blind, and the acceptable year of the Lord, may be dated the start of that movement which thrilled Italy, which brought forth the greatest splendours of art and literature, the first wave of which is spent, but which is only gathering new force, and which cannot rest until it accomplish the complete emancipation of the intellect from every form of tyranny. With Francis the age of dogmatism ends. In his entire recoil from every form of it, in his penetration into the genuine simplicity of Christ's Gospel, in his naturalness and his feeling for nature shown so marvellously in his songs, the new era is found awakening. As Sabatier truly observes: 'The thirteenth century was prepared to understand the voice of the Umbrian poet; the sermon to the birds closed the reign of Byzantine art, and of the thought of which it was the image. It is the end of dogmatism and authority; it is the coming in of individualism and inspiration; very uncertain, no doubt, and to be followed by obstinate reactions, but none the less marking a date in the history of the human conscience.' From this time the stiff, conventional forms of Christ, seen in the mosaics of the basilicas, give place to new efforts after naturalness and truth; Cimabue and Giotto in painting, the Pesanos in sculpture, Dante and Petrarch in literature, all lent their aid to usher in the new day of light and attainment; but the first note of the Renaissance was heard on the hills around Assisi when Francis sang the 'Canticle of the Sun.'

One other characteristic of this revival is that it was of the people. All the great movements spring from thence, especially religious movements. For in the days of religious depression and indifference, it is the common people who suffer most. There is withdrawn from them the one consolation which makes their life bearable, and gilds the future with an immortal hope. And at the close of the twelfth century, as we have seen, their lot was unhappy indeed. Ground down by intolerable wrongs, the prey of the powerful, and the dupe often of the ecclesiastic, they lived in a state of terror unsoothed by those higher consolations which change the way of thorns into the way of the Cross. When, then, there came sounding down from the hills the joyous songs of the lovers of poverty and the lovers of men, these depressed ones of the earth looked up with a pathetic hope awaking in their dull eyes. It seemed too good to be true; and yet it was true. The old message of God's love had come back to earth, the old evangelical gospel was sounding its tidings of great joy to the shepherds abiding in the fields, and to the lowly ones of the earth, and as in the early days the 'common people heard them gladly.' From this hour can be dated that humanism which entered so conspicuously into literature and art, which deflected the eye away from the exclusive consideration of heaven to take cognisance of the things of earth, and in religion that humanitarianism which to-day is moving so mightily the hearts of men. Previous to this, theology was exclusively concerned with the relation of the worshipper to the world to come; in its contemplation of divine things it lost touch with life, with common needs; its mission was to get men into heaven, not to save them from present sorrows, or to fight for them the battle of their wrongs. But with Francis, love for humanity returned to the earth, the old love for the maimed, the halt, and the blind; the love which Christ bore toward His brethren, which made the wilderness rejoice, and the desert to blossom as the rose. Religion became once more connected with present sorrows, with the redressing of human wrongs, with the defence of the weak, and with the turning of this world into the kingdom of our Lord and His Christ. The success of the movement was instantaneous, first because of the long historic preparation, next because of the hunger for it in the people's hearts, and last of all because of the wonderful personality of its founder and leader. We close now with recalling some of the main characteristics of this personality.

### Saint Francis

To understand Francis at all we must first recognise him as knight, as summing up in himself the new romanticism of the age, and by his amazing spiritual genius, reinterpreting this romanticism, in the terms of the spiritual life. At this time the troubadours were roaming over northern Italy, and infecting all the gay youths with their 'love service,' their love songs, and dalliance. Frequently these gay troubadours attached themselves to the court of a prince or famous knight, whose martial honour they sang, and whose victories in love and war they celebrated; more frequently, however, their theme was some fair lady, to whom, under a fanciful title, they addressed their complaints, their entreaties, and their songs. In addition to this influence the whole of Christendom was at this time affected by the Crusades. The desire to wrest from the possession of the infidel the tomb of our Lord fired the ardent and romantic minds of that day with a burning fervour. Kings forsook their kingdoms, nobles their castles, bishops their sees, and the peasantry their ploughs, to cross the seas, and to wage war against the heathen around Jerusalem, from which the shattered remnant returned with the conquest unattained but with hope undaunted. The times, thus, were full of the spirit of romance; visions of glory filled the dreams of every youth; nothing was too extravagant for the blithe spirits of such an age.

The effect of all this upon the mind of Francis, upon the bent of the movement which he initiated, will be immediately recognised. It gives the clue to his whole life. For in the early days he differed from the other youths with whom he mixed only in the greater intensity with which he conceived the prevailing spirit, and the way in which he interpreted it. His early excesses were the outcome of a highly romantic nature throwing itself with vehemence into a mistaken conception of what knighthood meant. 'Tortured with the desire of that which is far-off and high, Francis had conceived a sort of passion for chivalry, and fancying that dissipation was one of the distinguishing features of nobility, he had thrown himself into it with all his soul.' The disillusionment when it came was no less violent; falling from such a height he seemed, as we have seen, to have plunged into the very abyss of despair; slowly, and with immense effort, he lifted himself out, and when at length in the little chapel at Portiuncula he found again his ideal, he was transfixed with joy, the old gaiety came back to him, once more was he the radiant knight, laughter came back to his lips, joy to his heart, only now his leader was Christ, his lady Poverty. To his lady he vowed his vows; he promised to be true lover and true follower, to defend her and to serve her with his life; and from that first moment when he cast off the garments he wore in the streets of Assisi, to that last when lying upon the earth he relinquished his soul to death, he remained true, the very perfect knight, *sans peur et sans reproche*.

This relinquishing of every form of material wealth, and the voluntary embracing of poverty as the chief good, appeared to Francis's generation, as it would appear even more to ours, as the ultimate reach of misery. In his day the rapacity of the strong made the struggle for possession the supreme passion of life. It has become more than ever so to us. So affected have we become by this spirit that all our ideas of well-being are estimated by material standards. 'What shall we eat, what shall we drink, wherewithal shall we be clothed ?'—these are the topics of consuming interest and importance. Happiness to the great majority of those around us consists in the possession of wealth, and to possess it they enter upon a struggle which, more than any other, makes happiness impossible to them. So consumed do they become with the passion of possessing, that they lose the power to enjoy what they possess. To such an age, poverty has become the unpardonable crime, and entails the last banishment. Here was one, however, who gave up, and gave up with a smile, every vestige of material possession; who turned away from everything which we have been taught to believe as necessary to our comfort; who voluntarily relinquished every one of those things without which, we are told, happiness cannot be attained. Contrast the life of Francis with the prevailing life of to-day. Has our greedy pursuit of material gain brought us happiness ? One need only look on the faces of the men and women whom we meet, to see in their restless eyes, their strained look, the haggard discontent of their lives. And this other life, which we expect to be wretched through the loss of those things we so ardently desire as good, is, we see, full of an unaccountable radiance. It was this which amazed the heathen of the first century as they beheld the lives lived by the early Christians; it was this which amazed the thirteenth century as it saw the character of the lives lived by Francis and his followers. They saw that in giving up all things for Christ, Francis had gained some new and unaccountable wealth. They saw the unclouded gladness of his daily life, and then they realised, at length, that in renouncing the world he had gained it; that by asking nothing from it he possessed all things; that by cutting the bonds which bound him to it he attained a freedom more priceless than rubies, and a peace more precious than pearls.

This outbreak of joy, which is characteristic of all revivals of religion, is specially prominent in Francis and his followers. They became the happy troubadours—'Joculatores Domini,' God's jongleurs, they were called—as up and down the valleys and the hills they took their way, singing their songs, the most famous of which was Francis's 'Canticle of the Sun,' declared by Renan to be the most perfect utterance of modern religious sentiment, and showing how closely the heart of Francis was wedded to nature and to God. The following is the well known translation of Matthew Arnold:

'O most high, almighty, good Lord God, to Thee belong praise, honour, and all blessing!

'Praised be my Lord God with all His creatures, and specially our brother the sun, who brings us the day and who brings us the light; fair is he and shines with a very great splendour: O Lord, he signifies to us Thee!

'Praised be my Lord for our sister the moon, and for the stars the which He has set clear and lovely in the heaven.

'Praised be my Lord for our brother the wind, and for air and cloud, calms and all weather by which Thou upholdest life in all Thy creatures.

'Praised be my Lord for our sister water, who is very serviceable unto us and humble and precious and clean.

'Praised be my Lord for our brother fire, through whom Thou givest us light in the darkness; and he is bright and pleasant and very mighty and strong.

'Praised be my Lord for our mother the earth, the which doth sustain and keep us, and bringeth forth divers fruits and flowers of many colours and grass.

'Praised be my Lord for all those who pardon one another for His love's sake, and who endure weakness and tribulation; blessed are they who peaceably shall endure, for Thou, O Most Highest, shalt give them a crown.

'Praised be my Lord for our sister, the death of the body, from which no man escapeth. Woe to him who dieth in mortal sin! Blessed are they who are found walking by Thy most holy will, for the second death shall have no power to do them harm.

'Praise ye and bless the Lord, and give thanks unto Him, and serve Him with great humility.'

Immediate as was the success of his mission, passionate though the love was with which he was entertained by others, neither success nor failure affected the noble simplicity of Francis's nature. He served God 'with great humility.' One day Brother Masseo, looking earnestly at Francis, began to say:

'"Why thee? Why thee?" And this he repeated again and again, as if to make a mock at Francis. "What are you saying?" cried Francis at last. "I am saying that everybody follows thee, every one desires to see thee, hear thee, and obey thee, and yet for all that thou art neither beautiful, nor learned, nor of noble family. Whence comes it, then, that it should be thee whom the world desires to follow?"

'On hearing these words the blessed Francis, full of joy, raised his eyes to heaven, and after remaining a long time absorbed in contemplation he knelt, praising and blessing God with extraordinary fervour. Then turning to Masseo, "Thou wishest to know why it is I whom men follow? Thou wishest to know? It is because the eyes of the Most High have willed it so; He continually watches the good and the wicked, and as His most holy eyes have not found among sinners any smaller man, nor any more insufficient or more sinful, therefore He has chosen me to accomplish the marvellous work which God has undertaken; He chose me because He could find no one more worthless, and He wished here to confound the nobility and grandeur, the strength, the beauty, and the learning of this world."'

The personal magnetism of Francis appears in the intense devotion of his disciples toward him, but also in the influence his preaching exerted upon the multitude. His words were of the simplest character, so simple that men could hardly remember what he had said; but the effect of his speech upon his hearers was almost miraculous. He swayed them as the wind sways the ripened corn. Multitudes, as they listened to his entreaty, turned for ever from a life of sin, and, in deep contrition, sought salvation from its power. His sermons, too, bore no marks of learning, contained no fixed dogmas, but, like his Master, he spoke 'as one having authority, and not as the scribes.' With Francis evangelical simplicity came back to the earth, and with it that primitive joy which enabled the disciples of the early church to eat their bread with abounding gladness and singleness of heart.

So, as we close this chapter, and turn away from him in whose companionship we have for a little while been dwelling, let it be with those beautiful words of his which explain all that is best in his life, and which will inspire all that is best in ours:

'Above all the gifts and the graces which the Holy Spirit gives to His friends is the grace to conquer oneself, and willingly to suffer pain, outrages, disgrace, and evil treatment, for the love of Christ.'

## SAVONAROLA AND THE FLORENTINE REVIVAL

THE conviction that those movements in history known to us as revivals are not mere sporadic outbreaks, but are governed and regulated by laws which lie deep in humanity, will readily impress itself upon the student of history. Some of these laws we have attempted to decipher. First we recognise a law of identity which reveals the underlying similarity of all such movements, which shows how they are correlated the one with the other, which declares their common origin, and the identity of the hopes and emotions which they evoke. But along with this identity of cause and effect there exists a law of variety, which, within this prescribed circle, permits of those modifications which come through environment, through locality, through nationality, and through those changes which come over men's minds in the changing centuries, and in the progress of humanity. History, we see, never repeats itself. It uses the same alphabet, but it breaks up the type after each impression, and with the old letters writes ever something new. Thus, while the underlying laws which called it into being are the same, each great movement stands out vividly from all others, it has its own distinguishing features, its own outstanding characteristics both in relation to the appeal which it makes and the effect it produces.

The underlying law of identity in the causes which gave rise to the revival which we are about to consider will emerge as we proceed; but the fact of diversity will become immediately apparent by contrasting for a moment the saint of Assisi with the monk of Florence. It would be difficult to find a single point of contact between those two men, except in their common hatred of iniquity, and their passionate and unflinching devotion to Jesus Christ. In all else—in temperament, in character, in mental equipment, in intellectual outlook, in the lives they lived, and in the deaths they died—they offer the most startling contrast. The life of the saint of Assisi was like one of those radiant days of spring, beginning in cloud and trailing mist, but breaking at last into sunny splendour, and calling all things to song and gladness; continuing thus through the short day, and closing in a great tranquillity of light—all the hills steeped in purple—all the land steeped in peace. The life of the reformer of Florence was like a turbulent day in autumn, beginning with blinks of sunshine through tattered mist, then darkening down in trouble and tempest, with intermittent gleams here and there through torn and startled cloud, but closing in at last with leap of lightning and roar of thunder—the day dying in conflagration amid the raging of the elements, and the fear of men. Nature offers these startling contrasts, and so does human history, and we seem to need them for the education of our minds, that we may be taught to recognise the deep and awesome things of life.

The differences are no less wide when we turn from the leaders to the conditions under which they did their work, and to the times in which they lived. During the two centuries and a half which intervene, profound changes had taken place in Europe. We saw at the end of the twelfth century human society just emerging from the darkness of the middle ages. These were the days of papal absolutism, when the human mind was imprisoned, when man's will was fettered, when his imagination was haunted by superstition, and when the thought of the dissolution of the visible universe gave a terrible sanction to the threats of the priesthood. Now, much of the old conditions of life had broken up. During the interval the feudal system had risen to its prime and had disappeared. The disintegrating process. which followed the dismemberment of the Empire under Charlemagne had been arrested; a new movement towards centralisation had sprung up, and the influence of the Crusades, which, by weakening the influence of the nobles, elevated that of the middle classes, began to be felt. Out of the chaos, nations were arising conscious of a vigorous, national life; kings were extending their authority, and were gathering around them courts and armies; a gradual process of consolidation was in process which was to map out Europe into modern geographical and national divisions. At the same time commerce was largely on the increase; towns and cities, receiving royal charters, were growing in wealth and in importance; a new life was breaking over Europe, the old order was changing, giving place to new.

No less profound were the changes coming over the human mind. In the history of human thought no period, perhaps, is of intenser interest than that with which we are now dealing. Italy, at this time, was blazing with the light and glory of the Renaissance. The human mind had thrown off the gloom and depression which had so long overshadowed it; instead of the haunting fear of death men became possessed by the joy of life; they awoke to find the world a beautiful place, and life a gladsome and radiant experience. It was like that day in spring of which Wordsworth sings, when secretly through all the earth there moves the quickening pulse of life, when the sap moves at the roots, and gives to all living things the promise of the festive pomp of midsummer. So through men's hearts there passed a thrill which woke them to newness of life, which called them forth to see, with undimmed eyes, the splendour of the world. In literature, in painting, in sculpture, in all the branches of human activity, new doors were being burst open, and through them pressed an eager throng curious after discovery, impatient at delay, and intensely eager to possess the treasures which lay beyond. The monasteries of the West were ransacked for ancient manuscripts; scholars revived the philosophies of ancient Greece and Rome; painters and sculptors sought to revive the lost beauties of classic art, architects vied with each other in building those stately cathedrals and monasteries which are the glory of Italy, and princes rivalled each other in their patronage and recognition of genius. Two events gave an immense impetus to the movement. Ten years before Savonarola saw the light, the first printing press was put up, and the world entered upon its era of the diffusion of knowledge. When Savonarola was one year old, Constantinople, which had so long withstood the assault of the Turks, at length succumbed. The result was the scattering through Europe of the scholars of the Byzantine Empire, who, taking their books and manuscripts with them, carried their scholarship to the different courts of Europe, and immensely quickened the intellectual movement wherever they settled.

Of all this seething, intellectual life, Italy was the centre. Francis, the precursor of the Renaissance, saw but little of that stream, which at first made its way with gentlest movement, but which, widening out, swept on with exultant rush for full three hundred years.

The progress of the Renaissance in Italy is marked out into three distinct periods. Through the first, which lasted from 1250 to 1400, known in art as the Gothic period, progress was slow and laborious. During the Dark Ages knowledge had been buried in the monasteries, and the traditions of art had been lost. Through painful effort these had to be regained, but men brought to their efforts the most eager resolve, and the most intense joy of heart. Through this period the religious idea still dominated the mind and efforts of the artist; their subjects were solely biblical, or were restricted to the lives of the saints. The second period, which stretches from 1400 to 1500, is known as the Early Renaissance. During this period, Art, while remaining religious in subject, began to widen its outlook; greater technical excellence was attained, and the ascetic ideal began to disappear before the growing opulence of life. The period from 1500 to 1600 is termed the High Renaissance. It was during this period that the Arts, throwing themselves into all the joy and abandon of the world, reached their dazzling heights of splendour; when the religious idea was thrown aside, and men revelled in the beauty of the physical universe, and in the intoxication of the senses.

When now we compare the external conditions of Italy in the period with which we are dealing, with those which existed in the days of Francis, we perceive that the most momentous changes have taken place; a new era has arrived; the modern world has emerged.

Vast though the changes be, then, which separate the two movements under Francis and Savonarola, and which give them their distinctiveness, we have only to look beneath the surface to discover the identity of the laws which brought them into being. The revival under Francis was preceded by a long period of reaction and of spiritual indifference, when evil flaunted itself in the streets and derided the good, when the Church itself had become corrupt, and when all sections of society had become infected by the prevailing scepticism, when even the godly had begun to faint and fear, and cried out day and night for a Deliverer. A close examination of the condition of life at the middle of the fifteenth century discloses an identical condition of affairs within the Church and without. The wave of religious emotion awakened in Europe through the preaching of Francis and his followers produced effects of the most far-reaching importance. As we have seen, it initiated a movement which overlapped the boundaries of its early history ; it not only awakened a new religious enthusiasm, and brought men back to the simplicity of the evangelic faith, but it helped to emancipate the human mind, it gave the first shock to the power of the priestly class, it opened the door to art and learning, and set agoing the first hesitating efforts toward religious freedom. This movement was to obtain a new impetus from the hand of Savonarola, but meanwhile the religious side of it had spent itself, and the student of religious history of the middle of the fifteenth century has to survey a period of almost unparalleled iniquity. Over Italy a profound change of manners had taken place. 'The ancient simplicity of life disappeared as wealth increased ; culture took the place of piety, habits of life became more and more luxurious, dress more costly, entertainments more lavish, worldliness more pronounced. Along with this outward refinement there arose a decay of morals ; the standard of rectitude began to oscillate ; the sanctities of home began to be invaded ; language, while becoming more polite, became charged with double meanings, and in the midst of elegant courtesies men looked for concealed impurities. Beneath the outward polish, too, there began to grow, with startling rapidity, that cruelty which all men possess, and which only the fear of God imprisons; in the decay of faith these evil instincts, no longer chained, began to prowl abroad. Men could no longer be trusted; beneath the velvet tunic peeped the dagger, and in the sparkling cup men expected the deadly poison. Murder and incest, lust and cruelty, haunted alike the palaces of the great and the hovels of the poor. Italy was full of bravos and cut-throats, who, before they struck down their victims from behind in the quiet street, did not think it incongruous first to visit the cathedral and, kneeling down, ask God's protection.'[1]

Such was the condition of society in the middle of the fifteenth century. What now was the condition of the Church? how did the religion of Jesus Christ fare in those days of cruelty and corruption? Alas! the story is a terrible one. Hardly before in all its history, perhaps, had the Church sunk so low as it did during the latter half of the fifteenth century. For long the popes had contemptuously thrown aside the pretence of piety; they were not only privately vicious, they were openly and blasphemously wicked. They scandalised Europe by their luxury, their avarice, their unblushing nepotism, and their crimes. Before the cupidity of Paul II., the cruelty of Sixtus IV., the unnatural passions of Alexander VI., and the infidelities of Julius II., the whole head reels, and the whole heart grows faint. They had become, indeed, Italian princes, intent upon the establishing of the fortunes of their families and unnatural offspring, using the authority of the Church to ruin neighbouring states, and not pausing even at murder itself to accomplish their ends. No better illustration, perhaps, could be given of papal morals than what is

[1] *The Christ Face in Art*, p. 40.

known as the Pazzi conspiracy, which occurred as Savonarola began his career. This conspiracy, by which a brother of Lorenzo the Magnificent lost his life, and which aimed at the murder of Lorenzo as well, was planned at Rome; the chief agent was the Pope's nephew, the murderer himself an archbishop. The place chosen for the murder was the Cathedral of Florence, the time selected by the murderers was the celebration of the Mass, the moment chosen to strike was that in which the Host is elevated, and while a layman could not be found to do the deed because of the sacredness of the time and place, no difficulty was found in securing the service of a priest. When the deed was done, though but half done, no condemnation of the murder proceeded from the Vatican, but a Bull of excommunication was hurled at those who had put the murderers to death. This act of barest justice was denounced as a crime which would meet with the most dreadful punishments both here and hereafter.

With this example shown to them, it is not to be expected that the rank and file of the clergy would exhibit habits of earnest piety, or that the age, which saw these excesses, would be one of spiritual earnestness. The condition of spiritual life has been summed up by Machiavelli. 'To the church and priests of Rome,' he says, 'we Italians owe this obligation—that we have become void of religion and corrupt.' Machiavelli can hardly be claimed as a Christian moralist, and when such as he were shocked, little more need be added to illustrate the fact that either the Christian Church must be reformed or perish.

Here, then, we have a repetition of the conditions which we have already met with preceding the revival under Francis of Assisi. In that dissolute age, as in the other, there must have been many devout souls praying for better things, for some mighty tide to arise which would cleanse the Church from its intolerable woes, and bring back to wearied hearts the joys of salvation. In that wicked age there was needed a voice to speak for righteousness, to condemn the sins which were defiling the Church, to warn men that the axe was laid at the root of the tree, and to call them everywhere to repent. That voice at length was heard; it was the voice of Savonarola, and we turn now to listen to its thunders, and to trace his brief and tragic history.

## Early Life

Savonarola was born in Ferrara on September 21, 1452. He was the third of seven children, his parents being of good family. Italy, at this time, was broken up into small and independent states, ruled over by tyrants who were engaged in constant strife, and who vied with each other in their pomp of circumstance and love of display. This internecine conflict proved ultimately the ruin of the country. It destroyed its commerce, weakened its powers of resistance, and made it an easy prey to the armies of Europe. Ferrara, at this time, however, was at its gayest; Borso d'Este, its Marquess, was famed throughout Europe for the dazzling luxury of his court, and for the splendour of his festivities. Popes and prelates, princes and nobles, were his constant guests, and the city was plunged in a ceaseless round of gaieties.

In the midst of all this outward pomp a young lad, lonely and dejected, walked the streets torn by emotions he could not quell, and by longings he could not name. To him, unlike other youths, the path of pleasure, and the gay excesses of sin, had no attraction; he had nothing of that gay abandon of character which made

Francis, even in his unregenerate days, the leader of every frolic, and the admired of all his companions. From his youth upward, Savonarola felt the call of God upon him, the hand of destiny weighed heavily upon his soul, and he could not shake it off. While others deplored the prevailing wickedness and then abandoned themselves to it, or made only feeble efforts to restrain it, this lonely youth spent hours before the altar, his heart torn by strange and conflicting emotions, his long vigils ever ending with the pathetic cry: 'Lord, make known to me the path my soul should tread.' To that young and lonely soul there had come the agony of the world's lost condition, the shame and corruption of the Church, and men's heedless rejection of Christ and of His salvation; and with the consciousness of these things there came the bitter call to separate himself, to become a voice for God in the midst of a crooked and perverse generation; to agonise and give himself for others, that the terrible sickness of the world might be healed.

The plan of forsaking the world and devoting himself to a religious life early presented itself to him, and hearing a sermon by an Augustinian friar, his destiny, he tells us, was settled by a single word. This one word he never forgot, though regarding it, he kept throughout his life a mysterious silence, refusing to reveal it even to his dearest friends. On the 24th of April 1475 he secretly left his home, fled to Bologna, and there entered the Dominican Monastery. He was impelled to take this step, he declares, by the impossibility of any longer tolerating the gross corruption of the world, and by seeing vice exalted, and virtue degraded, throughout Italy. From his retreat he wrote a noble letter to his father, entreating him to forgive his flight, and to send him his blessing. 'Never since I was born,' he says, 'have I suffered such bitter mental torments as at the moment when I abandoned my own father to make the sacrifice of my body to Jesus Christ, and to surrender my will into the hands of those I have never seen. You complain of the secrecy of my departure. In truth I suffered such grief and agony of heart when I left you, that, if I had betrayed myself, I verily believe that my heart would have broken, and I should have changed my purpose. In mercy, then, most loving father, dry your tears, and add not to my pain and sorrow.' Thus the step was taken, not with the dramatic intensity which characterised the abandonment of the world by Francis, but after a like prolonged agony, with the same consciousness of a call from God, and with a like realisation of the awful condition of sin of the world around him. The differences between the two men are differences of temperament, but the Spirit of God, moving in their hearts, awoke them to the same agony of repentance, the same consciousness of a burden imposed upon them by God, the same sense of the world's awful need, the same consecration of themselves to Jesus Christ and to His cause. Differing much in outward temperament they were united in their spiritual experiences; they stand together in that great roll of great men who hear the Voice and obey it, and who give up everything for the sake of Christ.

In the monastery of Bologna, to which Savonarola had fled, he remained for seven years. During this period he gained fame for his extraordinary piety and religious zeal. His learning and his remarkable mental gifts were early recognised, and immediately on his entering the monastery he was given the instruction of the novices. Through these silent years, however, a great change was taking place in his mind as well as in his character, for here, by prolonged and intense study of the Scriptures, he was laying the foundation of that tremendous power which he afterwards revealed. The Scriptures, at this time, were practically unopened; all knowledge of them was denied to the common people through the scarcity of the manuscripts, and through the wide-spread illiteracy. Even when they were openly read their meaning was obscured by excessive allegorising; they were overlaid with the subtleties of the schoolmen, or the refinements of Greek philosophy. For long Savonarola's own mind was clogged by his training, but gradually he shook himself free and brought to the study of the Word of God a flaming imagination, an almost oriental delight in imagery, and, above all, a faith which flamed at white heat. More and more he began to realise that it was the messages of this Book, with their startling images, with their awful denunciations of sin, with their exalted and throbbing pity, which alone could break up the corruption which abounded, and bring back to earth the peace of God, and the recognition of the sovereignty of Jesus Christ. So he pored over them day and night until it was declared that he knew the Scriptures by heart from beginning to end. While residing in the monastery, Savonarola wrote a canzone entitled 'De Ruina Ecclesiæ,' which reveals the agitated state of his heart, and the direction in which, even at this time, his thoughts were tending. In this poem he represents the Church as a pure maiden, and asks her where the ancient purity, the learning and love, the ancient doctors of the law, and the saints who once inhabited her courts have gone. And she replies that when contamination entered she fled, and showing the wounds upon her beautiful body, she reveals her terrible sufferings at the hands of those who claim to be her friends. When the youthful poet asks, Who has brought these things to pass? she answers, referring to Rome, A false, proud harlot. Then cries the poet in burning wrath, O God, O Lady, alas! would that I could break those spreading wings!

For a while he was sent to his own town, Ferrara, to preach. He was now twenty-nine years of age, and fearful lest he might awaken his dormant affections, he lived in complete retirement. His preaching did not prove extraordinarily effective; Savonarola had not yet come to his own, his mind was still groping, the mantle had not as yet descended upon him.

This same year—1481—war broke out in Ferrara, largely fomented by the cupidity of the Pope, who, when peace was concluded on terms which he regarded as humiliating to himself, died of rage. On the outbreak of the war, Savonarola was sent to Florence, which he entered for the first time, and there took up his residence at the famous monastery of St. Mark's. Nowhere in Italy, perhaps, was there a retreat which offered so satisfying a home to one of the temperament of Savonarola as this monastery. Given over to the Dominican Friars in 1436, it was rebuilt on a lavish scale at the command and at the expense of Cosimo de Medici. The valuable collection of Niccolo Niccoli, the greatest manuscript collector of his day, found there a home, and St. Mark's became the first public library established in Italy. Not only was the monastery famous, therefore, for its learning, it was no less venerated for its traditional piety. Here the saintly Antonine had lived, one of those characters, as it has been truly said, who are the true glories of the human race; who, amid all the spiritual degradation of the times, kept his heart pure from all offences, and offered in daily life to the eyes of the people an illustration of the beauty of holiness. Though dead for over twenty years, his name was kept in grateful remembrance, and his spirit of saintliness seemed still to give an odour of sanctity to the monastery itself. One other name lives in the hearts of all who have visited St. Mark's: it is the name of Fra Angelico, the saint of artists, who never took his brush in hand without prayer, who never painted the Cross without tears. Here, in the quiet cloisters, and in the narrow cells, with quiet eyes and heart unencumbered of the world, he wrought, covering the cold walls with warm and living colour, and making the monastery for all time the home of saintliness in art. Here one dwells in the company of angels and saints, of the 'bright seraphim in burning row,' but ever and changelessly in the company of the Saviour whom Angelico adored with all the fervour of his pure and saintly heart. For as you enter, He meets you; in the cloister He greets you from the Cross; He welcomes you as the pilgrim Christ as you pass from the cloisters into the cool Refectory; His pierced hand is stretched out to you as you enter the narrow cells; here He is born, here He does His mighty works, here He wrestles and prays in the olive shade, here He bears the bitter Cross; and here, majestic over death, He bursts its bonds, and rises into deathless life. Yes! here, as nowhere else in all the world, Jesus lives; He is everywhere, He meets you at every corner, the monastery vibrates with His presence, and He is ever gracious, ever the pitiful One, with hands stretched forth to heal and save. And these first days in Florence were to Savonarola amongst the happiest of his life; he saw the soft beauty of the Tuscan hills, he felt the charm of this city of renown, and in the monastery itself was there not all that his heart longed for—learning, and piety, and peace! But these days were few; they were but the quiet before the tempest, the stillness which precedes the storm.

## The Prophet

Up to this time Savonarola had shown no sign of those transcendent gifts which have made his name famous in history. Some curiosity was felt on his entrance into Florence, but it was aroused on the ground of his piety, not on account of his power as a preacher. Shortly after his arrival he was appointed Lenten preacher at the Church of San Lorenzo. The church was crowded at first, but his preaching failed to attract. His rough accent and his uncouth gestures displeased the fickle Florentines, who were much as the Athenians of old. The congregations rapidly thinned until they had almost entirely disappeared. Meanwhile, the sorrow and anguish which, from earliest days, had gnawed at Savonarola's heart on account of the state of the Church, were not abated but increased. And good reason had he, and all who loved and served the Christ, for such anguish. At the death of Sixtus iv., which happened at this time—1484—it was hoped that a successor would be found who would free the Church from her calamities, and save her from her woes. But in Innocent viii. the papal chair received one who made even the infamous character of Sixtus appear excusable. No longer disguising the character of his life, he openly acknowledged his offspring as his sons. 'He was not only a parent, and a dissolute parent, but so lenient to all descriptions of vice, that the Roman court became the headquarters of vice and scandalous living. All men were revolted by actions, equally threatening to religion and dishonouring to humanity; nor was it possible to foresee to what fate Italy might be doomed, under the deepening misrule of the Papacy.'

Deeply the woes of the Church, and the sorrows of Christ's people, burned into the heart of this lonely monk. He fasted and prayed, he cried aloud to God day and night, he pored over the Scriptures, and in its startling prophecies heard the note of coming doom. On a sudden, like a meteor from heaven, he burst upon his hearers at Brescia, where he had been sent to preach. At last he had found his message ; at last those enormous powers, lying so long dormant, blazed into fierce and inextinguishable flame. In the Apocalypse, amid the flaming images of the prophet evangelist, his imagination awoke, his message came to him, the fire of the prophet descended upon him. He applied the terror of the Book of Revelation to the events transpiring around them ; with awful voice he prophesied the coming doom ; fathers would see their children massacred in the streets—for the day of the Lord was at hand, the cup of iniquity was full, the patience of the most High God was exhausted. The effect of these sermons upon his hearers was overwhelming : men already heard the tramp of the avenging host, and saw the flaming sword of the angel of destruction. As the burning words of the preacher poured forth, their faces blanched, their lips trembled, their eyes were glazed with terror.

Soon the fame of this preacher began to be noised abroad ; his name became known through Italy ; devout souls, who were waiting for the light, heard with gladness of a mighty voice raised in fearless condemnation of sin, and to Savonarola himself there came the consciousness of an authentic message given him of God which he must needs deliver to his day and generation.

For some time he remained in Lombardy, preaching from place to place until, at length, in the summer of 1489, he received the ominous message which summoned him back to Florence—a summons which was issued, strange to say, by desire of Lorenzo de Medici himself. Savonarola instantly obeyed ; but, even as he went, a heavy presage of coming woes burdened his heart. Near Bologna his strength suddenly failed him, and he sank upon the ground unable to proceed. Overwrought in body and in mind, it is not surprising that to his excited brain there should have appeared visions warning him of the dangers which confronted him, or that strange voices should have been heard by him calling him to faithfulness and courage. Weak and ill, he entered the gates of that city with which his name was to be for ever associated, and passing through its streets once more, entered St. Mark's, which was to be his home until the end of his short and troubled life.

It will be necessary for us to pause here for a moment to survey the Florence of that day. The famous city was at the very height of its glory; it was the city of light, not only of Italy, but of the whole of Europe. For here the Renaissance had borne its most glorious fruits. Only two hundred years had elapsed since, in the first dawn of the new spirit, Cimabue's Madonna had been carried through the streets, and amid the waving of banners and rejoicing of the populace, had been deposited in the Cathedral. From that day until the hour when Savonarola passed through her gates, her history had been one of effort and glorious attainment. From being a town of mean streets, without a single great building of which its citizens might be proud, it passed into a city of architectural splendours, the home of poetry, literature, and art. For, in days gone by, had not the immortal Dante paced her streets dreaming of Beatrice? had not Niccolò Pisano wrought out in matchless beauty the imaginations of his fertile brain, and Ghiberti produced those marvellous gates which Michael Angelo pronounced as worthy to be the gates of paradise? Everywhere were noble buildings, churches, and palaces, and amidst them all, like a rose of dawn, her glorious Duomo. And in the realm of art what names of the mighty dead were inscribed upon her roll of honour! Giotto, the friend of Dante, and the liberator of painting from Byzantine conventions; Orcagna, whose shrine of the Madonna in San Michele is still one of the wonders of the city; the youthful Masaccio, master of his craft, who at the early age of thirty, leaving the city for Rome, perished miserably on the way; Fra Angelico, whose heart was set on heavenly love, and Fra Lippi, who, notwithstanding his monkish dress, loved too much the things of earth. But great as these names were which adorned its past, they paled in presence of the mighty men who then walked the streets of Florence. Never, perhaps, at any single time in the world's history, has there been a greater galaxy of genius than that which was gathered in this Italian city during the closing years of the fifteenth century. Benozzo Gozzoli, Andrea Verrocchio, Cosimo Rosselli, and the Pollajuolo were still alive; Botticelli, Ghirlandaio, Filippino Lippi, Leonardo da Vinci, and Luca Signorelli were in their prime; Michael Angelo, and Fra Bartolommeo were entering into manhood; Raphael and Andrea del Sarto were just about to take up the brush, and already were beginning to enter into the spirit of the age. Scholars and poets, goldsmiths and sculptors, painters and designers, thronged the city streets, for it was the golden age of the Renaissance, and, with the Renaissance, a new spirit had entered into the world. With a recovery of the Greek manuscripts, there had come a recovery of the Greek spirit; humanism had entered into the world and was challenging for supremacy the ascetic ideal. The cry on every lip was, 'Let us enjoy life; open our heart to its seductions, our eyes to its beauty. Why mourn? Why lament? Let us be happy while we may.' And so men flung restraint aside, and in joyous abandon stretched forth greedy hands to pluck the pleasures of the world.

In Florence there was one name which, above all others, expresses the spirit of the Renaissance at its best. This name is that of Lorenzo de' Medici, known as the Magnificent, himself a scholar and poet, the patron of scholarship and poetry, of music and art, of refinement and culture. Around his court gathered all the great and blithe spirits of the age; his wealth, the brilliance of his gifts, the courtesy of his manner, his generous patronage of the arts, his zeal for scholarship, his love of splendour and of gaiety made his name famous throughout the world. Florence was not at this time more wicked as a city, perhaps, than any other city of Italy; nor was Lorenzo an evil man. He was in this respect, if not a model to his age, at least in advance of it. But he represented to Savonarola a spirit of evil; he exhibited, in his own personality, that abandonment to the world which to the intense and ascetic spirit of the eager reformer seemed to lie at the very root of the age's spiritual declension. So in these two men were summed up those two forces, humanism and asceticism, which in the years to come were to enter into conflict for the possession of the souls of men. From the eventful moment when Savonarola entered the gates of Florence that conflict was begun.

## Savonarola as Preacher

On taking up his residence at St. Mark's, Savonarola was appointed, as before, to give instruction, and there in the cloisters, beside a damask rose bush, which has been regrafted down to our own day, he began his expositions of the Apocalypse. At first only the friars attended, but soon the general public clamoured for entrance, and the lectures took on more and more the character of sermons. Urged to enter the pulpit, he hesitated long before the way seemed open to him. At length his decision was made, and on the 1st of August 1489 he occupied the pulpit of St. Mark. Then began those sermons which shook Florence to its centre, and which have made his name immortal. He wasted no time, and he did not beat the air ; he struck at the vices of Florence ; he contrasted its outward culture with its hidden crime and sensuality ; he dragged into light the scandalous sins which were done of them in secret who occupied high place in civic life ; nor did he fail to lash out against the impurities of the Church, or contrast its glaring immoralities with the splendour of its ceremonial, and the sumptuousness of its ritual. At last, in that land given over to licentiousness and crime, righteousness had found a voice. Here at last was a man of God, fearless, incorruptible. Here, once more, appeared the prophet, confronting the vicious of his age with unflinching courage, crying aloud in voice resonant with indignation, passionate with pleading, 'Repent ! Repent ! for the day of vengeance is at hand.'

The year following his settlement in Florence, Savonarola was made Prior of St. Mark's. It was customary for the newly-elected Prior to pay homage to the head of the house of the Medici in recognition of the indebtedness of the monastery to the generosity of their patron. Savonarola, however, took no notice of this custom. The surprised monks took occasion to expostulate with their Prior ; they pointed out the value to the monastery of Lorenzo's good-will, and recommended bowing to the powers that be. 'Is it God or Lorenzo de' Medici that has made me Prior ?' asked

Savonarola. 'God,' they replied. 'Then shall I render thanks to God alone,' replied the intrepid monk. Lorenzo took no notice of this slight, and in visiting the monastery on one occasion, sought to appease the Prior by placing a number of gold coins in the alms chest. Savonarola instantly gave them to the poor. Next, an influential deputation waited upon him, warning him to modify his tone, and declaring that they came of their own good-will, in the interest of the Prior, and for the public good. 'You say that you are come of your own accord,' replied Savonarola, 'I say that you are not. Go, make answer to Lorenzo: "Let him repent of his sins."' Harsh as this may seem to be, it is clear that no man can do the work of reformation in evil times who tampers with conscience, or has fear in his heart for the great ones of the earth. Lorenzo, with all his qualities, represented to Savonarola's mind the sum of all the evils then afflicting Italy and Florence. To bend to him, to deviate from his course, even by a hairsbreadth, was to weaken the defences of his own soul, and tamper with the most solemn dictates of his conscience. Nor can one fail to admire the noble constancy, the fearless demeanour of this lonely monk. Arrayed against him were all the forces of the world. It was easy for Lorenzo to make advances, but the only platform on which this man of God could meet him was that decreed by all the heroic prophets of old: 'Let him first repent of his sins.'

Shortly after, Lorenzo was taken suddenly ill. Feeling the shadows of death gathering around him, terror seized his soul. He desired absolution, but had no faith in the sincerity of the priesthood—they were all his minions. Suddenly he recalled the name of Savonarola, and instantly dispatched a messenger for him, declaring as he did so, 'I know no honest friar save this one.' What actually happened at this famous interview can now never be known. The evidence of those actually present, or of those who relate the incident, differs. According to one report Savonarola refused absolution unless Lorenzo would promise to restore to Florence her liberties, but a more credible account declares that to Lorenzo, now in deepest penitence, Savonarola spoke kind and comforting words.

Meanwhile Savonarola was attracting ever larger and larger congregations, and his fame was swiftly spreading throughout Italy. So large was the concourse gathered to hear him that he had to transfer himself to the Cathedral. Here, day after day, the population of Florence thronged to see and hear him. Many were drawn by curiosity, but even the most superficial became awed as they listened to the burning words of the preacher. The crowds thronged and pressed each other so close that there was hardly room to breathe; they built seats against the walls in the form of an amphitheatre, and still the space was insufficient. And how is it possible at this date to describe the preacher? the deep, resonant voice, the flash of his deep-set, penetrating eyes, the impassioned gestures, the marvellous flow of his oratory as, swept along with the fiery vehemence of his great soul, he discoursed to men of the eternal verities, of the awful facts of death and judgment to come? First he would begin in measured and tranquil tones, taking up the subject, turning it quietly round, suggesting some scholarly exposition, advancing some interpretation, dealing with it casually, critically, suggestively; then, suddenly, often without warning, he would change; the meditative style was flung aside as the mantle of the prophet fell upon him; fire flashed from his eyes, the thunder came into his voice; now in passionate entreaty, now in scorching indignation, the sentences rushed out, never halting, never losing intensity or volume, but growing and growing until his voice became as the voice of God Himself, and all the building rocked and swayed as if it moved to the mighty passion of his words. And what of the hearers ? They were as clay in his hands. Tears gushed from their eyes, they beat their breasts, they cried unto God for mercy, the church echoed and re-echoed with their sobs. Those who report his sermons suddenly break off and add : 'Here was I so overcome with weeping that I could not go on.' Pico della Mirandola, one of the most learned men of the day, says that the mere sound of Savonarola's voice was as the clap of doom ; a cold shiver ran through the marrow of his bones, the hairs of his head stood on end as he listened. Another tells that these sermons caused such terror, alarm, such sobbing and tears, that every one passed through the streets without speaking, more dead than alive.

From the first a deep vein of prophecy mixed itself with the friar's preaching ; but as the dangers which were now menacing Italy increased, this prophetic note became more prominent, and his prophecies more detailed. They were all summed up, however, in the three famous propositions :

I. That the Church would be renewed in their time.
II. That before this renovation God would strike Italy with a fearful chastisement.
III. That these things would happen shortly.

These threats of coming ill profoundly moved the city, for even the most callous could not dull their ears to the mutterings of the storm ; but they also gave great offence to those in high position, so much so that Savonarola tells us that he began to reflect whether or no he should leave out of his exhortations all mention of coming events. ‘I remember,’ he says, ‘when preaching in the Duomo, I determined to leave out all mention of them, and never to recur to the subject again. God is my witness how I watched and prayed the whole of Saturday and throughout the night; but all other ways, all doctrines save this were denied me. Towards break of dawn, being weary and dejected by my long vigil, I heard, as I prayed, a voice saying unto me: “Fool, dost thou not see that it is God’s will thou shouldst continue in the same path?” Wherefore I preached that day a terrible sermon.’ In this sermon, portions of which are still extant, we gain some knowledge of the fearlessness with which this solitary monk attacked the abuses of the day, and those who had entrenched themselves in them. His most vehement condemnation is reserved for the clergy, who, with all the semblance of piety, are ‘ravening wolves, who enter into widows’ houses in greed of gain, and who rob the poor.’ ‘Fathers make sacrifice to this false idol, urging their sons to enter the ecclesiastical life, in order to obtain benefices and prebends; and thus ye hear it said: “Blessed the house that owns a fat cure.” But I say unto ye, A time shall come when rather it will be said: Woe to that house; and ye will feel the edge of the sword upon you. . . . In these days there is no grace, no gift of the Holy Spirit that may not be bought and sold. . . . Bethink ye well, O rich, for affliction shall smite ye. This city shall no more be called Florence, but a den of thieves, of turpitude and bloodshed. Then shall ye all be poverty-stricken, all wretched, and your name, O priests, shall be changed into a terror. I sought no longer to speak in Thy name, O Lord; but Thou hast overpowered me, hast conquered me. Thy word has become like a fire within me, consuming the very marrow of my bones. Therefore am I derided and despised of the people. But I cry unto the Lord day and night, and I say unto ye: Know that unheard-of times are at hand.'

Not content with condemning these sins in others, Savonarola attacked them in his own convent. Notwithstanding the terrible curse which St. Dominic had pronounced against the holding of property, the convent of St. Mark's had become a wealthy fraternity. Savonarola began by reviving the old rule. He sold its possessions, reduced expenses by clothing the monks in coarse garments, forbade all superfluities, and brought back poverty to its ancient home. Instead of driving men away, this drew to the Convent of St. Mark's many of the finest spirits of the day; members of the noblest families in Florence sought admission, nor did any find the burden too heavy, for the strictest, the most unselfish, the most humble and devout was their beloved Prior, Savonarola himself. But these days of quiet and prayer were to be ruthlessly invaded by the momentous trials which were now at hand.

### Savonarola as Tribune

The unrest in Italy, instigated and kept alive by the cupidity of the popes and the tyrants of the various cities, broke out at last into open conflict, and began that series of disasters which devastated the land, and ruined her civilisation. At his death Lorenzo was succeeded by his son Piero, a weak and dissolute youth incapable of government. Affairs within the city were at their worst when the alarming news was brought that Charles VIII. of France had crossed the frontier and was descending into Italy. While Italy, broken up as she was into many separate kingdoms, had remained weak, the other kingdoms lying around her had slowly consolidated their forces, and were beginning to regard their rich but distracted neighbour as offering a convenient prey. On the pretext, then, of asserting his rights to the kingdom of Naples, Charles, instigated by Ludovico of Milan, gathered his army together and marched into Italy. The policy pursued by Lorenzo had been that of friendship with the French, but this line of policy had been abandoned by the foolish Piero in favour of support to the King of Naples. The news, therefore, of the approach of Charles, threw the city, and Piero himself, into the deepest alarm. So intense was the anxiety that the magistrates sent for Savonarola, entreating him to allay the anger of the people. Savonarola obeyed, but not without reiterating his note of warning that the sword of God was upon the land, that dire ills were to fall upon Italy. Dragged thus into public affairs against his will, Savonarola appears now as the tribune of the people, the one hope of Florence in the hour of her despair.

Meanwhile, Piero de' Medici, filled with terror, recalling how his father had averted disaster by appearing in his own person at the court of Naples, sought, by imitating the act, a like success. Possessing, however, neither the courage nor the dignity of his father, he cast himself as a suppliant at the feet of Charles, who extracted from him the most degrading terms. So enraged were the Florentines that Piero had to flee the city, and when Charles marched in at the head of his troops, the utmost disorder prevailed. Again it was to the Dominican monk that Florence had to look for safety. 'I spoke to the king,' he says, 'as not one of you would have dared to have spoken, and by the grace of God he was appeased. I said things which you yourselves would not have endured, yet he heard them patiently.' Another instance of the many in history in which the tyrant stands helpless before the man of God. Through the influence and courage of Savonarola a treaty was signed, and Charles left the city.

Florence was now virtually in the hands of Savonarola. He was the one strong man within her gates, the one man whose character was unimpeachable, the one man in whose unselfishness the people implicitly believed. So circumstances gathered together to force him into the realm of political interference, so dangerous because of the fickle affections of men, still more dangerous to the preacher since it arouses the hostile passions of the selfish and the unworthy. Savonarola was not ignorant of the dangers which assailed him through the new position which circumstances had forced upon him, but he took upon himself the burden in the name of God. Right gladly would he have escaped from it and retreated into the peace of the cloister. 'I have entered into a vast sea,' he says, 'and with great desire I long for the haven, and I see no way to return. Oh, my sweet haven, shall I ever find thee more? Oh, my heart, how hast thou suffered thyself to be taken away from so sweet a haven? Oh, my soul, look where thou art; surely we are in the midst of a deep sea, and the winds are adverse on every side. . . . I would be at peace and speak no more, but I cannot, for the word of the Lord is as fire in my heart. His word, if I utter it not forth, burns my marrow and my bones. Well, then, Lord, if Thou wilt that I navigate this deep sea, Thy will be done.' It was with this heavy burden upon him, conscious of the dangers that beset his path, but driven by the sense of a divine call, that Savonarola entered that career which was to end in bitterness and in death.

Having responded to the call which came to him from without, and to which he seemed to be driven from within, Savonarola, with characteristic courage, set himself to the task of saving Florence from the dangers which beset her from within and from without. From the first his ideal was to make her a city of God, a city where Jesus Christ would be adored, where He would, in all its public and private acts, be acknowledged king. Amid the gross licentiousness of the age, against the worldliness and impiety of other cities, and especially of Rome, that city of harlots, that modern Babylon, as he called her, Florence was to rise pure and unspotted, a new Jerusalem, a pattern for the nations. A great council was formed, a new republic arose from the ashes of the old, but the ruler of Florence was Savonarola, and the place from which he governed was the pulpit. Here, day after day, through times of crisis and danger, he asserted and reasserted those principles for which he was ready to lay down his life. And that ideal which he longed for, that city made clean and prepared as a bride of Christ, seemed actually to become a reality. The most startling changes in the manners of the people took place. 'On the days when the Prior of St. Mark preached,' says Milman, 'the streets were almost a desert; houses, schools, and shops were closed. No obscene songs were heard in the streets, but low or loud chants of lauds, psalms, or spiritual songs. Vast sums were paid in restitution of old debts, or wrongful gains. The dress of men became more sober, that of women modest and quiet. . . . Nor were the converts only of the lowly and uneducated. Men of the highest fame, in erudition, in arts, in letters, became amongst the most devoted of his disciples; names which in their own day were glorious, and some of which have descended to our own.'

Not content with reforming the lives and manners of the elders, Savonarola sought to influence the youth and children of the city. These he invited to the

Cathedral to hear sermons addressed especially to them. They responded in such numbers that he was bound to restrict the attendance to those between the ages of ten and twenty. The youth he enrolled in a sacred militia who bound themselves to observe the following rules :

I. To observe the commandments of God and His Church.

II. To attend with constancy the sacraments of penance and the Eucharist.

III. The renunciation of all public spectacles and worldly pleasures.

IV. To recognise the greatest simplicity in manners, conduct, and dress.

On the day of the Carnival in 1496, which in previous times was an orgy of drunkenness and debauchery, in which all sense of decency and restraint was thrown to the winds, a procession of children took place ; clad in white, they went through the streets singing their hymns, and making a collection for the poor. Of the change which this effected, Savonarola himself makes mention. 'Thou knowest,' he says, 'that many sins were committed in carnival, and now even children go to confession ; and this carnival hath been like unto Lent, the which must surely be the work of heaven.'

Wonderful as the change wrought by Savonarola's preaching upon the people of Florence was, it is not to be conceived that the rigid rules which he enacted could be aught but galling to a large section of the community. In some the love of the world was banished, in others it was curbed, in others it lived as strong as ever, and only waited opportunity for outbreak. The populace began to divide itself into new sections according to their love or hatred of the new doctrines. There were the Piagnone, loyal adherents of the Prior's ; the

Tiepidi, who were lukewarm; the Arrabbiati, who opposed, and the Compagnacci, who hated Savonarola and all his works, who looked back to the old and dissolute days with longing, and vowed to revenge themselves on him who had curbed their joys. Hushed for a time, owing to the ascendency of the Prior in the councils of Florence, and his popularity with the people, these unruly spirits hid themselves, nursing their wrath. Gradually, however, as the first wave of his popularity spent itself, as popular fears subsided, and new dangers arose to assail this champion of righteousness, these evil and antagonistic spirits began to assert themselves; faint murmurs gave place to open discontent, to fierce denunciation, and to an implacable hate which could find no satisfaction save in the destruction of that victim whose voice was a daily accusation of their misdeeds.

### Savonarola and the Pope

From those enemies who were menacing him in his own city, we have to turn now to a more terrible enemy who was menacing him from without. In the papal chair at Rome sat one whom the world unites to execrate, Alexander VI., bearing the infamous name of Borgia. He was of Spanish birth, and by favour and astonishing capacity for intrigue, had at last reached the papal chair. 'One of his strongest passions,' says Villari, 'was an insatiable greed for gold, and he accordingly formed intimate relations with Moors, Turks, Jews, regardless of all the prejudices and customs of his age. In this way he was able to accumulate the immense fortune that served to raise him to the Papacy. Addicted to licence and sensuality, he was always the slave of some woman. At the time of his election he was the lover of the notorious Vannozza, by whom he had several children. This woman's mother was said to have been his former mistress, just as he was afterwards accused of a shameful connection with his own and Vannozza's daughter, Luerezia, known to all the world as the cause of the many scandals and sanguinary jealousies by which the name of Borgia became a disgrace to humanity. Such was the character of the man now raised to the papal chair.'

To such a man, the life lived by the Prior of St. Mark was a direct challenge. Licentious Rome could not exist with a regenerated Florence. Either the one or the other must fall, and Alexander prepared himself for the fight. It was not for the first time in history that the organised head of the Church should regard a preacher of righteousness as its most dangerous enemy; nor was it for the first time that the Church should set in motion its machinery for the silencing of the voice which condemned the iniquities of the age. Nor, indeed, in this case could Alexander help himself. From the pulpit of St. Mark there thundered through Italy the accusations of this monk, who hurled the most bitter maledictions against his sins, and who, with awful voice, foretold the disasters which were about to be poured out upon the land on account of these iniquities. All the sorrows of the times, the sickness in men's hearts, the misery that was abounding, he traces, step by step, up through the iniquitous lives lived by the clergy to the feet of the Pope himself. Here was the heart of the cancer, here the source of all the age's woes, here repentance must begin, let the occupant of Peter's throne repent in sackcloth and in ashes.

Reports of these sermons were sent to Rome. Alexander could neither close his ears to them, nor hinder the public movement which they were beginning to set in motion. He must, at all costs, silence this voice. At first he tried flattery, and then a bribe. So little did he understand the character of the man he was dealing with that he actually sent him the offer of a cardinal's hat. This roused Savonarola to intensest indignation. 'I will have no hat but that of a martyr,' he cried, 'red in my own blood.'

Finding blandishments unavailing, Alexander had recourse to wiles to bring Savonarola to Rome where quickly he would be silenced. In July 1495 he was courteously invited to go thither, but Savonarola excused himself. In September came another summons, less laudatory and more peremptory in tone; in the following year the glove was thrown aside, the mask put off, and the knife unsheathed. If obedience to the Pope's command were not observed, Florence would be laid under interdict. But Florence was too independent a city to be lightly moved, and Savonarola, still the idol of the great mass of the people, continued his sermons.

The next move made by the wily Alexander was the appointment of a theological commission to inquire into the orthodoxy of the friar. All, with one exception, condemned him as guilty of heresy, schism, and disobedience to the Holy See. It was not until May of the following year, however—1498—that the long-threatened bull was launched against him. It contained three charges: 1. The refusal to obey the summons to Rome. 2. The teaching of heretical and perverse doctrines. 3. The refusal to unite St. Mark with the Tuscan and Roman provinces. Savonarola had long expected this dread hour to arrive; he had prepared himself and his hearers for it, and when it did arrive, it found him collected and undismayed. In letters addressed to the Pope, he denied the impeachment of heresy, and defended his action in declining to visit Rome. For some time, also, he desisted from preaching, contenting himself with holding conferences in St. Mark's. Soon, however, his partisans began to clamour for his voice. In January of 1498 was elected a Signory made up mainly of his partisans, and entreaties addressed to him to resume his preaching became more and more insistent. At length, on Septuagesima Sunday, in the Cathedral of Santa Maria dei Fiori, he resumed his ministry, and began a series of sermons on Exodus. He at once addressed himself to his resistance to the Pope, and we hear in his words the first rumble of that thunder which broke out finally at the Reformation.

'I lay down this axiom,' he says; 'there is no man that may not deceive himself. The Pope himself may err. You are mad if you say that the Pope cannot err! How many wicked Popes have there been who have erred: if they have not erred, should we do as they have done, should we be saved? You say that the Pope may err as man, but not as Pope. But I say that the Pope may err in his processes and his sentences. How many constitutions have Popes issued, annulled by other Popes; how many opinions of Popes are contrary to those of other Popes? He may err by false persuasions; he may err by malice, and against his conscience. We ought, indeed, in this case to leave the judgment to God, and charitably suppose that he has been deceived.'

He declined to seek absolution at the hands of Alexander. Why should he seek absolution?

'I should think myself guilty of mortal sin if I should seek absolution,' he says. 'Our doctrine has enforced good living, much fervour, and perpetual prayer, yet are we the excommunicated, they the blessed. Yet their doctrine leads to all evil doings—to waste in eating and drinking, to avarice, to concubinage, to the sale of benefices, to many lies, and to all wickedness. Christ! on which side wilt thou be?—on that of truth or lies? of the excommunicated or the blessed? The answer of Christ may be expected. . . . The Lord will be with the excommunicated, the devil with the blessed.'

These sermons, reported to the Pope, roused him to fury. Briefs were instantly forwarded to Florence full of threats; the city was menaced with interdict unless it yielded up the insolent priest, and so fierce was the passion of the Pope that only with the utmost difficulty could the ambassador secure a brief delay in the launching of the dread interdict. The Signory of Florence sought to appease his wrath; they reminded him of the blameless life lived by their friar, of the changed life of the city, of all that Florence had benefited through his untiring and unselfish labours. But the Pope would not be appeased; it was not the majesty of the Church which he was defending, it was his own scandalous life. By a religious mind the appeal of the Signory would have been met with an instant response; in the case of Alexander it only added fuel to the flame. It was the accusing voice, not the recalcitrant monk, which aroused his fury.

At this juncture Savonarola boldly appealed to the whole of Christendom. He wrote letters to the great sovereigns of Europe calling upon them to convene a council to depose the Pope. He claimed that the wickedness of Alexander made his possession of the holy office a scandal to the faithful; that he had bought his preferment by sacrilegious simony; that he was himself an atheist, and was guilty of such monstrous vices as to make the whole Christian world shudder. One of these letters was intercepted and shown to the Pope. After this there could be no truce or mercy. It was the last act.

### Closing Days

The net which now was closing around the life of Savonarola began to be closer drawn. Within the city his enemies grew in power, the Signory began to waver, and the crowd, ever fickle, were in that state of excitement in which a trifle would suffice to arouse their passions or win them either way. In addition to these circumstances, Savonarola's popularity was menaced by an outbreak of plague in the city ; the times were bad, and famine was rife. At such times the judgment of the populace is warped ; sullen and revengeful, they seek some victim upon whom they can vent their wrath. For long, too, a feud had existed between the rival Orders of the Dominicans and Franciscans, and in the heated passions of the hour this feud broke out afresh. The whole city was in that state in which a trifle was enough to feed the flame of passion, and make it leap into conflagration ; when even peaceable men lost their accustomed quietude and gave way to anger and excitement. The jealous hatred, which had so long separated the two Orders, was blown into fiercest flame by an offer of the Franciscans to submit their differences to the judgment of God. Such ordeals were not unknown, and that demanded was a trial by fire. Savonarola personally rejected the proposal, but he could not allay the excitement or curb the passions of his followers. Champions on either side were found. On April 7, 1498, the ordeal was appointed to take place. A huge pile was erected on the Piazza forty yards long, and through this, when set on fire, each champion was to pass. On the day appointed a huge and excited crowd gathered to see the ordeal ; the wildest passions were let loose ; men expected the miraculous to happen. But the ordeal never took place. At first the Franciscans objected to the follower of Savonarola entering the flames wearing his sacerdotal robes, next to his bearing in his hands the Host; so prolonged were these altercations that the day waned, and a downpour of rain falling, the Signory declared that no ordeal would take place. The Franciscans quickly disappeared, but Savonarola, who bore in his hands the Host, had to make a more dignified retreat. The passions of the mob, however, had been worked up to their utmost tension, and, now balked of their desires, the whole force of their wrath was levelled against Savonarola. In frenzied rage they pursued him; hurling out imprecations they threatened his life, and he was saved from being trampled to death only by the devotion of his followers, and by the popular reverence for the Host. When the gates of the monastery swung to that night, the power of the friar was broken, the die had been cast, nothing but his blood could now slake the ferocious passions of his enemies.

With the morning came a meeting of the Signory, and an instant decision to arrest the friar. Instantly a rush was made by the crowd to the convent, but the devoted friends of Savonarola were not so easily to be overwhelmed, and for long they held it against his enemies. Warning after warning reached them from the Signory, threatening them with the utmost penalties if they persisted in the defence, and at length an order was issued for the apprehension of Savonarola and several of his more prominent supporters. Even then escape might have been effected, but Savonarola refused to avail himself of it. In a quiet and affecting speech he bade farewell to his disciples, and then, permitting his hands to be bound, he walked forth into the piazza. His appearance was the signal of a frenzied outburst of hate; only with difficulty could the soldiery prevent him from being torn to pieces. As he went, the mob, who but a few weeks before hailed him as the Saviour of Florence, now hurled at him the most insulting epithets. In mockery they adapted to him the words of Scripture; striking him from behind, they shouted, 'Prophesy who it was that smote thee!'

When news of these events reached Rome, Alexander burst out into a paroxysm of delight. Brief after brief was sent to Florence. He congratulated the Signory on their justice; he absolved every one, even those guilty of homicide, who were concerned in his arrest; he congratulated the Franciscans on their success in unmasking the impostor; and he offered a plenary indulgence to all the followers of Savonarola who would return to the true faith as embodied by himself.

The remaining acts of this pitiful tragedy are only too well known to need recording. The examination of the prisoners was begun the following day, and continued during ten days more. While this examination proceeded, Savonarola was submitted to excruciating torture. Possessed of a singularly delicate and sensitive frame, he broke down under the terrible agony of the torture applied to him; no sooner was the torture withdrawn than he revoked what he had confessed. For a month Savonarola lay in prison, and then, a new Signory having been appointed, permission was asked of the Pope to proceed to capital punishment. Alexander was eager to glut his passions by having him sent to Rome where he himself would preside at the spectacle; but the Florentines, while thanking his holiness for his 'divine virtue and immense goodness,' represented to him the absolute necessity of disabusing the public mind by having the deed committed in Florence itself. Yielding to their importunities, the Pope sent as his representatives two legates who entered

Florence amid the enthusiastic acclamations of the populace. 'It is the frate's deception,' they said to each other, 'that has brought upon us all our misfortunes. Let him be burned, and our troubles will cease.' So 'Death to the friar!' was the cry with which the legates were received, who smilingly replied, 'He shall die without fail.' Indeed letters had already been received from Rome demanding the friar's death 'even if he be another John the Baptist.'

Of the confession which under excruciating torture Savonarola made, and which he was forced to sign, little need be made. Its character can be gauged by the report sent to the Pope by his own legates, from which we quote:

> 'He has been guilty of crimes so enormous that it does not seem right to make them known at present. He confessed, moreover, to have been the cause of sedition among the citizens, of scarcity of provisions, and thereby of deaths among the poor, and of the slaughter of many citizens of rank. He declared also that he had abused the Sacraments of the Church. . . . He has confessed also that by letters and messages he has sought to incite many Christian princes to a schism against your Holiness. Moreover to such a pitch of wickedness did this friar, or rather this nefarious monster, proceed, that all his appearance of goodness was but a pretence, and a cloak for ambition, and for his desire to attain to worldly glory. He has been wont to turn to the crucifix and say to our Lord, "If I lie, Thou liest." In a word such is the enormity of his crimes that the hand shrinks from writing them, and the mind from thinking of them.'

Amid the infamous documents which stand in human history to reveal the depths to which human nature may sink, there are few to equal this.

Along with Savonarola, Fra Domenico, and Fra Silvestro, two of his most faithful friends and supporters, were condemned to death. On the evening of the 22nd of May the news was brought to them that on the morrow they would suffer the penalty of the law. According to custom, a certain Nicolini was appointed to pass the night with the person condemned in order to encourage him. Entering the friar's cell he said, 'I come not to urge resignation on one who has converted a whole people to virtue.' After spending a long time in prayer, Savonarola laid his head on Nicolini's lap, and peacefully slept. And as he slept the weariness and pain seemed to slip from his face, and he was seen to smile as if it were his bridal morn.

When he and his companions were led forth on that fatal morning which opened one of the dark days in the history of the world, the Piazza della Signora was crowded with spectators. Here, in this splendid square, is found an epitome of all the city's turbulent history, of its splendid past and sordid present, of all the city's glory and of all its shame. Here the Duke of Athens was expelled from Florence, here the Ciompi rose against the Ghibellines, and in later times Alessandro de' Medici made himself Duke ; underneath the Loggia de' Lanzi, where Cellini's lovely Perseus stands, and Donatello's Judith, the laws were proclaimed ; and there, in the open space, the children made their bonfire of vanities, and Jesus Christ was proclaimed King of Florence. But another king sat triumphant over this tribunal, and out of the city gates, with bowed heads, had long since departed Love, and Justice, and Truth.

The appearance of the three monks was greeted with execrations from the crowd. 'On the marble terrace of the Palazzo were three tribunals—one near the door for the Bishop, who was to perform the ceremony of degradation ; another for the Papal Commissioners, who were to pronounce them heretics and schismatics, and deliver them over to the secular arm ; and a third for the Gonfaloniere, and the Eight who were to pronounce the sentence of death.'[1] Standing in front of the Bishop the religious habit of the three monks was stripped off. 'I separate you,' said the Bishop, 'from the Church militant, and from the Church triumphant.' 'Not from the Church triumphant,' said Savonarola, with a loud voice ; 'that is beyond thy power.' As the prisoners were led forward to the gibbet it was noted with awe that it had the form of a cross. Like his Divine Master, as he approached the place of execution Savonarola was assailed with coarse jests and curses, but on the outskirts of the crowd were men and women whom he had saved from sin, who were faithful to him, and to whom this terrible act was as the last clap of doom. 'The Lord hath suffered as much for me,' he said, as the noose was placed around his neck. A moment more and the deed was done, and that voice which had swayed the city was for ever still.

Thus died Savonarola, 'firm, calm, without the least acknowledgment of guilt, with no word of remonstrance against the cruelty of his enemies, at peace with himself, in perfect charity with all.' No sooner were his ashes thrown into the Arno than the people began to wake to the enormity of their crime. Gradually, as their fury subsided, the true lineaments of the man they had so brutally done to death appeared. They saw that the forces of hell had triumphed, and that they had been its agents. Almost instantly he became a saint. The Church even proposed to canonise him whom they had so foully condemned as a corrupter of the people. Thousands who, during his life, had remained obdurate, were brought to repentance through his death. But the death of Savonarola marks the downfall of Florence.

[1] *Romola*, by George Eliot, ch. lxxii.

Her glory had already departed, and the ills which her prophet had warned her must surely take place, came rushing with devastating swiftness upon her. 'Florence,' as Dean Milman says, 'fell to the Grand Dukes of the House of the Medici, than whom no more odious or crafty tyrants ever trampled on the liberties or outraged the moral sense of man.'

### The Movement and the Man

Turning now to survey the movement itself, we are at once cognisant of the differences which it presents when compared with that initiated under Francis of Assisi. These differences seem such as to characterise the Franciscan movement as purely a religious one, while the spiritual character of that under Savonarola seems to be dimmed, if not largely destroyed, by the interference of its leader in secular affairs. This, however, is only partly true. The words of St. Paul, that 'no man that warreth entangleth himself in secular affairs,' cannot be applied to mean that there are no circumstances in which a religious man may not intervene in times of strife or danger. The rule is one that admits of exception under exceptional circumstances, and the question is not so much whether it would have been better for Savonarola to have stood apart from the political strife of the city, as whether it was possible for him to stand apart. Being what he was, occupying the position of authority which he did, suddenly confronted by imminent dangers which he alone could avert, appealed to by every section in the city, conscious of the danger and anxious to avoid it, but urged onward by an inner impulse which seemed to him divine, which at last drove him with such certainty that resistance seemed to be impious, we are confronted with just that combination of circumstances which silences all criticism save that of the intemperate, the prejudiced, or the misinformed. Inasmuch as he suffered from the popular fury which makes its hero an idol one day, and burns him the next, he suffered as the greatest have done, and as his Master Himself.

Nor is there much to be made of the charge brought against Savonarola that he was blinded by his fanaticism, and deluded by his prophecies. Doubtless he was often carried away beyond the bounds of reason, and often failed to distinguish the thin dividing line between the man who speaks for God in condemning present iniquity, and the man who seeks to give his words a terrifying sanction by forecasting the future. The point to remember, however, is, that it was not because his prophecies were unfulfilled that he was hated, but because they were unwelcome. In these days his claim to prophesy was not considered impious; if he had prophesied smooth things, he would never have been hated. The reason he was hated was that he spoke the truth about men's sins, and made the future black with their overthrow. It has been the fashion from the beginning to silence such men by means of the stake and the gibbet, and Savonarola's was only another name added to a long noble list.

It is just possible, too, that the tragedy of the great Prior's death may dim for us the real glory, and the vast influence, of his life. It is a common error to think that, with the leader violently put to death amid popular fury, the cause is likewise extinguished. Men thought so around the Cross; the death of the Founder was to them synonymous with the extinction of the heresy. But the Truth once spoken, evil once unmasked, righteousness once set in motion, the consequent activity can no more be arrested than the sweep of a tidal wave, or the coming of the dawn. The voice of Savonarola —sounding through Europe, condemning abuses, holding up in the glare of the day the sins done in secret, fearlessly tearing the mask from the lives of those who claimed sanctity because of their holy office, while their lives were a profanity and a sham, preaching to men repentance, and that the kingdom of God was at hand —was not raised in vain. It hurried on, and made possible the crisis. It forced men to reconsider claims which before they had accepted without question ; it was the herald of the Reformation. As with all others who have suffered at the hands of evil men, his death did more for the cause of righteousness than his life. After the dementia passes, the world wakes to the truth ; and to the bitterness of being mistaken, there is added the rage at being fooled. So remorse sets in, and with it rage against those by whom they have been deluded. At Savonarola's death men turned to look at the claims of Pope and priest with a new light in their eyes, and with something in their hearts which boded ill for all hypocrisies in the days to come. He was thus the herald of a new movement, the John the Baptist of the Reformation. 'When Savonarola, degraded and unfrocked, ended his life on the gallows, his cause seemed irretrievably lost, and his enemies triumphed. Nevertheless, he died a conqueror, and he died for the noblest cause for which a man can give his life—for the spread of God's kingdom on earth. The future belonged to him, and he to the Church.' So writes Dr. Schnitzer, and we may make his words our own.

The more immediate result of the friar's life, however, is to be found in Florence, in that city for which he gave his life. That he awakened a genuine revival of spiritual religion, a revival which did not pass with his life, but grew and deepened in thousands of hearts, is not for a moment to be doubted. He not only influenced for good the lives of unknown citizens, but he profoundly affected the lives of some of the greatest men of the day. Sandro Botticelli, Fra Bartolommeo, and others gave up painting for love of him; the two Robbias and Lorenzo di Credi entered the Church through the effect of his preaching upon them; some of the greatest scholars of the day sat at his feet; Michael Angelo, to the day of his death, pored over his sermons and drew inspiration from them; while to the monastery of St. Mark the friar had drawn men from all the noblest families of the city. Nor was his influence confined to those of maturer years, since his love for the children produced in their lives the most wonderful change. 'Words fail me,' says a contemporary writer, Cinozzi, 'when I try to set forth the change, the wonderful, stupendous, and almost incredible conversion, of so many thousands of boys of every condition of life. What they were, how deeply plunged in every kind of vice, every one knows who has lived in the city. Their dress bespoke both pride and a shameless lack of modesty. . . so that Florence had become another Sodom, a thing horrible to think of; they were gamblers, blasphemers, and given up to every kind of vice. But under the influence of the friar's preaching they became entirely changed, laid aside their vain and unbecoming modes of dress, desisted from the vices of which I have spoken, and became so fervent as to be an example to all Florence. In their faces there shone the radiance of divine grace, so that by their means a great work was achieved.'

Of Savonarola's character little need be said. No one doubted the noble sincerity of the man. Even in his own church he was regarded with the deepest veneration by such saints as Philip Neri, and Catherine de' Ricci, and by Benedict xiv. was deemed worthy of canonisation. Through the darkness of these dark days, in which it was his sorrowful lot to have been cast, his character shines in undimmed splendour. He bore on his heart the sorrows and the sins of men. He sought nothing for himself; his days and nights he spent in prayer, and in laborious study of the Word of God. He rediscovered the Bible, and in this respect also was a precursor of the Reformation. As a preacher he has never been surpassed, perhaps has never been equalled, in the history of the Christian pulpit. The visitor to the Duomo to-day, as he walks the marble floor of its vast solitude, and listens to the echo of his footsteps, recalls those days, when, crowded to its utmost extent, and filled with a vast sea of faces intently gazing upon the preacher, its walls echoed with that deep and resonant voice which sounded to many as the voice of doom, and which, in its notes of passionate entreaty, brought thousands of hardened sinners to the Cross. Never before, perhaps, never since, have there been heard eloquence so sustained, earnestness so intense, passion for righteousness so concentrated, as were heard in those days, when, from the pulpit in the Duomo, Savonarola ruled Florence in the name of His Master, Jesus Christ. He died amid the execrations of those he tried to save. He died a martyr's death after having been delivered into the hands of evil men. And now, when persecutors and persecuted long have gone, and the dust of controversy has passed away, we look again upon his face, and remembering all that he was, all that he did, all that he suffered, we bow our heads, and say: 'Truly this was a great and noble man.'

# LUTHER AND THE REVIVAL IN GERMANY

RELIGIOUS interest swings now away from the Latin to the Teutonic races. There, in these northern lands, whose population was regarded as barbaric long after Rome had reached its zenith, that mighty revival, which for centuries had been preparing, was to have its birth. No more important event has happened since the birth of Christianity ; none more volcanic in its effects ; none more vital in its issues. According to some writers it owed its existence ' to a certain uncommon and malignant position of the stars, which scattered the spirit of giddiness and innovation over the world ' ; to another class it had its origin ' in Luther's desire for a wife.' Such explanations can be dismissed with amusement and with contempt. All great movements which profoundly affect human life have their origin, as we have seen, in causes which lie far back in history. They are the result of many influences—some of them obvious, some of them hidden, many of them too minute to trace, but all contributing to the great end, and combining at last in the great upheaval. It is the duty of those who would understand such movements patiently to seek the causes which gave them birth. When this is done, men see, behind these events, not the evil influence of the stars, but the purposes of the Almighty.

The Reformation may be regarded from two aspects. First it may be viewed from its intellectual side, as the dawn of a new period in history, marking the emancipation of the human mind, and the first great step in the march of freedom. On the other hand it may be regarded from the religious side, as a revival of spiritual life after a long period of darkness; as a return to Biblical Christianity in opposition to the sacerdotal system which had grown around it. It is with the latter —the Reformation as a revival of spiritual religion—that we have to do; and whatever further steps the movement once initiated was forced to take, it is well to remember that the reformers had this at first solely in view. No break with the Romish Church was contemplated. The reformers sought a reformation from within; they sought to cleanse the Church from its offences; they sought to regain for the Church its primitive life and faith. The abuses which the reformers sought to remedy, however, were found to be so inextricably wedded to the system, that nothing was left to them but to separate themselves from it. Beginning by condemning abuses, they went on to denounce errors, and finding that reformation could not be effected from within, they were forced to attack it from without. The supreme fact with which we are concerned is that the Reformation was supremely a revival; that it marked, for a vast multitude, the recovery of faith; that it was a rebirth in the world of primitive and evangelic Christianity, and lighted myriads of human hearts with the flame of spiritual joy.

### Causes of the Revival

The cause of every revival, either in the history of the individual or the community, is the mysterious action of the Holy Spirit operating in the heart. Yet in the action of the Holy Spirit there is no reason for expecting that which is arbitrary or capricious. We have already seen that there is a certain similarity in the experience of the individual and the community. In neither is the pressure of the consciousness of the presence of God uniform. There are long times of seeming withdrawal. These are times of lethargy and spiritual insensibility, when the heart of man seems dead to the unseen, when the spirit of levity and worldliness creeps into and corrupts society, and invades even the sanctuary of the Church, and infects her priests and ministers. So prolonged is this state often, that it seems as if society had become so hopelessly corrupted that it could not live, as if in the prevailing wickedness God had forgotten to be gracious, and had finally cast us off. Then gradually, almost imperceptibly, a change takes place ; new emotions and longings arise ; there is a soul-weariness, a craving for something deeper than the world can give, a disposition to pray, a hunger for God. Scarcely audible at first, the cry increases, it mounts up to Heaven, it beats against the gates of the Most High, in unwearied importunity it knocks, and seeks, and asks ; and then, at length, in response to the vast need, the gates are flung open, and poured down upon the world there falls a shower of blessed revival and spiritual quickening.

Of all such movements the most momentous, because the most widespread, is that which we are now to consider. At this point of history, conflicting forces which had been gathering from widely different centres, clashed together. Vast changes, which had been silently gathering shape, seemed at this point of time to emerge. The Reformation, therefore, marks a crisis in the history of civilisation as well as in the history of religion, and it is the meeting of these various movements which gives to it its peculiar significance. It marks, for instance, the end of mediævalism and the birth of the modern spirit. The discovery of printing revolutionised letters; the discovery of gunpowder revolutionised the art of war; the Papacy had become a secular as well as a spiritual power, the Pope a possessor of Empire; nationalism had arisen on the ruins of feudalism.

It is with the Church of Christ, however, that we are mainly concerned, and the causes within it which cried out for cleansing and renewal. 'Never,' says Froude, 'has mankind thrown out of itself anything so grand, so useful, so beautiful as the Catholic Church once was.' This is a great declaration, but no one will doubt that it is a true one. After passing through centuries of the most terrible persecution the Church of Christ arose in the world—imperfect, no doubt, and containing many excesses, but nevertheless the one safeguard of law and order, the refuge of the weak and oppressed, a terror to evil-doers, and the last hope of the wretched. For centuries it remained so, and while it remained so it was the noblest thing that the world possessed. It stood for liberty against oppression; for mercy against might; for law against disorder; for the protection of the weak and defenceless; and for the defence of every righteous and worthy thing. Even the Church of Christ, however, sacred as it is, cannot claim exemption from the influences which make for corruption. When once apostolic simplicity gave way, when wealth began to pour into the Church, when her priests began to taste the sweets of luxurious living and of power, the days of moral decline set in. This is the history of all institutions. Prosperity kills the spiritual in them; they grow fat and worldly; the ideals which called them into being, and for which men willingly lay down their lives, cease, in days of wealth and ease, either to quicken the imagination or move the heart. The successors of the martyrs sit at ease; they wax gross and heavy; their ears are dull of hearing; their eyes are sleepy through indulgence; they remain inert and tolerant while corruption is eating away the defences of the Church and of society. When this happens in the Church—and we have seen that it does—the disaster is immeasurable. The corruption of the best is the worst, and it is this corruption which confronts us as we survey the condition of the Church in the beginning of the sixteenth century.

Something of the condition of the Church in Italy we have already seen, for Luther was born when Savonarola had entered Florence for the first time, and when he died, Luther was a youth of fifteen. For the Church's corrupt condition two things are mainly responsible.

1. *The love of Wealth.*

In the ruthless days of the Middle Ages men could only be restrained by terror, and the Church alone could terrify their minds. It did so by the penalties of excommunication, and by holding before them the frightful punishments which awaited evil doers in the future world. A glance at the art of the period is sufficient to indicate with what gross and terrible realism the sufferings of the damned were conceived. To propitiate the Church, to gain pardon for their misdeeds, and to win a safe-conduct through the dark and terrible regions whose fires were ever lighted below, men readily parted, especially at death when they had no more use for them, with their ill-gotten gains. This custom of leaving wealth to the Church increased in those days when the fall of the Roman Empire gave to men a terrible sense of insecurity; and still more when they thought that the end of the world was approaching. Hastening to divest themselves of their wealth and property, the wisest investment, it seemed to them, was to hand it over to the Church. Nor was the Church found unwilling to accept such treasure, though she would have been wise had she refused it; for the effect was disastrous upon her spiritual witness. Great churches began to be built; monasteries, discarding the austerities imposed upon them by their founders, became wealthy corporations. The monks possessed of the richest lands, having all things and abounding, without occupation to employ their time, became first lax in their duties, next indifferent to them, and finally abandoning even the outward pretence of piety, plunged into the utmost excesses of vice. So corrupt, indeed, did the Church become, that escape from every earthly penalty was possible to those who could pay for it. Not only so, but the gates of entrance into the kingdom of heaven were made to open and close at the clink of gold. Money became increasingly necessary as the Papacy extended its secular dominions and sway. So, by extortion, by the threat of penalties, by the exercise of all kinds of trickery, by terrorising their victims, by offering drafts upon the future world, by every device, almost, which avarice could devise, money was raised; the poor were robbed of their possessions, and held down in an embittering bondage.

2. *The love of Power.*

If the love of money is the root of evil, the love of power must be a not inconsiderable branch. The power of the popes, as we have seen, was of the most unlimited character. They were the dictators of Europe. The proudest monarchs had to bow to their commands. So helpless was the secular power that it could not be applied to those over whom the Church flung its mantle. A priest was not punishable at the hands of the law. He was a sacred person, and in the event of his committing a crime, could only be judged and punished by his ecclesiastical superiors. While thus the secular courts were helpless to reach the ecclesiastic, there was no realm, however sacred, into which the arm of the Church could not reach. With the growth of its worldly power there followed, almost in exact ratio, a decline in its spiritual testimony. The lust of power became the second great passion of the clergy, and having almost unlimited opportunity to exercise it through their hold upon the consciences of the worshippers, their superstitious terrors, and their ignorance, it is not in human nature to possess such power and not abuse it. With the ambition of the popes to raise the Papacy to temporal power came the final step. The Church of Christ has no other reason for existence save that of creating a holy society in which the life of Christ, its Founder, shall be reproduced, and acting through that society upon the world. With the entrance of the Church into competition with secular powers came an instant deterioration of morals, and the loss of the one thing which gave it a reason for existence.

In the interval which separates Luther from Savonarola, Alexander, the Pope at whose instigation the prior had been done to death, had also gone to his account, and had been succeeded by Julius II. 'More of a soldier than a pope,' says Sarpi. Under his martial rule, in which things spiritual were almost entirely neglected, the Papacy reached its culmination as a temporal power. Julius was succeeded by the sceptic, Leo X., whose nature was a combination of intellectualism and sensualism, and who would have been a complete Pope, says the historian already quoted, 'if he had only added some knowledge in things that concern religion, and some propensity unto piety, of both of which he seemed careless.'

With the condition of the Church in Italy during the

fifteenth century we have already dealt, and as it was in Italy, so was it over the whole of Europe. Pope and priest became the subject of jest and ridicule. Their scandalous lives induced imitation in those who were not naturally vicious, and gave a horrible sanction to the excesses of those who were. All respect for the Church as a divine institution vanished. Its condition became the subject of mockery to the flippant, of indignation to the serious, and of agony to the devout.

Yet, even in that age, God was not without His witnesses. The spiritual life within the Church was kept alive by religious mystics, such as Tauler and Eckhart, Gerson and Thomas à Kempis. Even in those dark days there were men in lonely cells bowing in agony of prayer for the Church's restoration, and for a revival of spiritual religion. Gradually there settled down upon men's minds a fever of unrest. Sects began to arise, such as the Albigenses and Waldenses; in almost every land the cry for reform was raised; Savonarola fanned the flame in degenerate Italy; Wycliffe in England, Huss in Bohemia; and these were joined by thousands of less notable men. At the same time a passion for religious pilgrimages broke out. Men and women, and even young children, were suddenly seized with a sort of frenzy of devotion, and joining together in companies, which swelled as they advanced, they journeyed to some famous shrine, hoping there to gain deliverance from their fears, and the remission of their sins. Strange cults sprang up bearing curious names; the worship of the Virgin increased enormously; while fraternities and religious associations were formed amongst the common people—often independent of the clergy. Everywhere there was feverish dissatisfaction, a bitter distaste of life, a craving for something that would satisfy their intense spiritual hunger. Everywhere there was darkness, the lowering of the tempest, the hoarse mutterings of the storm. We have met with these phenomena in our previous studies, but here they are on a vaster scale. While Italy was being weakened by internal discord and the growing Paganism of the Renaissance, vigorous nations, independent in mind, and uncorrupted by a decaying civilisation, were growing up around her. This movement, therefore, previously restricted to Italy, the home of culture and piety, had burst its ancient barriers; into it there entered the robust, freedom-loving peoples of the north, unencumbered by traditions, naturally fretful under restraint. Amongst them this soul-weariness was fast becoming intolerable. While the Latin race, accustomed to the separation between sacred rank and scandalous living, looked on with comparative complacency, the Teutonic found the dissonance unendurable. The hour had come. The pent-up waters, fretting and chafing behind their barriers, were groping for an outlet. They waited for the hand of one who could open the gates and let them free. In the fulness of the times he appeared, and out of a humble German home there comes to meet us the rugged form of Martin Luther.

### Early Days

Luther was born in the town of Eisleben in Prussian Saxony on November 10, 1483. His parents were poor, his father a miner; from his earliest days he knew the pinch which comes from want. Of his humble origin he had too much healthy common sense to be ashamed. 'I am,' he said with pride to Melanchthon, 'a peasant's son; my father, grandfather, all my ancestors were genuine peasants.'

His youth was spent in scenes and amid conditions

of hardship, and in a home in which the discipline was stern,—too stern, as he afterwards declared. His mother flogged him so severely for stealing a nut that the blood came; nor was his father less strict a disciplinarian. The recollection of his own early experiences at home and at school made him compassionate toward the young of his own generation. 'Be temperate with your children,' he was wont to say; 'punish them if they lie or steal, but be just in what you do.' In these early days he was taught to pray to God and to the saints; but his imagination was inflamed by terrible stories of warlocks and witches which haunted him to his dying day. At school he learned the Creed, Catechism, Ten Commandments, and several hymns; but his intercourse with the common people educated him in their needs, and stored his mind with their shrewd and kindly wisdom. Much of the power of popular expression came to him through his ancestry of the soil, and his early education in the lore of the people. To pay for his education he had to sing through the streets—not an uncommon practice in those days—and attracted the notice of a wealthy lady, who invited him to her table 'on account of his hearty singing and praying.' This lady has been made a chief subject in the well-known novel entitled *Chronicles of the Schönberg-Cotta Family,* and through his intercourse with her, Luther learned 'that there is nothing dearer in all the world than the love of woman.'

When eighteen, Luther entered the university of Erfurt, then one of the best in Germany. Here Scholasticism still predominated, tempered in a slight degree with Humanism, that product of the Renaissance. He was regarded with great good-will by his fellow-students, both for his gifts as a musician, and for the geniality of his character. His mental gifts, however, were even more apparent, since he was able to graduate as Bachelor of Arts in 1502, and take his degree as Master of Arts three years later. His father, who by this time had improved his position, was anxious for him to follow the profession of the law, and with this in view he began to prepare himself, when an event took place which changed his whole career, and which, it is not too much to say, changed, in its ultimate effects, the history of Europe.

### Luther's Conversion

From earliest days Luther had been of a devout mind without being conscious of a divine call. Though in obedience to his father's desires he took up the study of law, his main interests were directed toward theology. Then a sudden circumstance brought before him the awful needs of the soul. A friend, whom he deeply loved, was struck dead by lightning at his side. Shortly afterwards, in returning from his parents' house, he was overtaken by a violent thunderstorm. This seemed to have filled him with an unaccountable terror. To his overstrained nerves it appeared as if God were directing His bolts against him, and falling upon his knees he cried: 'Help! beloved Saint Anna! I will become a monk.' This indicates the direction in which he had secretly been travelling, and on the 16th of July 1505 Luther entered the Augustinian Convent at Erfurt.

The condition of the monasteries, as they existed in Italy, Germany, and England at this time, was, says Froude, 'so shocking that even impartial writers have hesitated to believe the reports which have come down to us.' These reports, however, are alas! too well authenticated to be denied. The practices permitted within them are such that they cannot be published, and with every disposition to believe the best, and to make allowances for the changed character of the times, the reader turns from the reports of their condition with nausea and disgust. ‘A monk's holy obedience,’ says Erasmus, who had reason to know monastic life well, ‘consists in—what? In leading an honest, chaste, and sober life? Not the least. In acquiring learning, in study, and industry? Still less. A monk may be a glutton, a drunkard, a whoremonger, an ignorant, stupid, malignant, envious brute, but he has broken no vow, he is within his holy obedience. He has only to be the slave of a superior as good for nothing as himself, and he is an excellent brother.’

The monastery into which Luther entered was a model of piety in those days. It was presided over by John von Staupitz, a mystic, and a devout writer, for whom Luther retained both affection and admiration. But even in this monastery Luther quickly revealed himself to the monks as a strange anomaly. His intense seriousness amazed them; for he practised every austerity which the rule devised—he fasted and prayed; he assumed the most menial offices to subdue his pride; he begged from door to door in the public streets. ‘If ever a monk got to heaven by monkery,’ he said long afterwards, ‘I would have gotten there.’ But with all his self-mortification he could not gain peace of conscience. The more he struggled the deeper he seemed to sink in wretchedness and in self-loathing. He could not convict himself of any one transgression above another, but he felt sin weighing him down; sin in its infinite subtlety, sin as alienation from God, corrupting his nature, defiling the world, casting him adrift with the wrath of God resting upon him. In deepest agony of soul he increased his austerities; he fasted and prayed; his tears were his meat day and night. Bitterly did he enter into the experience of the Psalmist:

> 'The pains of Hell gat hold upon me:
> I found trouble and sorrow.'

He saw sin in everything he did, but he could not rid himself of it; 'O wretched man that I am! who shall deliver me from the body of this death?' he continually cried; but he had not learned to say, 'I thank God through Jesus Christ our Lord. . . . For the law of the Spirit of life in Jesus Christ has made me free from the law of sin and death.' He could not rid himself of the awful words, 'I the Lord thy God am a jealous God.' Weak and trembling he went to his confessor, and besought his advice; but the jovial friar had never known a case such as his. 'Don't make a mountain out of trifles,' he said. But sin, guilt of conscience, the burden of the unforgiven heart—these were no trifles to Luther. Shallow men can be satisfied with shallow evasions, but men like Paul, and Francis, and Savonarola and Luther, and all men of profound character refuse to be fed on sophistries. Sin to them is a terrible thing; in the hour of soul distress they see in it alienation from God, an awful power menacing the world, lifting itself up in impious defiance of God's holy Law.

Through the advice of Staupitz, Luther was led to the study of the Scriptures, and especially to the study of the Epistles of St. Paul. Gradually there dawned in his heart the victory of justifying faith; he came to realise that God, out of His infinite grace, and not through any merit of the sinner, is willing fully and freely to forgive all who in faith come to Him. This truth flashed into his mind with all the swiftness and power of a divine revelation. It brought to him that radiant peace which comes from conviction, and that joy which is born of spiritual certainty. To the end of his life it was to be the rock to which he clung for safety, the place of joyous refuge for his soul in every tumult. No longer a slave enchained by fear, the Gospel had set him free ; he was now a son in his Father's house.

The first step in Luther's spiritual experience now was taken. He had entered into possession of a truth which cut at the root of much of the traditional belief of his day, and still more of its abuses. He held it, however, without for a moment realising whither it would lead him. The new truth seemed to accommodate itself at first with the old practices, but an experience through which he passed drew him a step nearer to that position in which separation became inevitable.

### The Preparation

In the autumn of 1510 Luther was sent on a mission connected with his convent to Rome. He went with heart glowing with devout expectation. 'Blessed Rome !' he cried, as he entered the gate, 'Blessed Rome ! sanctified by the blood of the martyrs !' But his emotion was short-lived. Instead of a holy city, full of piety and religious observance, he found it wholly given over to idolatry. Julius, the Pope, had just returned, flushed with victory, after a sanguinary siege of a town, which he had conducted in person. Priests he found saying mass, and mocking the elements in the midst of their sacred duties. In saying the Mass himself he was told to 'hurry up, and send her Son home to our Lady.' In Rome he learned the truth of the awful stories of the previous Pope, stories circulated in Germany, but believed to be incredible. 'If there was a hell,' he was told, 'Rome was built upon it.' For himself, he ran like 'a crazy saint,' from church to church, adoring relics, and worshipping at the shrines of saints; he toilsomely crawled up the steps of the Scala Santa in order that he might possess the indulgence promised to the faithful; but even as he did so, the words of the new evangel came sounding in his ears, 'The just shall live by faith.' To Luther the whole city became a place of horror. He turned and fled from it as if pursued by the furies. 'Adieu, Rome!' he cried. 'Let all who would live a holy life flee from thee. Everything is permitted of thee except to be an honest man.'

Recalling his bitter experiences in after years he declared 'I would not have missed seeing Rome for a thousand florins; for I might have felt some apprehension that I had done an injustice to the Pope; but as we see, so we speak.'

Returning to Wittenberg, whither he had been sent as lecturer, he completed his scholastic training by taking the degree of Doctor in 1512. Soon afterwards he began to deliver exegetical lectures on the Psalms and the Pauline Epistles, and here the theological preparation for the revival may be said to have been made. The effect of these lectures was profound. Those who listened to them realised that some new force had awakened, without being able to analyse what the force was. 'This monk,' said Dr. Pollich, 'will revolutionise the whole scholastic teaching.' And with Luther's sturdy and homely eloquence, the flippancy of the schools and their petty trivialities began to look ridiculous. His burning earnestness, his intense convictions, his consciousness of having got possession of a living truth, and of not playing with a mere shibboleth, profoundly surprised and profoundly affected his audience. 'There is here a divine,' says another learned doctor, 'who explains the epistles of the man of

Tarsus with wonderful genius.' 'This monk,' said another, 'is a marvellous fellow. He has strange eyes, and will give the doctors trouble by and by.'

Along with the theology of Augustine, whose writings had profoundly influenced his mind and shaped his thought, a new influence at this time entered, not so much to formulate his opinions, as to deepen his piety. Happening to read a few sentences of a book by the mystic Tauler, he was at once arrested by its teaching regarding the submission of the individual will, and the absorption of the soul in God. Luther was too sane and practical to be carried far into the passivity of the mystic temperament, but he drew from Tauler's writings much that was spiritually valuable. They left a definite impression both upon his piety and upon his theology.

Thus, gradually, Luther's mind was ripening. The peace and comfort, which he had derived from the new conception of being justified by trustful faith, gave him a confident message to his day and generation. But his powerful and original mind began to work on the discovery he had made. He could not leave it as a mere emotion, he had to formulate it into a theology, to give it its place in the logical sequence of his matured convictions. Slowly and imperceptibly thus there was being built up within him a system of belief which, when carried to its ultimate issue, was not only likely to give the doctors trouble, but which undermined the whole system in which they had been trained. Yet all this time Luther was a devout and loyal son of the Catholic Church. His last thought was of separation, or even of reformation. He still offered prayers to the Virgin and the Saints; still believed and taught the doctrine of Transubstantiation; still performed, without offence, the daily office. Yet there was growing up at the same time within him an ever deepening detestation of the frauds perpetrated upon the simple by the clergy. His keen and independent mind saw through them ; his own transparency and sincerity of character made him rebel against them ; and never lacking in courage or outspokenness, he could not help smiting them when occasion arose.

Thus, through these formative years, was Luther being trained for the work he was called to do. Forced by a combination of circumstances over which he had no control, impelled by his spiritual discoveries, by intellectual convictions, and by righteous indignation, he was gradually converging upon the inevitable goal. To the same goal, and by many different routes, many of the best spirits of his age were moving. There, blindly, but led by an unfailing instinct, the mass of the people had already arrived. For the hour of destiny had struck. The old order had become corrupt, and threatened the health of the world. The hour had come, and with it the Man.

### The Dawn of the Revival

'Behold!' says the Apostle James, 'how great a matter a little fire kindleth.' What follows is an apt illustration of the truth of this reflection. The times were such that it needed only a spark to cause a conflagration, and that spark was supplied by one John Tetzel, emissary of the Pope, past master in the sale of indulgences.

At this time a great church was in process of erection at Rome. Leo the Tenth had imbibed the spirit of the Renaissance in its love of art, as well as in its Paganism ; and his ambition was to build, like Constantine, a church that would outshine that of Solomon and his successors.

Plans for the building had been furnished by Michael Angelo himself, and all that was needed for the completion of the scheme was money, much money, for the Papal exchequer was at this time not overflowing. But how was this money to be raised ? The building of a great cathedral in Rome was not likely to arouse the enthusiasm of the faithful, and Rome itself was impoverished and indifferent. A promising scheme for the raising of money was ready to hand in the sale of indulgences.

In the ecclesiastical use of the word an Indulgence means the remission of the temporal punishment for sin. These indulgences were technically only available in the case of those punishments, not of mortal sin, but of such penalties as extend into Purgatory. They were only to be considered valid also when accompanied by penitence, and the payment of a certain sum of money to the Church or some charitable object. Represented by the hawkers of the Pope, however, they were considered as nothing less than 'letters of credit upon heaven.' On the one side debited against them were the sins they had committed, on the credit side the money they had paid by way of compensation. Did a man want to marry a forbidden relation ? gratify a secret indulgence ? escape the penalty when the deed was done ? get his relations a swift release ? then all that had to be done was to drop his money into the box provided for it, and surely as the money tinkled, release would be obtained.

Of those who carried out the Pope's design the most successful, because the most brazen and audacious, was this John Tetzel already mentioned. He travelled throughout Germany in state, and gathering crowds wherever he went, he, with cool effrontery, described his wares and charged the people to buy. And buy the people did, encouraged as they were by their priests and spiritual advisers. So terribly had the future been presented to them that escape from it on such easy terms was not to be neglected. So in crowds they passed up the aisles of their churches, paid their money, and went away rejoicing with their free passports for heaven.

At length, in his triumphal procession, Tetzel arrived at the borders of Saxony, only a few hours from Wittenberg. Luther was on the outlook for him. This thing was a lie and could no longer be tolerated. The remission of sin, he had learned, was not to be given by Pope or priest; it is God's free gift of grace to all who by faith apprehend it. How could he sit in silence and see this travesty of divine truth perpetrated, and the people deluded by their spiritual guides? He must speak, and speak he did. First of all he addressed a letter of remonstrance to the Archbishop of Mayence. This worthy prelate, though a friend of Luther's, did not deign even to reply, and perhaps silence was golden in his case, since he was promised half of the spoils. Denied redress by his ecclesiastical superior, Luther struck the first note of the Reformation by appealing away from such authorities direct to the people. On the church door of Wittenberg he nailed his ninety-five propositions, challenging the Church to defend its action, denying its power to take away sins, to remit penalties other than those which the Church itself inflicts. At twelve o'clock, on the 31st day of October 1517, he nailed his theses to the door, and his act has been truly regarded as marking one of the great epochs in human history.

The effect of this publication by Luther was of the most extraordinary character. News of it seemed to be borne on the wings of the wind. Copies were printed and went through the entire land, it was said, in fourteen days. The wildest excitement prevailed. The voice, which men had waited for so long, at length had spoken, and at the first sound of it the people rose up in welcome. For, as Froude has truly observed, 'It is with human things as with the great icebergs which drift southward out of the frozen seas. They swim two-thirds under water, and one-third above; and as long as the equilibrium is sustained, you would think that they were as stable as rocks. But the sea water is warmer than the air. Hundreds of fathoms down the tepid current washes the base of the berg. Silently, in those far deeps, the centre of gravity is changed; and then, in a moment, with one vast roll, the enormous mass heaves over, and the crystal peaks, which had been glancing so proudly in the sunlight, are buried in the ocean for ever.' Such a process had been silently going on, unconsciously to him who sat in Peter's chair, or to those whose interest it was to maintain the old order. 'The people that sit in darkness shall see a great light' is everlastingly true, and is fulfilled in every revival in human history.

## Luther as Reformer

The publication of his theses had thrown Luther unwittingly into the leadership of a movement of vast dimensions. His bold stand was welcomed by liberal minds amongst the theologians, but most of all by the devout, who saw in the awful degeneracy of the times an insult to the faith, and in the declaration of Luther the dawn of a better day for Christ's people. But he was denounced with the vilest reproaches on all sides by the defenders of the Pope, and especially by those whose income was threatened were indulgences withdrawn. The Pope himself was not alarmed. Looking over the pages of Luther's indictment he smiled in amusement. 'A drunken German wrote them,' he said. 'When he has slept off his wine he will be of another mind.'

Luther was still a loyal member of the Church of Rome, but the discussion which his theses had awakened drove him to examine, with more care than he had yet done, the ground of the Papal claims. To his intense surprise he discovered how weak was their foundation; the decretals upon which much of the Papal power had been established he discovered to be forgeries; this threw him back upon the Scriptures, and to the further discovery that they gave no sanction to the claims of the Papacy. Thus the one step led inevitably to another. In considering the grounds upon which the practice of selling Indulgences should be condemned, he was forced to consider the grounds of the Church's authority; denying its authority in the one case, he had to justify it in others, and finding the whole superstructure crumbling, had to set about reconstructing it. The movement thus branched into channels, which the originators of it least expected, but which they were helpless to avert. Beginning by seeking to reform from within, without questioning the claims of the Church which had been slowly built up through the centuries, the movement next forced its leaders to examine those claims, then to reject them, and finding reformation impossible from within, they were forced to seek it from without. While regretting the necessity, it is difficult to see how it could have been obviated. Ecclesiasticism, which had imposed increasing servitude upon the lives of men, and which had become corrupt through abuse, was bound to come into conflict with primitive Christianity, unless primitive Christianity were finally to be buried under a marble sarcophagus, and the spirit of man finally enslaved. As neither is possible, as every religious movement is a liberating of the human spirit from the bondage of ecclesiasticism, and a return to the primitive evangelical faith, and as the fight for freedom plays a necessary part in the evolution of the individual and the race, the struggle was inevitable. The form which it took depended upon its leaders, upon circumstances over which men have control; the extent of its success depended upon the temper, the spirituality, the earnestness of the men who led it; but the movement itself, when once begun, could no more be stopped than the avalanche when loosened by the breath of spring. Into this movement, therefore, unlike the others we have been considering, there entered elements of a complex character. The upheaval was so vast that it affected not only religious life but social and political life as well. It was an intellectual movement marking a new dawn in the history of human thought; it was a political movement marking a new development in human freedom; it was a theological movement marking a reconstruction of belief and of Church government, but most of all, and first of all, it was a revival of evangelical Christianity; it was a movement which brought men back to Christ, to a living faith, and to a new and blessed realisation of Christ's mercy toward sinful men.

Into all these various movements it is not our duty here to enter. We seek to follow but one channel, and in doing this it will be necessary to deal only slightly with the various conflicts in which, through the complex character of the movement, Luther had to engage.

If the Pope at first saw no cause for alarm as he read the theses of Luther, he soon found cause to alter his mind. With incredible speed the movement was taking shape; in every city and university, Luther's name was known, and his action discussed. The Pope, therefore, commanded him to appear before him at Rome, a command which Luther was not anxious to obey. Rome had not the best of names as a centre for free discussion, and the justice and mercy of papal judgments were not at that time to be relied upon.

It happened, in the providence of God, that Saxony was ruled at this time by a man of sterling worth. Prince Frederick was a good Catholic, and a good man, and because he was both he viewed with pain the prevailing corruption. To the amazement of every one, Frederick intervened. Before agreeing to hand over Luther to Rome, he sent for Erasmus, who represents the movement on its intellectual side, and asked his opinion. 'Luther,' said Erasmus laconically, 'has committed two sins; he has touched the Pope's crown and the monks' bellies.'

Hearing of Frederick's delay, the Pope wrote a threatening letter, and Frederick, while he dared not openly refuse, temporised. At length it was arranged that Luther's case should be dealt with at Augsburg, and a papal legate was sent from Rome to deal with it. Thither Luther willingly went, the crowd shouting as he left Wittenberg: 'Luther for ever.' 'Nay,' said the great Reformer gravely, 'Christ for ever.'

At Augsburg he met the papal legate, who commanded him in the Pope's name to recant. But Luther suggested, as a preliminary condition, the duty of the legate to prove him wrong. Finding threats of no avail, bribes, and then entreaties were tried, but nothing would shake the fearless monk. Losing his temper at length, the legate cried: 'What! do you think that the Pope cares for the opinion of a German boor like you? The Pope's little finger is stronger than all

Germany. Do you expect your princes to take up arms to defend *you* ? I tell you, No. And where will you be then—where will you be then ? ' 'Then, as now,' replied Luther, 'in the hands of Almighty God.' So another step was taken. The legate returned to his master, Luther to the safety of his own city.

We enter now the storm and stress period of Luther's life, and of the movement. Low mutterings of the coming storm began to be heard, and around the head of this solitary and daring monk the lightning began to play. Enraged at the report given him of Luther's obduracy, the Pope promptly excommunicated him, demanding again from Frederick that he be sent to Rome. But Frederick still temporised. 'There is much in the Bible about Christ,' he said, 'but not much about Rome.' Meanwhile, at the Elector's instigation, Luther made overtures for peace. These were contemptuously rejected. 'My being such a small creature,' said Luther afterwards, 'was a misfortune to the Pope. He despised me too much. What, he thought, could a slave like me do to him—to him, the greatest man in all the world ? Had he accepted my proposal he would have extinguished me.' Certainly had Luther once reached Rome, no more would have been heard of him. The respect of popes for human life can be gauged by recalling the words used by Gregory XIII. with regard to our own Queen Elizabeth : 'Whosoever removed such a vile monster from the world would be doing God service.' Finding that he could not entice him to Rome, the Pope hurled a bull at him, excommunicating him, and condemning him and all his works. This bull Luther burned in the great square of Wittenberg, and this public act marks his definite break with the Catholic Church. Influenced and helped by Melanchthon, a young scholar of great sweetness of character, and of vast erudition, Luther began in rapid succession to issue his appeals to the nobility, to the clergy, and to the people. 'The time for silence is gone,' he declared, 'and the time for speaking has come.'

In his *Address to the German Nobility* he condemns the exclusion of the laity from control in the Church, declaring that the only difference between the two is not of estate, but simply of office. He condemns, also, the evil lives of pope and cardinals, their greed and extortion, and advocates the burning need of reform. In his next work, *The Babylonian Captivity of the Church,* in which Rome is likened to Babylon, he attacks the whole of the Church's sacramental system, which he represents as a captivity, refutes the withdrawal of the Cup from the laity, transubstantiation, and the sacrifice of the Mass. He closes with these words: 'I hear a report that fresh bulls and papal curses are being prepared against me, by which I am urged to recant, or else to be declared a heretic. If this is true, I wish this little book to be a part of my future recantation, that they may not complain that their tyranny has puffed itself up in vain. I shall also shortly publish, God being my helper, such a recantation as the See of Rome has never yet seen or heard, thus abundantly testifying my obedience in the name of our Lord Jesus Christ.'

The tract which Luther refers to is that on *Christian Freedom.* This has been called 'the pearl among Luther's writings.' It is free from that polemical bitterness which is almost inevitable in one who is attacking abuses, and doing the work of reformation, and full of measured convictions and helpful practical wisdom. Although battling for freedom, Luther realised the danger of licence, and his tract is a treatise on true Christian liberty in Christ.

The burning of the Papal bull brought matters to a

crisis. In 1519, Charles v. of Spain had succeeded to the throne of Maximilian. The heir of four royal lines, a devout Catholic, but by disposition a warrior, the descendant of a line of gloomy and despotic rulers, Charles became the most imposing figure in the concert of Europe. The Pope, who had opposed his election, sought his assistance when his succession to the crown had been made absolute, urging him to put Luther under the ban of the Empire. The German princes, however, demanded for Luther a fair hearing, and yielding to their representations he cited Luther to appear before him at a Diet he was convening at Worms, promising him a safe-conduct. Even with this promise the prospect for Luther was not a promising one. A safe-conduct had been given to Huss, but that had not hindered him from being burned alive. From the first, however, Luther regarded it as a call of God, and few men who have ever lived have shown more personal courage than Martin Luther. 'You may expect from me,' he said on leaving, 'everything save fear or recantation. I shall not flee, still less recant. May the Lord Jesus strengthen me!'

He left Wittenberg on the 2nd of April 1521, and his journey to Worms was a long series of triumphs. Ofttimes, however, his friends sought to dissuade him, warning him of the grave dangers he ran. But Luther would not be dissuaded. 'Not go to Worms!' he said. 'I shall go to Worms though there were as many devils there as tiles on the roofs.' And to Worms he went, this noble man; alone, without friends who could support him, without means of defence, strong only, as all great souls know themselves strong, in defending the right at whatever cost.

Luther arrived in Worms on Tuesday, April 16th. On the following day he appeared before the Emperor and the Papal legates. It was a memorable occasion. The hall was crowded, princes and nobles, cardinals and prelates were there, and the greatest of the land had gathered to see this notable monk who had convulsed Europe and shaken the Papal chair. Representing privilege and constitutional law, the gathering was hostile to the Reformer; yet even in this assembly the new cause had its secret champions. 'Pluck up thy spirit, little monk,' whispered one as he passed; 'some of us here have seen warm work in our time; but by my troth, neither I, nor any other knight in this company ever needed a stout heart more than thou needest it now. If thou hast faith in these doctrines of thine, little monk, go on, in the name of God.' 'Yes, in the name of God, forward,' said Luther, and up the narrow way, his head thrown back, his deep eyes flashing, alone, the one man fighting in God's name against all the forces of privilege and corruption, forward he went, until he stood before the king. There are few incidents in history more inspiring than this; few which have more deeply moulded or influenced the progress of the Christian Church.

Standing before the Emperor, Luther was called upon to recant. They insisted that he should say, in a word, whether he would recant or no. 'Unless convinced by Holy Scripture, or by clear reasons from other sources, I cannot retract,' he said. 'To councils or to Pope I cannot defer, for they have often erred. My conscience is a prisoner to God's word.' Again given an opportunity, he folded his hands, 'Here I stand,' he said; 'I cannot do otherwise. God help me.'

This was the last word. The Council broke up. Many, on the ground that faith is not to be kept with heretics—a Jesuitical doctrine born before the time—urged that Charles should seize Luther and burn him;

but to the amazement of every one he allowed him to go free. Long afterwards, when he had retreated to the convent of Yuste, he expressed regret at his action; although standing at Luther's grave, and being urged by the bloodthirsty Alva to dig up his ashes and scatter them to the winds, Charles showed again his toleration, saying, 'I make war on the living, not on the dead.' Recalling the incidents a few days before his death, Luther thus described his feelings on this great occasion: 'I was fearless,' he said; 'I was afraid of nothing; God can make one so desperately bold. I know not whether I could be so cheerful now.'

The result of the Diet, though outwardly favourable to the Papal cause, marks the moment of definite separation from it. 'From the moment that Luther left the Emperor's presence a free man, the spell of absolutism was broken, and the victory of the Reformation secured. The ban of the Pope had fallen; the secular arm had been called upon to interfere; the machinery of authority strained as far as it would bear. The Emperor himself was an unconscious convert to the higher creed. The Pope had urged him to break his word. The Pope had told him that honour was nothing; morality was nothing; where the interests of orthodoxy were compromised. The Emperor had refused to be tempted into perjury; and in refusing had admitted that there was a spiritual power upon earth, above the Pope, and above him.'

On his way back to Wittenberg a plot was formed to assassinate Luther; but the Elector heard of it. He sent a company of horse, who waylaid Luther, and carried him to a safe retreat in the castle of Wartburg.

### The Movement and the People

Only three years and a half have now elapsed since Luther nailed his theses to the door of the church at Wittenberg. The extraordinary commotion which that act created is an illustration of the state of public feeling. The minds of men were like fuel only waiting for a spark to set it ablaze. When Luther supplied the spark the conflagration was immediate, and it swept with incredible swiftness over Europe. Although the result differed in different countries, being stamped by national characteristics, yet over the whole it made for reformation in morals, for a cleansed Church, and for a purified spiritual vision. Even within the Catholic Church itself the result was to regenerate and to revive.

In Germany, however, partly because of Luther's massive personality, partly because of the natural independence of the Teutonic race, the Reformation was carried through with a thoroughness which necessarily led to many complications, but which freed the people from every yoke of bondage. Even in the days of its pride, Rome found the impassable forests of Germany, and the dauntless independence of its tribes, a check to its conquests, and even a menace to its peace. The Teutonic differs from the Latin temperament in being less romantic, less imaginative, but also less tolerant of superstition and of ecclesiastical or political tyranny. Its characteristics are manly independence and solid common sense, and in these, and all other respects, Luther was a typical German. It was natural then that when the blow was struck, it would be driven home with decision. Even before Luther nailed his theses to the door and challenged the conduct of Rome, the laity in Germany were beginning to deny the claims of the ecclesiastical authorities for immunity on account of their sacred office, and to insist upon reformation. The natural piety of the people also revolted at the corrupt state of the Church, and already a deepened feeling after spiritual things had arisen; men were groping for the light, and crying out for God.

So great, however, was the upheaval when it did come, so many-sided was it, so full of fury were its political, intellectual, and theological conflicts, that the reader is in constant danger of having obscured for him the real spiritual awakening which took place, and which lifted the whole Church of Christ into higher spiritual levels. Such conflicts were inevitable in the nature of the case, and are not to be put down to the evils incurred by the Reformation; they are the inevitable accompaniments of disintegration and reconstruction. The new-found freedom of the individual, for instance, before it could attain a form definite and also restrained, was bound to be claimed by some as a defence for licence and the casting off of all restraint. This is seen in many of the conflicts which followed, and which engaged the attention of the Reformers, and distracted their lives. This new-born sense of freedom sent a thrill of hope and energy into the hearts of the poor and the down-trodden, but it produced also the ill-fated Peasants' War, with all its attendant sufferings. So vast a movement, so radical a transition, could not be effected without suffering, without intense and embittered conflicts, without much that is to be regretted on both sides. The whole of the ecclesiastical edifice having been laid in ruins, and much of the doctrine entwined around it having been uprooted, the task of reconstruction was one of the most difficult that could have been conceived, and considering the state of Europe, the surprise is that it was done so thoroughly and so well. For this Germany has mainly to thank Martin Luther, and in regarding his immense personality it is difficult to know whether to admire most his intense religious sincerity, his indomitable courage, or his massive and penetrating intellect.

When in his hiding-place at Wartburg, Luther completed a task which, more than any other, was to bring men back to the evangelical faith. This was the translation of the New Testament. For such a work Luther was eminently endowed. He himself was so ardent a student of Scripture that he was intimately acquainted with its style, and breathed its spirit. Previous translations had been effected, but these were inaccurate as to scholarship and pedantic in language. Luther, however, had another gift which fitted him in a preeminent degree for such a work—he knew German; not the German of the schools, but the German of the people. Born amongst them, breathing to the last days of his life something of their virtues and their vices, he spoke to them out of their own hearts. Terse, rugged, idiomatic, yet full of tenderness and a noble simplicity, Luther gave to the German people at once a legacy of divine truth which was to be their dearest spiritual guide, and also a new language which was to recreate their literature, and to unify the whole German race. On his return to Wittenberg, he began the translation of the Old Testament, his scant acquaintance with Hebrew rendering this a task of great difficulty. He humorously describes his difficulties with the Patriarch Job, who resisted, he said, his efforts to translate him, with as much ill-nature as he exhibited in receiving the consolations of his friends. The work, however, was finally completed in 1532.

Like all great popular movements, the revival was borne from place to place on the wings of song. The reformation of public worship demanded a simpler form in which the people might engage. Luther began by translating hymns and chants previously sung only by the choir; but he followed this up by composing hymns of his own, and himself set these to tunes. These hymns bear the same popular note as his translations of Scripture. They are full of the evangelical faith, full of fervour, and couched in language which goes straight to the heart of the people. His greatest hymn, 'Ein feste Burg ist unser Gott,' with its inspiring tune also written by himself, Heine has called 'The Marseillaise of the Reformation.' It at once caught the popular ear, and sweeping over Germany, was sung by tens of thousands whose hearts had been liberated by the evangelical message, and who found in this noble hymn an outlet for their joy. His hymn, also, 'Nun freut euch lieben Christen gemein,' which expresses his own Christian experience, and gives expression also to the joyous liberty which the message of the Gospel brings, became immensely popular. 'Through this one hymn of Luther's,' says Hesshusius, 'many hundreds of Christians have been brought to the true faith, who before could not endure the name of Luther.' These hymns undoubtedly did much to awaken in dormant hearts a new desire for spiritual things; they created new emotions; they brought into common life an intimate acquaintance with some of the most tender and affecting thoughts of God; they brought religion down to live with the people in their common tasks, to cheer them in their hours of drudgery, console them in their hours of loss, and to their troubled and burdened hearts gave solace and ease. Instead of being regarded as something distant and mysterious, religion became to tens of thousands something intimate and precious; Christ had come down from the clouds in which He had been hidden, and now tabernacled amongst them.

### Luther's Closing Years

On June 13, 1525, occurred an event which more than others reveals how completely Luther had emancipated himself from his past. On that day he married Catherine von Bora, a nun who had embraced the new truths, and had escaped from her convent. This was no affair of passion, it was a deliberate act carrying with it, as Luther knew, the gravest issues. For more than a century the impurity of the monastic life had been a cause of ribaldry to the satirist, and of anguish to the devout. The dissolution of the monasteries had further complicated the problem. Immorality had become so common as almost to pass unnoticed, and since the monks were hindered by their vows from marrying, and yet were members of no community, concubinage became almost a recognised necessity. Luther saw what was happening, saw that all eyes were fastened upon him, and saw his duty. 'We may be able to live unmarried,' he said, 'but in these days we must protest in deed as well as in word against the doctrine of celibacy. It is an invention of Satan. Before I took my wife, I had made up my mind that I must marry some one; and had I been overtaken by an illness, I should have betrothed myself to some pious maiden.'

The union thus begun in mutual respect deepened into rich affection. Nothing is more delightful in its playful wit, in its drollery, and yet in its marks of deep affection, than the account of Luther's home life. He tasted its joys, but also its deep and tragic sorrows in the loss of his daughter Margaret at the age of fourteen.

In his home life his tastes were of the simplest. He rejoiced in company, and his table was open to all. Nowhere was the genuine simplicity of his character more in evidence than when, surrounded by his friends at his own table, he poured forth a rich stream of pungent talk, and delighted all by his humour and his insight.

The remaining years of his life were years of absorbing work, full of anxieties, and never free from danger. In addition to the troubles around him he entered into a controversy with Henry VIII., with Erasmus, and with the Swiss Reformers. His vehemence, the intensity of his nature, and his extraordinary vocabulary, made him a dangerous, and not always a wise controversialist; but these things have to be taken as part of the man, and everything about Luther was built on a massive scale.

The labours through which he had passed, the intense strain which these imposed upon him, at length began to tell their tale upon a naturally strong constitution. On January 23, 1546, he went by invitation to his native town of Eisleben, as arbiter in some dispute. Just as he was entering the town, Luther was seized with sickness, but this passing off, he was able to preach on the following Sunday. He remained until the dispute was settled, and on February 16th the agreement was signed by the disputants. On the following day, however, he was seized with sudden sickness, and a consciousness that the end was near seemed to possess him. 'Dr. Jonas,' he calmly said, 'here in Eisleben, where I was born and baptized, I think I shall remain.'

All was done that human skill could suggest, but his pain increased. In the midst of his paroxysms he was heard to offer up the following prayer:

'I thank Thee, O God, the Father of our Lord Jesus Christ, that Thou hast revealed Thy Son unto me, on Whom I have believed, Whom I have loved, Whom I have preached, and confessed, and worshipped, Whom the Pope and all the ungodly abuse and slander. O Lord Jesus Christ, I commend my poor soul to Thee. O Heavenly Father, I know that, although I shall be taken away from this life, I shall live for ever with Thee. "God so loved the world that He gave His only-begotten Son, that whosoever believeth on Him should not perish, but have everlasting life." Father, into Thy hands I commend my spirit.'

Around him, as he lay dying, were gathered many of his friends and comrades. 'Reverend Father,' said one, 'do you die in the faith of your Lord Jesus Christ, and in the doctrine which you preach in His Name ?' The answer came clear and distinct : 'Yes.' Soon after he breathed his last.

News of his death was flashed through Germany, and caused the most profound grief. Even his enemies, embittered though they were, could not but confess that there had died a man who had followed the light, and who had followed it without fear.

### Character of the Revival

The Reformation, we have seen, marks a crisis in the history of civilisation. It is that point where the human spirit, meeting the combined forces of reaction, burst the fetters so long imposed upon it. Under the smashing blows of Luther we see mediævalism, with all its blind and slavish submission to authority, collapse. A new era now dawns for the human spirit, an era having freedom as its watchword. No movement possesses all the truth ; it centres upon one great aspect of it, and in the violence which in human affairs seems necessary to obtain it, much that is good in the old has to be sacrificed. The Reformation is no exception to this truth. The rending from the old tore up by the roots many beautiful traditions ; it engendered bitterness and strife ; it bore the bitter fruit of cruelty and bloodshed. These facts are grievous, but they were inevitable under the conditions and in the times in which the Reformation took place. When all the bitterness, the noise of the combatants, the passion of opponents, the recriminations of the partisans, and the dust of the conflict, however, had died down, it was seen that the gain to the human spirit was immense; that the penalties imposed were not too severe for the progress attained. The religious life of humanity had set out upon a new road of travel, and had left the old for ever behind.

When we look for the main factors which produced this, we see first of all that the success of the movement lay in the intensity and sincerity of the protest made by the Reformers against the degradations of religion. They protested against men, however immune from criticism on account of their sacred calling, using the awful mysteries of religion for material ends, and by thus adding to their wealth, endowing themselves only with means for further corruption. They pointed out that the priestly office was in danger of being used, and in many cases was being used, for the practice of the worst excesses; and they condemned, at the same time, the protection given to these evil practices, by an organisation whose only right of existence lay in her struggle to put an end to them.

To us, reaping what they have sowed, such a protest seems easy, and its success natural. To do it, however, in the sixteenth century, as it was done by the Reformers, demanded a courage of conviction, and a faith in God, which is given to few men in history. 'It required no great intellect,' says Froude, with truth, 'to understand that a Pope's pardon, which you could buy for five shillings, could not really get a soul out of Purgatory. It required a quality much rarer than intellect to look such a doctrine in the face—sanctioned as it was by the credulity of the ages, and backed by the pomp and pageantry of earthly power—and say to it openly: "You are a Lie."' When an evil becomes once entrenched and the monopoly of a favoured class; when its continuance offers to that class ease of living and immunity from danger, then whosoever attacks it engages in a conflict which will arouse the fiercest passions and the most implacable persecution. For an acquaintance with the facts of human nature shows, that when men are fighting for their personal ease, or for practices that are morally indefensible, though long practised, they call to their defence the worst excesses and the basest human passions.

Luther's attack on the corruption of the Church met with all this hatred from those who practised it, or whose interest it was to maintain it. It is not too much to say that every day he carried his life in his hand, and one of the wonders of history is that he did not lose it.

But the Reformation was more than a protest against admitted evils. Had it been no more than this, it would have perished with the wreck of the existing order. On its intellectual side the Reformation saw a reconstruction of dogma; on its spiritual side it saw a revival of evangelical and practical religion.

In the reconstruction of dogma the chief place must be given to the recovery of the doctrine of the Person of Christ. The development of sacerdotalism naturally obscured the ease of approach, and the nearness of the Saviour to the suppliant. The more the priestly power became augmented, the more Christ became a lay Figure who could only move at the bidding of His earthly representatives; or He became the awful Judge whose wrath could only be appeased through the mediation of the priesthood. Luther tells how, when a boy, his imagination was inflamed by gazing at a stained-glass picture which represented Christ, not as Saviour, but as Judge ; seated on a rainbow, with sword in hand, He looked down with burning and threatening eye upon the awed worshippers below. Men had thus come to believe that Christ could not do His own work in the world ; that He had either delegated entirely His duties, or helplessly yielded His authority, to the priests. The Reformation, however, reinstated the doctrine of the Person of Christ exalted in Heaven, yet graciously active in the work of man's regeneration and redemption.

From the human side the Reformation theology was founded upon the rediscovered doctrine of justification by faith. The educative value and spiritual efficacy of faith had become buried under a superincumbent mass of tradition, of the value of relics, of the intercession of saints, and of the accumulation of merit through masses and indulgences. By these means the Gospel was made of none effect, they only appeased the conscience by deadening it. The moment the soul awakes, trust in such merit becomes impossible. 'Miserable creatures that we are,' cries Luther, 'we earn our bread in sin. Till we are seven years old we do nothing but eat, and drink, and sleep, and play. From seven to twenty-one we study four hours a day, the rest of it we run about and amuse ourselves ; then we work till fifty, then we grow again children. We sleep half our lives ; we give God a tenth of our time ; and yet we think that with our good works we can merit heaven ! What have I been doing to-day ? I have talked for two hours ; I have been at meals three hours ; I have been idle four hours ! Ah, enter not into judgment with thy servant, O Lord.' This is the true cry of the heart of man in its bitterness and self-abasement.

In the struggle for light, however, which went on in

Luther's own soul, emancipation came not by trusting in any merit of his own, but by his throwing himself in utter trustfulness upon the mercy of God, and believing that poor and unworthy though he might be, God's great love would respond to this act of trustful faith. Belief in this doctrine cut at the base the vast edifice of priestly mediation ; it clothed the individual believer with a new dignity ; it made the humblest a priest unto God, and called him forth to that education of the soul which comes from the acceptance of responsibility. The immediate consequence of the Reformation, therefore, was to immensely quicken the intellectual side of man's nature. It promoted a thirst for education ; it gave a new impetus to the pursuit of knowledge ; it let loose that spirit of intense inquisitiveness which wrests the secrets of the universe ; above all, it made man surer of himself, and of his rightful place in the world.

On its spiritual side the Reformation was a revival of evangelical and practical religion. Like all other spiritual awakenings it broke with the formalism and deadness of the schools, and brought men back to the primitive faith, and to simple trust in Jesus Christ. For the first time in history the Bible became the possession of the people. Men went straight to the source of truth ; the beautiful and tender words of Jesus became familiar to the poorest ; the peasant, as he ploughed the soil, the weaver, as he spun his cloth, the housewife, as she performed her common tasks, or rocked her babe to sleep, could repeat the sustaining messages of Him of Nazareth, and feel Him the daily Companion of their toils.

Through the change which was effected in worship also, the laity were brought into intimate connection with the Church, and trained in its government, and in the conduct of affairs. Most of all were they trained to realise that religion consisted, not in obedience to outward observances, but in the trustful service and humble adoration of the soul toward God.

## LUTHER

Of the character of the great leader of this revival little need be added. We see at once how he differs from those great leaders whose life and work we have already considered. Francis was a poet; Savonarola was a preacher; Luther was both, but in addition, there was his broad and massive personality. About him there was something elemental, something of that volcanic energy which we connect in our minds with the forces of nature. 'I am rough, boisterous, stormy, and altogether warlike,' he says of himself. 'I am born to fight against innumerable monsters and devils. I must remove stumps and stones, cut away thistles and thorns, and clear the forests.' In the hour of battle Luther's voice is like a hurricane; he gathers the fury of the tempest around him, and shakes the earth with the fury of his indignation. 'Courage,' he cries to his enemies, 'swine that you are! Burn me then, if you can and dare. Here I am; do your worst upon me. Scatter my ashes to all the winds—spread them through all the seas. My spirit shall pursue you still. Living, I am the foe of the Papacy; and dead, I will be its foe twice over. Hogs of Thomists! Luther shall be the bear in your way—the lion in your path. Go where you will, Luther shall cross you. Luther shall leave you neither peace nor rest until he has crushed in your brows of brass and dashed in your iron brains.'

It is easy for us to condemn the violence of such language, but the times were wild, were full of fury and conflict, of persecution and bloodshed, and in the centre of the whirlwind stood the fearless figure of Luther himself.

Of courage, that pre-eminent gift of the great leader, he was supremely possessed. He was, perhaps, the most fearless man who ever lived. It would be a disgrace to the Pope, he used jokingly to say, if he died in his bed. He did die in his bed, but fear of death never brought from him the tremor of an eyelid. Entreated once not to enter Leipsic for fear of Duke George who, it was known, was evilly disposed to him, Luther swept his friends aside. 'I shall go to Leipsic,' he cried, 'though for nine days it rains Duke Georges.' He was not afraid even of the devil, in whose existence he intensely believed, and whose power to do him physical harm he did not for a moment doubt. Disturbed one night by a noise in his room, he rose, lit a candle, and found nothing. At once he concluded who had made it. 'Oh!' he said, 'it is you, is it?' and returning to his bed, he went quickly to sleep.

To his enemies the most terrible of foes, Luther to his followers was the most gentle of friends. He was of the number of those for whom men would willingly have laid down their lives. Easy of approach; totally without personal vanity; so simple in his tastes that men wondered how he could sustain life on so little; abounding in solid sense, in playful humour, and in mirthfulness; honest as the day, and transparently sincere, it is not to be wondered at that he bound men to him with bonds of steel.

But the central pivot upon which his whole life swung was his life in God. Luther was a great Christian. On that side of the spiritual life which demands the prostration of the being before the awful majesty of the Most High, Luther was supreme. He carried in his heart an awful sense of the presence of God; of the fearfulness of sin; of the need of divine grace; of that infinite love which, out of the fulness of its grace, and in mercy toward sinful men, gave itself for our redemption. He knew the Scriptures, and loved them, as no other man in his day and generation. He was a man of prayer, spending hours of each day alone with God, carrying his soul apart from the world's busy thrall.

'I will call this Luther a true Great Man,' says Carlyle, 'great in intellect, in courage, affection, and integrity; one of our most lovable and precious men. Great, not as a hewn obelisk; but as an Alpine mountain—so simple, honest, spontaneous, not setting up to be great at all; there for quite another purpose than being great! Ah, yes, unsubduable granite, piercing far and wide into the heavens; yet in the clefts of its fountains, green beautiful valleys with flowers! A right Spiritual Hero and Prophet; once more a true son of Nature and Fact, for whom these centuries, and many that are to come yet, will be thankful to Heaven.'

## CALVIN AND THE SWISS REVIVAL

So vast was the upheaval caused by Luther and his supporters that it was impossible to confine it to the vicinity in which it took place. A wave of spiritual awakening swept across Europe, agitating nations, threatening dynasties, arousing joyful acceptance or implacable opposition wherever it went. We propose to trace this awakening in two widely separated lands, and under the two great leaders—Calvin and Knox.

In the first act of this great movement the form of Luther towers high above all others. In the second act it is the form of Calvin. The two offer an interesting contrast. Luther was a typical German—stout, thick-set, rough in manner, with something of the shagginess as well as the courage of a lion. Calvin was a typical Frenchman—small, thin, with a glittering logical mind, hardly less courageous, but less daring; with more self-restraint, but with less humour and natural gaiety. The one was like a volcano, all fire within, liable at any moment to burst into terrifying energy, and with roar and conflagration hurl forth its devastating flood; yet when quiescent, majestic and beautiful. The other was like a great mountain peak—calm, immovable, with glittering heights which seemed cold and forbidding, save when the rising or setting sun steeped them in splendour, and changed the glistering whiteness of their snows into deep and glowing crimson.

In the second act of the great Reform movement, the

real troubles of the Reformers began. When Luther struck the first resounding blow, it met with an instant response from the most unexpected quarters. Indignation at existing abuses was wide-spread, the demand for amendment almost universal; it seemed therefore as if reform could be effected without difficulty, and radical changes made without resistance. Men soon found, however, that reform was not the easy thing they imagined, and that in every attempt to introduce the good, evil meets it with an embittered and entrenched resistance.

Nor was it to be expected that Rome would sit passively by and see her power wrested from her, her priests defied, and her august authority trampled in the dust. Luther owed his life, and the opening acts of the Reformation their success, to the supercilious contempt with which the Pope treated both; but when the true nature of the movement was discerned, when the fears of the Vatican were once aroused, then the whole machinery of Rome, its vast and secret resources were put into operation to stamp it out.

In such circumstances Rome has always known how to act. No authority on earth has proved itself more astute in dealing with cases of discipline or insurrection; none in which knowledge of human nature has combined with more unlimited resource in adapting itself to sudden emergencies, than in that venerable authority, which, seated in the city of the seven hills, defies the assaults of the ages. Whether by mutual compromise the movement might have been guided into channels which would have made for reform within the Church, without rending it asunder—as the absence of the spirit of compromise certainly helped to do—it is difficult to say. It may be that the differences were too great to be bridged over by compromise, and that separation, with all its attendant evils, has done more for the spiritual enrichment of Europe, and for its true progress, than a unity gained at the sacrifice of the essential features of the revolt. It is possible to gain peace at too heavy a cost, and compromise on vital issues means often the destruction of the vital thing in them.

However this may be, it remains for us now as a mere academic discussion. With the neglect of the early opportunity for compromise no second opportunity was afforded. Men seemed almost instantly to rush into hostile camps, and war was declared almost before men were thoroughly awake to the cause of the conflict. In such a war it stood ill with the Reformers. For when once fear aroused the occupant of Peter's chair; when it was realised that the Church's most valued possessions were being wrested from her; when the denunciations of the Reformers aroused that conservative instinct which, in the realm of religion, is so potent a factor, and which calls to the defence of the existing order those who either fear progress or hate it; then the whole of that mighty engine of repression which the Church possesses was set in motion against them, and peace could only come through exhaustion or extermination.

The peril in which the Reformers stood was increased by the disunion which broke out in their own camp. Different voices were clamouring for different things. Some were conservative and hesitating; they did not want finally to break with Rome. Others saw that separation was inevitable, but wanted to retain as much of Roman practice and belief as they could. Others sought to make the breach deep and unbridgeable. In seeking to compose these differences a more serious cause of strife was disclosed. The Reformers found it necessary not only to define what they regarded as the errors of Rome, they had to define the basis of their own belief. It is always more easy to assail an evil system, than to erect a good one; always more easy to pull down than to build up; and this the Reformers were soon to realise. They all agreed that there was much in the teaching of Rome that was false, but they were not all agreed as to what was true; the moment they began to define their own position they met with irritating obstacles, and with opposition from the bosom of their friends. All this was inevitable; it was impossible that the reformed doctrines should exist in the air, they were bound to receive dogmatic statement, and to be subjected to critical investigation. It is unhappily the case, however, that no disputes are so interminable, so embittered, or so lacking in the Christian grace of charity, as those which belong to the domain of theology. This arises partly from the fact that the subjects discussed belong to a realm but partly and dimly lighted by revelation; partly from the fact that language is not a flexible enough medium to express, without possibility of misunderstanding, the abstract and subtle shades of meaning of the highly organised intellect; partly also from the fact that theologians, as a class, cut off as they are from the practical affairs of life, lose their sense of proportion, and attach often to the most trivial differences the most important values. When religious and deeply spiritually-minded men meet each other in friendly intercourse, and converse together on the deep things of the spiritual life, they find themselves united with each other in experience and in sympathy; but when they meet as ecclesiastics or theologians to define articles of the faith, agreement seems impossible; discord breaks out in which the combatants seem to lose all sense of proportion; they quarrel over words and delicate shades of meaning, and often break up with mutual recriminations, having made the breach wider than before.

Such was the character of many of the discussions carried on within the circle of the reform movement itself, and what the movement needed, if it was to weather the storms of persecution now lashing against it, was a man of supreme force of character, of earnest piety, and of peerless intellect, who would define the Protestant faith, and put an end to its hesitations and divisions. This man the Reformers found in John Calvin.

### Early Days

Calvin was born in Noyon in Picardy, on July 10, 1509. At this time Henry VIII. had ascended the throne of England; Erasmus was at the zenith of his powers; Luther had been called to Wittenberg; Ignatius Loyola, the Founder of the Jesuits, was a youth of eighteen, engaged as a soldier in the Spanish army; Melanchthon, though now only thirteen years of age, had just graduated at Heidelberg; and John Knox, a child of four, had not yet begun his education in the Grammar School of Haddington.

In common with most of the Reformers, Calvin was born in comparatively humble circumstances. Of his mother little that is authentic is known; his father had gradually risen to a position of comparative influence as fiscal agent, and as such procured for his son the opportunity of being educated with the children of a noble family in the district. It is related that even in these early days he showed an extraordinary aptitude for study, that the ordinary amusements of youth offered no attractions to him, and that along with the abnormal development of his intellectual powers the sentimental side of his nature remained unfostered.

When Calvin was twelve years of age his father, who had added to his fiscal duties that of secretary to the diocese, used his influence to get him appointed to a curacy, the revenues of which would be sufficient for his maintenance. This was a common practice in those evil days. Infants even, and children, were appointed to responsible posts in the Church, drew the revenues all their lives long, and pursued their own course of living with total disregard of their ecclesiastical responsibilities. Thus Jean, son of Duke René II. of Lorraine, a contemporary of Calvin's, in the course of his life entered into possession of no less than three Archbishoprics, at the same time drawing the emoluments of ten Bishoprics as well as those of nine Abbeys. The application made by Calvin's father proved successful, and he was appointed to a chaplaincy in Noyon Cathedral, receiving a few years later another benefice.

With his maintenance assured, Calvin was now, at the age of twelve, sent to Paris to pursue his studies, his father having destined him for the priesthood. The University of Paris had for long been rightly regarded as one of the greatest in Europe. Many illustrious names had appeared on its roll of honour, and its theological faculty, known as the 'Sorbonne,' founded in 1253 by Robert de Sorbon, had, in past days, won a deserved repute. In relation to the new learning, however, it remained on the whole uncommitted; Scholasticism still retained its hold, while to the Reform movement it constituted itself a determined enemy. It gave shelter, nevertheless, within its walls to three men who, in themselves, represent three widely different movements. Erasmus had passed through its classes before Calvin entered; and Calvin had scarcely left before Ignatius Loyola appeared.

The teaching of the University made up in severity

what it lacked in knowledge. The students began their tasks at five in the morning, and with the exception of four hours for food and relaxation, continued them until eight in the evening. The discipline was of the strictest, and the punishments severe.

Calvin was not long a student of the University before he impressed his teachers no less by the acuteness of his mind than by the seriousness of his character. This latter quality was somewhat rare amongst the students of his day. Erasmus describes the immorality which then prevailed amongst them, the language they used, and the lodgings they inhabited. To pass through such an ordeal, and to come out untainted, was to give proof of a strength and loftiness of character as rare as it was attractive. Beza informs us that as a student he was not only deeply religious, but was a strict censor of the vices of his associates ; while Vasseur, a not altogether kindly critic, relates that his fellow-students called him ‘ the Accusative Case.’ He seems even then, however, to have attracted to him many who already recognised him as a leader amongst men.

At the completion of his Arts course, his father changed his mind regarding him. Either on account of a personal quarrel, which he had with the ecclesiastical authorities at Noyon at this time, or being anxious to secure for his son a more lucrative employment, and one which would give more opportunity for the exercise of his rare gifts, Calvin's father determined that his son should enter the profession of the law. With this object in view he was sent to Orleans, then famous for its schools and legal erudition. Here again the young Calvin attracted the attention of his professors, and so zealous was he in his studies that his naturally weak constitution became seriously undermined. It was his custom, his biographers tell us, to work on late at night, recollecting and arranging the studies in which he had been engaged during the day; then waking early in the morning to recall what he had thus reduced to order. The strain of these early years so weakened his constitution that he never altogether recovered; it limited his powers of endurance and hastened his end.

### Calvin's Sudden Awakening

Somewhere about this time Calvin came into contact with the new movement which was awakening the foremost minds in Europe. Influenced by a relative who first translated the Scriptures into French, he brought his keen intellect to bear upon its pages, and soon there awoke in him that sense of discord which all deep natures realise when brought into contact with God's Law. Especially as he pored over the writings of St. Paul were the deep fountains of his being moved; in the pages written by the great Apostle of the Gentiles he came into contact with a mind and spirit of like temper with his own. During his university days, also, the props which maintained his faith in the doctrines of the Catholic Church one by one gave way. He had felt the deep abyss of sin, had realised the awful holiness of God, had sought deliverance along the prescribed paths, but peace he did not find. Of this period he speaks himself in the following passage:—'When I had performed all these things (*i.e.* obeyed the directions of the Church for the penitent), though I had some intervals of quiet, I was still far from true peace of conscience; for, whenever I descended into myself, or raised my mind to Thee, extreme terror seized me—terrors which no expiations nor satisfactions could cure. And the more closely I examined myself the sharper the stings with which my conscience was pricked, so that the only solace that was left to me was to delude myself by obliviousness. Still, as nothing better offered, I continued the course which I had begun, when, lo, a very different form of doctrine started up ; not one which led us away from the Christian profession, but one which brought it back to the fountain-head, and, as it were, clearing away the dross, restored it to its original purity. Offended by the novelty I lent an unwilling ear, and at first, I confess, strenuously and passionately resisted ; for (such is the firmness or effrontery with which it is natural to men to persist in the course which they have once undertaken) it was with the greatest difficulty that I was induced to confess that I had all my life long been in ignorance and error.'

Even when his judgment was convinced, however, the task of breaking with the past was found to be no easy one. One fear remained. By severing himself from the Church was he not severing himself from Christ? was he not by thus exercising the rights of private judgment assuming an awful responsibility ? was he not by separating himself from the Church rending asunder the Lord's Body ? What was his opinion, after all, compared with that august authority which claimed the sole right to interpret those Scriptures, and which warned men of the ease with which those were led astray who trusted in their private judgment ? And, if accepting those new doctrines, he were to be banished from the pale of the Church, what hope had he that he might not be banished from God's grace ? The Church rose before his eyes, august and venerable ; he saw her coming down from a remote past, clothed in majesty, pointing to her Apostolic descent, her noble martyrs, her ancient traditions, and her mysterious and awful authorities. He heard her voice speaking through popes and cardinals, through councils and priests, declaring that to separate from holy mother Church was to be separate from grace, was to commit sin unpardonable, was voluntarily to shut upon oneself the gates of Heaven. In that Church he had spent his earliest days; her services, her ritual, her mystic rites had been known to him since childhood; her doctrines and beliefs had entered into the warp and woof of his mind, had become part of the very texture of his being. What right had he to set himself and his puny intellect against her awful judgments and her venerable claims to obedience and submission?

No wonder that he trembled as others have done who have stood at the parting of the ways. Only those who have experienced it can know what it costs to tear up by the roots the ties which bind us to the past, and to go out by a lonely way, seeking for truth.

Calvin faced the whole situation, faced it with that unflinching courage which is one of his chief claims to the admiration of posterity. He possessed that intellectual honesty which follows truth at whatever cost. At length he came to this conclusion :—'There can be no Church where the truth is not. Here, in the Roman communion, I find only fables, silly inventions, and idolatrous ceremonies. The Society which is founded on these things cannot be the Church. If I shall come back to the truth as contained in the Scriptures, shall I not come back to the Church? and shall I not be joined to the holy company of prophets and martyrs, of saints and apostles? And as regards the Pope—the Vicar of Jesus Christ—let me not be awed by a big word. If without warrant from the Bible, or the call of the Christian people, and lacking the holiness and humility of Jesus Christ, the Pope place himself above the Church, and surround himself with worldly pomps, and arrogate lordship over the faith and consciences of men, is he therefore entitled to homage? and must I bow down and do obeisance? I will go on my way without minding him.'

The movement which was going on within him intellectually was consummated by a spiritual experience which happened about this time. This was what he himself terms his 'sudden conversion.' Finding himself embedded in superstitions, and experiencing the difficulty of tearing himself free from them, 'by a sudden conversion,' he says, 'He subdued and reduced my heart to docility, which, for my age, was over-much hardened in such matters.'

The date in which this took place is generally attributed to the year 1532, but the details, so plentiful in the lives of the others whose lives we have been considering, are singularly lacking in that of Calvin. It was not preceded with the same intense outward struggle, we see, or accompanied, when reached, by the same marks of excessive joy. This does not mean that the change was less profound, or less permanent. It is a mistake to judge of spiritual effects by their outward demonstrations, or to lay down hard and fast rules for the movement of God's Spirit in the lives of men. This is a folly of which many have been guilty in past days, and it is one that has borne exceeding bitter fruit. The truth is that Conversion is a word which covers a whole range of widely different spiritual experiences, and instead of there being but one way in which conviction is reached, there seem to be as many ways as there are individuals to tread them.

In the experience of Calvin we meet with an illustration of this, and of the variety of types which God uses to do His work in the world, and which the world itself needs. In him, we perceive, the intellect is predominant; his character could be changed less by sentiment than by reason. With such men the judgment must first be convinced before the heart capitulates. Before they can become free they must first 'know the truth'; and the truth comes, not always by swift and unexpected upheavals, but by slow accumulations, until at length the crisis is reached, and the mind being convinced, the will and heart submit. The anguish, thus, through which Calvin passed, did not arise primarily through consciousness of sin, for from earliest days the excesses into which his companions plunged seemed to have no attractions for him; nor did it come through a craving for the divine love, as often appears in deeply emotional natures; it came through that part of him which dominated his being. He had first 'to face the spectres of the mind, and lay them,' before he could make a 'firmer faith his own.'

The anguish of such a struggle, though less demonstrable than that which comes to the nature conscious of sin, or to the nature of strong emotions, is often, not less, but more deep; and the influence exerted upon character, though less outwardly apparent, is often more dependable, and more lasting.

To Calvin, his conversion ever afterwards appeared as the direct work of God. He believed that He had spoken to him out of the Scriptures, and this experience of their illumining power imprinted itself deeply upon his mind and teaching. They became to him the very word of God, the supreme source of all instruction, the authoritative and final source of appeal in teaching and in practice. To study the Scriptures, and to make them known, he regarded as an object worthy of his life's devotion.

Here, then, we find a supreme intellect awakened to the needs of the times, consecrated to the truth, and impelled by an inner impulse to seek to awaken others to a like sense of its joy and power.

### Calvin's 'Call'

It will be necessary for us now to pause for a moment and to inquire into the state of France at this time, to see its spiritual condition, and to estimate the forces running toward reform.

Already two movements for reform had appeared before the rise of Protestantism. In the South there had appeared the Cathari and the Waldenses, both condemning the abuses of the Church and crying out for reform. Though having passed through terrible persecutions, the Waldenses remained, and in 1532 adopted Protestant principles. In the fifteenth century a movement had arisen in France which sought to remove abuses, and to check the encroachments of the Papacy. This, however, had met with but little success. In France the conditions were different from those which obtained in Germany. Although the French Church had always remained determinedly orthodox, the Crown had for long claimed a certain power of jurisdiction over it, and was quick to resent undue interference on the part of Rome. Spiritually the Church of France was but little better than that of Germany. There were the same abuses, the same beliefs, the same gross superstitions, the same externalism, but the burden was made less intolerable through their independence; added to their other woes they had not to bear the crushing weight of Rome.

At this time there was on the throne of France a monarch whose personal gifts attracted to his court many of the same type which Lorenzo the Magnificent had attracted to Florence. Full of military ambition, Francis I. sought to widen the sway of France, and to win for himself influence and renown. His loose moral character, however, unfitted him to be the arbiter in a strife which concerned the deepest moral issues, although, by his love of learning, he helped to attract to his court men filled with the Renaissance spirit, and scholars eager to go back to the sources of learning.

The first to raise his voice for the new ideas was Lefevre. Like the others he found his inspiration in the study of Scriptures, and especially in the writings of St. Paul. As early as 1512 he said to Farrel, 'God will renovate the world, and you will be a witness of it.'

At first his writings, which were mystical and devout, remained unimpeached; but when, in 1521, the tidal wave of that great upheaval which had taken place in Saxony had reached France, the Sorbonne became alarmed, denounced Luther as a heretic, and at the same time condemned a dissertation of Lefevre's. For a while he, Farrel, and others whom he had attracted around him, found an asylum with Briconnet, Bishop of Meaux, but the authorities gave them no rest, and the Bishop, yielding to his superiors, recanted, and this early movement was crushed.

Francis himself was vacillating at this time in his attitude toward the movement, being influenced less by theology than by political considerations. It had, however, a firm supporter at Court in his daughter Margaret, who, after her marriage with the King of Navarre, continued to promote the evangelical doctrine, and to give asylum to its persecuted followers; and also a no less embittered opponent in the Queen-mother Louise, then under the influence of the Chancellor Duprat.

Such, then, were the conditions when Calvin, by a sudden conversion, stepped into the arena as a champion of the Protestant cause. At once he was accepted as a leader. 'Before a year passed,' he says, 'all those who had some desire for pure doctrine betook themselves to me in order to learn, although I myself had done little more than begin. For my part I commenced to seek some hiding-place and means of withdrawing from people.'

Soon after this, withdrawal from Paris became imperative. One of Calvin's friends, and a sympathiser with evangelical opinions—Nicholas Cop—having been appointed Rector of the University of Paris, took the opportunity, in delivering his inaugural address, to state the case for the Reformers. This drew upon him the wrath of the theological faculty, and he, along with Calvin, who was said to have had a hand in its preparation, had to flee the city.

For a time Calvin led a wandering life, being engaged upon a work which was destined to prove epoch-making in the history of opinion. There were many, Calvin realised, thirsting for the light, eager to know what the new opinions were about which they heard so much, yet unable to possess definite information. For the enlightenment of earnest seekers after the truth Calvin wrote his famous *Institutes*.

The publication of the *Institutes,* however, served another purpose, not intended when first begun. Francis, who at first was uncommitted in his attitude towards the Reformers, had thrown his weight at last into the opposite scale, mainly through the intrigues of the papal party. Persecution had followed on a scale which had aroused the indignation of the Protestant princes of Germany, and Francis, to shield himself, accused the French Reformers of the lawlessness and fanaticism of the Anabaptists. In a dignified and restrained preface, Calvin dedicated his *Institutes* to the King, and vindicated the cause of his persecuted subjects. His appeal, which better than anything else reveals the range and loftiness of Calvin's mind, concludes thus:

'Magnanimous King, be not moved by the absurd insinuations with which our adversaries are striving to frighten you into the belief that nothing else is wished and aimed at by this new gospel (for so they term it) than opportunity for seditions and impunity for all vices. God is not the Author of division, but of peace; and the Son of God, who came to destroy the works of the devil, is not the minister of sin. We are undeservedly charged with desires of a kind for which we have never given even the smallest suspicion. . . . Your good-will we are confident we would regain, would you but once, with calmness and composure, read this our confession, which we wish to serve with your majesty instead of a defence. But if the whispers of the malevolent so possess your ears that the accused are to have no opportunity of pleading their cause; if those vindictive furies, with your connivance, are always to rage with bonds, scourges, tortures, maimings, and burnings, we, indeed, like sheep doomed to slaughter, shall be reduced to every extremity; yet so that, in our patience, we will possess our souls, and wait for the strong hand of the Lord, which doubtless will appear in time, and show itself armed, both to rescue the poor from affliction, and to take vengeance on the despisers. Most powerful and illustrious King, may the Lord, the King of Kings, establish your throne in justice, and your rulership in equity.'

Calvin, at this time, was only twenty-seven years of age, but the learning and acumen displayed in the *Institutes*, no less than the restraint and dignity of the *Introduction*, marked him out as a leader of men. They marked him out as the kind of leader, also, which the times required. For the first wave of emotion was spent, and what the movement required, if it was to retain its spiritual value, was clear definition of its faith. An intellectual revival, indeed, was necessary in the sphere of religion; a revival which would awaken the mind to the conception of new truth, which would bring right belief into the sphere of personal religion, and which instead of blind acceptance, would add to belief the enormous strength of personal conviction. For as the Holy Spirit working in the individual does not crush down individual characteristics in order to reduce all to uniformity, neither is this done in those great movements which sweep into their sphere of influence large bodies of men. Each revival, indeed, is seen to differ from all others in some certain characteristic, and while the result in all is a quickening of the spiritual life, the path by which men are led to the goal often widely differs. There are whole races whose pathway to spiritual life can only lead through the reason, and who need not only to be convinced of sin in order to seek Christ, but who need also to be convinced of truth before they can accept Him. For such an age, and for such races, Calvin for long was to prove a leader and a guide.

After the publication of the *Institutes*, Calvin's great desire was for quiet in order to continue his studies. He felt himself inadequately prepared to take up the work of a public teacher, and so he betook himself to the life of a wandering scholar, visiting Italy, and other parts of Europe. In the course of his wanderings, while on his way to Strasburg, he stopped for the night in Geneva. Here for four years William Farrel, an intrepid Reformer, had been working, and the citizens had adopted Protestantism by an open vote. The discipline which followed, however, aroused bitter opposition, and Geneva was torn by strife and discord, when, on the 5th August 1536, Calvin arrived. Being recognised by some one who knew him, news of his presence was conveyed to Farrel, who immediately regarded it as the dispensation of God. Going straight to his lodgings Farrel revealed the state of things in the city, and invited him to remain. Calvin, however, had no inclinations toward mixing in public strife. He asked to be excused, pleading his devotion to scholarly pursuits, and to the need of quiet to continue them. The fiery Reformer, however, finding persuasion vain, assumed the garments of the prophet. Lifting up his hands he declared that the Almighty would blight him with a curse if he put forward his own inclinations before his immediate and manifest duty. Calvin was awed by the voice of his friend ; he felt as if the Almighty had actually spoken to him, and that to disobey would imperil his salvation. With a deep sense of responsibility he agreed to remain, and so was begun that union between the city and the Reformer which was only to terminate with his death, and which was to leave its deep impress upon both.

## Calvin and Geneva

Geneva, at this time, was one of the stormiest cities in Europe. Its government was distributed over three different classes, who divided authority amongst them. First was the Bishop, styled 'Prince of Geneva,' who had the nominal right of leadership in war, and the actual right of coining money, of hearing appeals, and of granting pardons. Next there came the Dukes of Savoy, who possessed a certain claim upon the city, and by right of that claim exercised a restricted judicial function. The citizens, however, who had in past days shown considerable spirit, and knew both how to demand and defend their independence, possessed powers of legislation which they applied through representative councils.

The character of the city and its people at this time has been thus described:

'The Genevans were not a simple, but a complex, cosmopolitan people. There was, at this crossing of the routes of trade, a mingling of French, German, and Italian stock and characteristics; a large body of clergy of very dubious morality and force, and a still larger body of burghers, rather sounder and far more energetic and extremely independent, but keenly devoted to pleasure. It had the faults and follies of a mediæval city and of a wealthy centre in all times and lands; and also the progressive power of an ambitious, self-governing, and cosmopolitan community. At their worst, the early Genevans were noisy, riotous, and revolutionary; fond of processions and "mummeries" (not always respectable or safe), of gambling, immorality, and loose songs and dances; possibly not over scrupulous at a commercial or political bargain; and very self-assertive and obstinate. At their best they were grave, shrewd, business-like statesmen, working slowly but surely, with keen knowledge of politics and human nature; with able leaders ready to devote time and money to public progress, and with a pretty intelligent, though less judicious, following. In diplomacy they were as deft, as keen at a bargain, and as quick to take advantage of the weakness of competitors, as they were shrewd and adroit in business. They were thrifty, but knew how to spend well; quick-witted and gifted in the art of party nick-names. Finally they were passionately devoted to liberty, energetic, and capable of prolonged self-sacrifice to attain and retain what they were convinced were their rights.'

For several years previous to Calvin's entrance Geneva had been in a state of unrest. An effort of the Duke of Savoy to curtail its liberties had been successfully resisted, and the sympathy shown by the Bishop to Savoy had rendered him so unpopular that he was forced to leave the city, and the syndics declared the See vacant. Just then the first wave of the reform movement was felt. Farrel appeared upon the scene, and assisted by delegates from Berne, a city which had already accepted Protestant opinions, began with his usual impetuosity to storm the citadel of Romanism. Meeting a procession carrying images, one day, he tore them from the grasp of their bearers, and contemptuously threw them into the river. A tremendous commotion followed in which Farrel almost lost his life; he had to flee the city, but soon was back again, and so intense was his zeal that in a few months the character of the city was changed; instead of being a stronghold of the Pope it began, timidly at first, but with ever-increasing momentum, to declare itself boldly on the side of the Reformers.

In the midst of the battle Calvin arrived, and almost immediately became the controlling figure. To understand his work it is necessary to keep in mind what had to be done. A new constitution had to be formed; the breakdown of the old form of government had thrown the city into confusion, and threatened it with anarchy or tyranny. With the collapse of the Catholic Church a further and even more serious problem had to be faced. Worship had to be reorganised in consistence with the new opinions, and the effort to do this not only met with the embittered opposition of those who still adhered to the old faith, but it aroused the greatest divergence of opinion amongst those who accepted the new. In addition, the aim of the Reformers was not only to sweep away abuses, they aimed also at the reform of morals, at the purifying of public life, at bringing discipline to bear upon the unruly, and at inculcating in the lives of individuals sobriety of behaviour, and purity of private life. The effort to attain this was of all others the one the Reformers had at heart, but it was of all others the one most likely to arouse bitter opposition toward their methods, and danger toward their lives. In this connection we cannot fail to recall the effort of a like character made by Savonarola. The two cities, Florence and Geneva, were like each other in the temperaments of their peoples, as they were like in their size, their importance, and their wealth. Savonarola's ambition, like Calvin's, was to change a sinful city into a veritable city of God, and it cost Savonarola his life. No sooner had Calvin begun his task than he was made to feel that the battle would be fought with naked weapons. The first effort to impose restrictions on the people's pastimes, to bring the discipline of the Church to bear upon the licentious, to enforce attendance at public worship, and to punish the refractory, aroused the most vehement indignation ; a party, called the Libertines, sprang up, and gaining the upper hand, both Calvin and Farrel were banished from the city.

The triumph of the Libertines, however, was short lived ; no sooner had the Reformers left the city than scenes of licentiousness and violence became frequent ; finding the camp divided, priests of the Catholic Church began to appear, seeking to restore their position, and regain what they had lost. At length the citizens grew alarmed for their freedom ; they entreated Calvin to return, and after an absence of three years spent in Strasburg, he once more entered the gates of the city to spend the remainder of his years within it.

The reforms which Calvin introduced into the city of Geneva have become famous, and have been condemned as infamous. If we are to pass judgment at all, however, it is necessary to do so with a full knowledge of the circumstances, and a generous recognition of the difficulties. It is easy for us to sit at ease, with the fury of the struggle long gone, and pass our sweeping condemnations on men who, in the stress of the times, have made mistakes, to condemn them as intolerant, to point out with easy phrases their inconsistencies and excesses. Every man, however, has a right to demand that he shall be judged from the standpoint of his own day and generation, and that, born in the sixteenth century, he shall not be expected to exhibit the virtues of the twentieth. The sixteenth century held erroneous views of the rights of conscience, of the value of coercion in things religious, of the right of the state to interfere in matters of religious opinion, and of the possibility of reducing all to one cast of theological belief. The modern ideas of the freedom of the individual, and the limited function of the state, had not yet arrived, and Calvin shared with his contemporaries the mistakes of his age.

Setting out with the intention of creating a city in which God would be adored, and His laws obeyed by every citizen, Calvin sought to bring to his aid the instruction of the Church, and the discipline of the State. The Church was to do its part, by instruction, by admonition, and by censure; but where this failed, the State, he declared, must step in, and by pains and penalties, not only suppress vice, but also inculcate piety, and insist upon uniformity. This was a fatal error, as we now perceive. It expresses an attitude of the State which to us is revolting, since it undermines individual liberty and founds a despotism. But it was the error of the age, and was not challenged by any of Calvin's contemporaries. They challenged the right of the Church to deny to applicants the right to sit at the Lord's Table, a claim of the Church which they had no right to challenge; but they accepted, without demur, the point most vulnerable according to modern opinion, namely the right of the State to interfere at all.

To attain the end he had in view, Calvin began by establishing his famous Consistory. This Consistory was composed of six ministers and twelve elders, one of the elders being president. It met every Thursday, and before it were brought all evil-doers, both rich and poor, learned or ignorant. It possessed the power of excommunication followed by civil penalties if the culprit proved impenitent. In addition to this tribunal, laws were enacted by the Councils, and these laws covered the whole public and private life of the citizen. Drunkenness and profanity, gambling and dancing, were condemned; teaching divergent theological doctrine was met with severe penalties; breaches of the moral law were rigorously dealt with, but also many innocent amusements were prohibited, and trifling offences received excessive punishments. The effort to set up this system, to maintain it, and to defend it from attack, called forth from Calvin the most unwearied industry. He believed that he was obeying the divine command, that his authority was strictly scriptural, and so he carried into the performance of his task a sincerity and loftiness of purpose which go far to redeem him from the attacks which the effort itself lays him open to. Needless to say, opposition was continuous and embittered. He was hated by the lawless, by those whose material well-being suffered under the new régime, and by those who rebelled against excess, or whose character led them to do evil. He was ridiculed and lampooned; dogs were set at him in the public street; he was in constant danger of his life, and he never knew rest. He declared that he never spent two hours without interference. Yet, for all this, notwithstanding his mistakes, his imperiousness, his rigid and unbending insistence upon discipline, he succeeded in making Geneva the most law-abiding city in Europe. Prosperity, such as it had not known before, was enjoyed by its citizens ; it became safe as no other city of that time was safe. But it became more than this ; it became the centre of light and freedom for the whole of Europe. Into it there poured all the rising spirits of the age ; sons of freedom ejected from other lands, or attracted by the illustrious name of Calvin, entered its gates, and sat down at the feet of its great scholar and teacher. First a city of refuge, welcoming within its gates the depressed, the persecuted, and the down-trodden, it became soon, to the whole of Europe, the city of light. Its schools, founded by Calvin, were thoroughly equipped, and its theological seminary, over which Calvin also presided, offered to the student the most thorough training in evangelical theology which the age could offer. Geneva, by these means, obtained a unique place amongst the cities of Europe ; the stamp which Calvin imprinted upon it seems indelible ; for centuries it has remained a centre of freedom, of learning, and of progress.

How Geneva under Calvin's rule appeared to a contemporary we learn from a letter written by John Knox. 'I neither fear nor shame to say,' he writes, 'that this is the most perfect school of Christ that ever was since the days of the Apostles. In other places I confess Christ to be truly preached ; but manners and religion to be so sincerely reformed I have not yet seen in any place besides.' It was characteristic of Voltaire that he should gibe at Calvin's reforms, but when he had to flee for safety it was to Calvin's city that he fled.

The success which followed Calvin's effort to reform Geneva, to make it a centre of evangelical faith and freedom, was not reached without heavy cost even to the cause of freedom, nor without at least one act of injustice which stains his name. For the death of

Servetus the enemies of Calvin are justified in using terms of the strongest denunciation. Servetus has been called the first martyr of modern science. He advocated theories of God and the world which were pantheistic in character, and mixed physical with theological speculations in a way which seemed to the Reformers blasphemous, and subversive of the faith. He was condemned to be burned, and though Calvin advocated a milder form, he supported the death sentence. The decision was carried out, and Servetus maintained his opinions and his courage to the last. On the three hundred and fiftieth anniversary of his death an expiatory monument was erected on the spot where he perished. This marks the judgment of posterity upon the act. Those who seek to defend Calvin can only do so on the ground that he was not in advance of the opinion of his age. Heresy, in these days, was the unpardonable sin; if men did not accept the orthodox faith it was not because they could not, but because they would not. And since the salvation of the many was of more importance than the personal safety of the individual, it was better that one should suffer than that many should perish. In this theory the majority of the Reformers believed; even the mild Melanchthon declared the burning of Servetus to have been 'justly done.' There were others, however, who declared that 'Christ would be a Moloch if He required that men should be offered and burned alive.'

The enemies of Calvin, within and without Geneva, made the death of Servetus the pretext for an embittered attack upon him, but so wholly did public opinion concur in the deed that they compromised themselves, and ruined their cause, which otherwise might have been successful. The Libertines, who had sustained the attack upon Calvin from the first moment he had entered into Geneva, finding all other methods of ruining him unavailing, at length, in 1555, took up arms, in a final effort seeking to get him banished from the city. This insurrection, however, utterly failed, and from this time forth Calvin enjoyed some measure of peace. The true magnanimity of the man who had so long battled for righteousness and truth in their midst began to dawn upon the citizens ; they began to see him in his true proportions, and to reverence him for his noble disinterestedness, his absolute fearlessness, and his unimpeachable integrity. But his life, spent in the most arduous labours, was now drawing to a close. It was impossible that a frame, naturally weak, could long endure the excessive strain and fatigue imposed upon it. By the year 1563 it became clear to all that his health was giving way. With his indomitable resolution he for some time longer made his feeble frame obey the commands of his imperious will, but at length nature rebelled. On February 2, 1564, he lectured for the last time in the Academy ; four days later he preached his last sermon. He felt that his end was near, and so worn out was he in body and mind that he was eager to go. 'O Lord, how long,' he was constantly repeating. His lips moved constantly in prayer; his thoughts were centred upon the things unseen. The City Council sought a last interview with him, and as they stood around his bedside, Calvin asked their forgiveness for any faults or excesses he had shown, expressed his gratitude for all their kindness, and commended them unto God. On the following day he received the Genevan ministers, and in bidding them farewell recalled his early experience and trials :

'When I first came to this Church it had well-nigh nothing. There was preaching, that was all. The idols were sought out and burned; but there was no reformation. All was in confusion. That good man Master Guillaume (Farrel) and the blind Coraud were indeed here . . . I have lived in marvellous combats here. I have been saluted of an evening by fifty or sixty gunshots before my door. Fancy how that could shock a poor student, timid as I am, and as I confess I have always been. After that I was hunted from this city, and betook myself to Strasburg. Having dwelt there sometime I was recalled, but I had no less difficulty than before in seeking to fulfil my office. They set dogs on me, crying "Scoundrel," and my cloak and legs were seized. I went to the Council of Two Hundred when they were fighting, and when I entered they said to me, "Sir, withdraw, it is not with you we have to do." I said to them, "No, I shall not! Go on, rascals, kill me, and my blood will witness against you, and even these benches will require it." I have had many faults which you have had to endure, and all that I have done is of no value. The wicked will seize upon that word, but I repeat that all I have done is of no value, and that I am a miserable creature. But, if I might say so, I have meant well, my faults have always displeased me, and the root of the fear of God has been in my heart. You can say that the wish has been good; and I beg you that the ill may be pardoned; but if there has been good in it, that you will conform to it and follow it. As concerns my doctrine; I have taught faithfully, and God has given me grace to write. I have done it with the utmost fidelity, and have not, to my knowledge, corrupted or twisted a single passage of the Scriptures; and when I could have drawn out a far-fetched meaning, if I had studied subtilty, I have put that temptation underfoot, and have always studied simplicity. I have written nothing through hatred against any one, but have always set before me faithfully what I have thought to be for the glory of God.'

Calvin ended his stormy life peacefully, passing away in his sleep. 'John Calvin went to God on May 27, 1564,' says the Genevan record. The next day his body, encased in a plain wooden coffin, without pomp or ceremony, according to his wish, was buried 'in the common cemetery called Plain-palais.' He was followed to the grave by all the most honoured citizens of Geneva, but for long no stone even marked his resting-place. An unpretentious slab marked J. C. is pointed out as marking the place where all that was mortal of the great Reformer was laid, but even this is conjecture. He expressly desired no outward marks of honour, but the public monument, which Geneva has erected to his memory four hundred years after his birth, marks her sense of gratitude, and the world's recognition of his greatness.

### Character of the Revival

The differences between the revival in Geneva and those others we have considered are more marked than the points of similarity. These differences are so apparent that they may obscure our vision, and tempt us to deny the term revival to this movement altogether. In Geneva there was not that outbreak of fervour which we naturally associate with the word; its origin seemed more political than religious, more moral than spiritual. This is a mistake, however. A revival is not to be recognised by its beginnings, but by its results. There may be, and there frequently have been, all the outward evidences of a revival—excitement, emotion, intense fervour, etc.—and the results prove that there was no revival whatever, that the hearts of men were unmoved, their lives unchanged. There may be, and there have been, movements which began in quite unexpected ways, which gave no evidences at first of profoundly affecting the lives of men, but which, when their results were rightly estimated, were found to have produced the most lasting gains to the kingdom of God.

Judged by results, Geneva was visited by a profound revival, and of the revival Calvin, under God, was the great leader. This revival was so great that it changed the whole character of the city. Before it began its inhabitants were torn by factions, and degraded by superstitions; they were totally ignorant of Christian truth, and sunk in the worship of relics and belief in miracles worked by the saints; in their private life they were given over to licentiousness, and had won an unenviable name for fickleness and deceit. When Calvin died, all this had changed. A new city had sprung up, with new characteristics and a new name. Geneva had in the interval become a city enjoying the priceless gifts of peace and good government; her citizens were free and law-abiding as were no other citizens of that century. Instead of being sunk in the darkness of mediæval superstitions she had become one of the greatest intellectual centres of Europe; to her schools and colleges came scholars from all nations, and in her pulpits were to be seen men who were the recognised leaders of the intellectual and spiritual life of the day. The coarse spectacles which had degraded her streets had vanished, the foul sins which had flourished unrebuked had either disappeared or were hidden away in shamed secrecy; in thousands of homes God was worthily worshipped, and in the public life of the city His will sought to be obeyed. Sneer as we will at some of these laws, condemn as we may the interference of the State in the private life of the citizens, assume as exalted and superior an attitude as we may in reference to the methods adopted, a work which resulted in the tremendous moral, civil, and religious gains which resulted to Geneva needs no defence. Calvin had only to say to his detractors 'Look around!' to silence them. The mistakes were mistakes of the time; they were such as were inevitable to men thrown into the midst of a great upheaval without precedents to guide them, conscious only of the mighty issues at stake; the gains were such as leave lasting imprints upon the lives of men, and help forward with swifter footsteps the progress of the Kingdom of God.

The most marked characteristic of the revival in Geneva we perceive to be, not its emotional, but its severely practical character. It had its inspiration, first of all, in a changed conception of divine truth. The revival of the spiritual life followed a revived interest in dogma, and a reconstructed theology. Belief in the authority of the Church, as built up in the Middle Ages, and conceived by the Schoolmen, completely collapsed under the swinging blows dealt it by the Reformers, and a completely new set of beliefs took their place. These beliefs, conveying first of all conviction of their truth, became the rule of faith, sunk down into the nature and actually produced an entirely new type of character—a type of character which was destined to write itself deep in European history, and which, wherever it appeared, was destined to be the most strenuous force in the world making for freedom of conscience, the rights of private judgment, and the purity of public life. The type produced was stern, was often narrow and intolerant, but it was heroic and God-fearing to an extent perhaps without parallel in history.

This interest in theology, which was characteristic of the Genevan revival, was in itself not surprising. The Schoolmen were absorbed in theological speculations. But there is this wide distinction to be recognised. The Schoolmen dealt with theological questions as mere speculations of the intellect; the Reformers as questions upon the solution of which depended their eternal salvation. The difference in disposition was that displayed by the fencer when exhibiting his skill to an admiring audience, and that which he displays when in deadly earnest he confronts his mortal enemy. Nothing could be more puerile than the subjects discussed by the Schoolmen, nothing more ridiculous than the gravity with which they discussed them, nothing more futile than the results they arrived at. They were mere jugglers with words. Truth had become a riddle to be discovered by the subtle, and, when discovered, flung wantonly aside. The connection between knowledge and conduct had so long been forgotten that it came to be at last denied. The Genevan revival pierced this dead realm with its shafts of light; it brought back the intellect into the sphere of religion, and made the reason the pioneer of faith. Theology became no longer a system of subtleties and speculations to be indulged in for the exercise of the faculties, or the amusement of the learned; it became a subject of intense interests, and of the most overwhelming importance. In a word, theology changed from being speculative to being experimental. Everything fell back upon the needs of the individual; theology became a personal quest—what is my attitude toward God? what is God's attitude toward me? what are my present hopes? what my future destiny? Before these deep and awesome questions the littleness of life vanished, and took on instead a solemn and even awful responsibility; they sobered the most careless-hearted, and gave to knowledge of the truth a grave and even terrible necessity. When such questions as these became—as they did in Geneva—the absorbing subjects of discussion, public life takes on a gravity and decorum, and private life, at least of great numbers, becomes permanently affected. To them the unseen becomes the great reality; their souls are caught in that mighty tidal movement which moves on, impelled by an indestructible faith, to those unseen shores where it believes it shall find eternal rest.

In the Calvinistic theology the infallible authority of the Word of God is set over against the infallible authority of the Church. The Scriptures are declared to be the only rule of faith and practice. The true Church is that which is modelled upon the New Testament, and is to be known by the right administration of the Sacraments, and the preaching of the Word. Within the Church visible is the Church invisible, composed of the elect, assurance being given by the Holy Spirit working in the heart and through the Scriptures. The essential features of a theology, however, lie in its teaching about God, about the nature of man, and in its doctrines of grace; and it is in connection with Calvin's teaching on these subjects that its most outstanding tenets are disclosed. The essential feature of Calvin's doctrine of the person of God is His sovereignty, His infinite holiness and exaltation. This is a sublime conception, but unmodified, as in Calvin's teaching, and applied with the Frenchman's remorseless logic, it led him step by step to that doctrine of predestination which has aroused more antipathy, perhaps, than any other doctrine conceived by the brain of man.

With regard to this characteristic tenet of Calvinism, however, it ought to be recognised that Calvin was not its first advocate. The doctrine was first enunciated by Augustine, though Calvin gave to it a stamp of his own. Nor was Calvin the only one of the Reformers who taught it. It was common to all, but while Luther set it in the background, Calvin set it in the forefront of his system.

The design of God in creation, says Calvin, is the manifestation of His glory. In the eternal plan man was created a free agent, and originally possessed holiness of heart. Through the Fall, however, this was lost, and God withdrawing His Spirit from man, the human race was plunged into such utter depravity that sin became a necessity, and man, incapable of holiness, lay under His wrath and curse.

Man being himself incapable of satisfying divine justice, God, in His sovereign will, prepared a plan by which His glory should be exalted, and those whom He chose should be saved from that eternal death which is the just punishment of sin. This scheme of redemption being the product of divine grace, God is free to extend it, or to refuse it, to whomsoever He will. In His immutable decrees He elects scme to eternal life, others He foreordains to eternal damnation. 'Predestination,' says Calvin, 'is the name we give to God's eternal decree, by which He has determined with Himself what He wills to be done with every man. For we are not all born alike; but for some eternal life, for others eternal death, is foreordained.' 'We assert that those whom He gives over to eternal death are by a just, and irreprehensible (though incomprehensible) judgment, excluded from all access to eternal life.' All this is traced back to the absoluteness of God's choice, for which no reason may or can be given, else the foundation of God's election 'would be in works,' says Calvin. Even Adam's fall he is forced to admit is part of the divine decree, for God could not have left anything doubtful as to the end of man, otherwise 'Where would God's Omnipotence be?' he asks. 'I grant you,' he continues, 'it is a horrible decree, yet no one can deny that God foreknew the end of man before He formed him, and foreknew it because by His own decree He had ordained it.' It follows, also, that the elect can never fall away, since man's will cannot be stronger than God's decree.

Such a system of belief, it will instantly be recognised,

opens itself to damaging criticism. Beginning with His conception of the Sovereignty of God, solely regarding His Omnipotence and excluding all other attributes, Calvin, to conserve His idea, pushed on to the depravity of man, and to still further uplift the divine and sovereign will, to his complete dependence upon divine grace as to his future destiny. Man's condition before the Fall is enriched in order that his condition after it may be depressed, and his election to eternal life or eternal death is the result of caprice—since all mankind is equally depraved—and is not due to the compulsions of justice or of mercy. To represent man as 'born unable to keep the commandments, yet as justly liable to eternal punishment for breaking them,' is to make a statement which is repugnant to the reason, which violates one's sense of justice, and of our conception of the wisdom and love of God. 'The doctrine,' says Southey, 'implies that an Almighty and All-wise Creator has called into existence the greater part of the human race to the end that, after a short, sinful, and miserable life, they should pass into an eternity of inconceivable torments, it being the pleasure of their Creator that they should not be able to obey His commands, and yet incur the penalty of everlasting damnation for disobedience.' To what purpose, it may be asked, is it for man to strive to obey the law if foreordained to fail, it matters not how earnestly he struggle; or what ethical value can it have if, it matters not now unfaithful his heart, he be foreordained to succeed? The whole conception, it is clear, lays itself open to terrible abuse; it saps the hope of the timid, and encourages the assurance of the self-righteous.

Burns, with his merciless power of analysis, and with his pen steeped in acid, depicted, in caricature, its effect upon character of a certain type, in 'Holy Willie's Prayer':

> 'O Thou, wha in the Heavens dost dwell,
> Wha, as it pleases best Thysel',
> Sends ane to Heaven and ten to Hell,
> A' for Thy glory,
> And no for ony guid or ill
> They've done afore Thee!'

Such criticisms are just, but it must not be imagined that Calvin was either ignorant of them or indifferent to them. The mysteries of predestination and election he did not pretend to fathom. He believed that in every decree of the Almighty there were reasons both wise and good which no man could fathom; which to our limited sense appeared to justify our arraignment of the mercy and love of God, but which, had we knowledge sufficient, would be found to be worthy of our highest praise. He said in effect: 'Here is predestination; here is election; they are written in Scripture; they are found in history; they cannot be denied without a denial of the Sovereignty of God, or without a limitation of His Being; they are part of God's dealings with His creatures. It is not mine to explain them away, it is mine to accept them and obey.'

It is easy, too, in describing their difficulties for belief, altogether to miss their strength, and the basis they have in spiritual experience. It may be taken at once for granted that a set of beliefs, which have been so widely accepted, and which have so profoundly affected human character, must have in them some elements of truth which make them 'doctrines of grace.' And first of all, what has proved more essential to practical religion than the sense of entire dependence upon God for salvation, for the guardianship of the soul, and for the preservation of the spiritual life? This thought, which brings the being prostrate before the Most High, which bends the will into submission, which clothes God in majesty and power, and makes His will supreme in the life of the believer, may lack some of the softer elements of belief, but, when unhesitatingly accepted, it enthrones character, and brings into it something of majesty and strength. Again, what has proved a more quickening aid to a deepened spiritual life, than the recognition of the deep-seated power of sin as it is found in the heart of the sinner, and as it displays itself in the misery of the world ? No theology, indeed, is worth a minute's purchase which makes light of this tremendous fact ; and the theology which stands appalled before it—which regards escape from it as the one thing to be desired, which in receiving salvation ascribes its possession as in no way deserved, but as solely the gift of free grace, and, through the mysterious election of God—has in it something which works at the root of man's being, and appeals to his deepest convictions.

The effect of these doctrines, also, upon the men who accepted them, has a right to be considered before they are ruthlessly flung aside. Did their acceptance cause men to lose hope ? Did they weaken or discourage them ? Did they produce character which was unreliable when confronted by the most terrible tests by which men can be tried ? Not at all. They turned out some of the strongest and grandest men the world has known. 'They attracted into their ranks,' says Froude, 'almost every man in Western Europe who hated a lie. They were crushed down, but they rose again. They were splintered and torn, but no power could bend or melt them. . . . They abhorred, as no body of men ever abhorred, all conscious mendacity, all impurity, all moral wrong of every kind, so far as they could recognise it. Whatsoever exists at this moment in England or Scotland of conscientious fear of doing evil is the remnant of the convictions which were branded by the Calvinists into people's hearts.'

On the Continent, amid the awful persecutions which the reformed movement had to endure, it was the Calvinists who bore the brunt of the fight, and who saved the Protestantism of Europe. They numbered more martyrs than all others put together. 'For one who disappeared in the flames, there appeared a hundred more; men, women, and children marching to their punishment singing the Psalms of Marot, or the canticle of Simeon:

> "Rappelez votre serviteur,
> Seigneur! j'ai vu votre Sauveur."'

But how, it may be asked, could such noble characters spring from such a creed? The truth is that it is not given to any man, or any body of men in any generation, to embody the whole circle of divine truth. Certain great truths emerge in certain epochs; they gain a ready acceptance because the minds of men are disposed to receive them; they suit the conditions of the times, and bring to needy hearts a new inspiration. These are truths for the times, but they are not, as they are originally stated, truths for all times. Sooner or later they lose their efficacy, because they are lifted out of touch with the wider range of divine revelation, and because the old order changes and truths have to be restated for every new age. That which was vital remains, becomes the permanent possession of the Christian consciousness, while that which was incidental and exaggerated is rejected. Only when this process is completed much of the original enthusiasm has vanished; the old words remain, but they are devitalised, and the principles, for which their fathers died, the sons lightly esteem or scornfully reject. This is what has happened with those extreme doctrines of the Calvinistic creed. In Calvin's day men were moved by the spirit of the doctrines, not by the logic of them; they corresponded with something which lifted them into strenuous sacrifice, and into an exalted conception of God, and of all that God required of them. When that early spirit passed away, the hard, relentless character of the doctrines remained. The period of criticism followed, in which fiercely assailed, and no less fiercely defended, that which was exaggerated silently dropped out, and the great shining truths which the Calvinistic doctrine incorporates were added to, and have enriched, the great body of Christian truth.

### The Influence of Calvin

No one can rightly consider this great religious movement begun in Geneva without perceiving how remarkably it bears upon it the impress of its great leader. This at once marks Calvin as a religious force of the first magnitude. This fact has been obscured for the present generation by the revolt of many from his theology; by their want of understanding of what was vital in it; and by the false perspective in which his character itself is viewed. He lacked the gracious sweetness of St. Francis, the impassioned, spiritual fervour of Savonarola, the massive grandeur and exuberant humanity of Luther. Yet, if greatness be measured by the power to impress his followers with his own personality, to imbue them with a loyalty and devotion which persecution only inflamed, then Calvin was not inferior to the greatest of these. The fact that the intellect also dominated his personality detracts from the graciousness of his character, but it does not follow that it detracts from the depth or range of his influence. A spiritual life nurtured on the emotions, no doubt exhibits graces which are warm and attractive, and, compared with its passionately devout moods, the repression of less emotional natures seems cold and forbidding. But it does not follow that it is less deep. Different parts of the nature are affected, and different forms of piety produced. The distance which separates the Irish Catholic worshipper, for instance, who lifts his streaming eyes in adoration to the crucifix, and the Scottish Calvinist, who, seated in an uncomfortable pew, in a building which scorns adornment, listens with penetrating intellect to a prolonged theological disquisition, is almost immeasurable. The worship of the one is as appealing to the senses as the other is forbidding. In the type of character produced, also, the Irish peasant, compared with the Scottish, is the more winning personality; both are intensely influenced by their religious belief, but when the question arises as to which type produces the more reliant character, when strength, and integrity, and moral uprightness are called for, he would be ignorant indeed of the facts of life who did not instantly turn to the latter. And it was to such men that Calvin appealed; men to whom the softer and more emotional doctrines would have made no appeal, but whose strong natures and massive intelligence started at once into life as they listened to his stern but august message.

Although representing, then, the less emotional type of character, it must not be concluded that Calvin failed to arouse affection amongst his intimates. Notwithstanding his natural acerbity of character, there was much that his contemporaries found lovable in him, and there was that strange quality which inspires devotion.

In appearance he was of medium height, of a rather pale and dark complexion, with eyes clear even to his death ; he had the emaciation of an ascetic, and the brow of a scholar.

Few men have ever lived more strenuously than he, and with more disinterestedness. Not only did he carry upon his shoulders the burden of civil and ecclesiastical affairs, but he ceaselessly engaged himself in preparing exegetical and theological works, and in writing commentaries on different books of Scripture. He slept little, rising from his couch each morning at four, and ate but sparingly. The work he accomplished was remarkable. In addition to the duties and pursuits already mentioned, he delivered three theological lectures to his students each week, besides doing the work of a city pastor, and on alternate weeks preaching every day in the Cathedral. In addition, he carried on a vast correspondence. He was consulted by the greatest men in Europe, and was regarded as the foremost champion of the Reformed cause. He corresponded with Cranmer, he inspired John Knox, and there was not a cause in Europe regarding which he was not consulted.

In the closing years of his life, his enemies having been driven out of the city, the true proportions of the man began to appear, and all voices died away save those which spoke in admiration and respect. Yet this brought no change to Calvin himself. He was still but one of the city pastors ; his salary was small, his dress was of the plainest, his house was scantily furnished. Large sums of money passed through his hands, but he sought nothing for himself ; he lived the simple life amid the most exhausting labours. When approached by the City Council and asked how they might reward him for his great services, the only thing he could think of was an overcoat to keep himself warm. Notwithstanding his defects and limitations, of which too much, perhaps, has been made, we perceive that he was a great man; great in the range and penetration, as well as in the clearness and accuracy of his mind; great in his unflinching zeal, in the loftiness of his ideals, and in the humbleness of his heart. But the noblest testimony of all as to what he was comes from those who knew him best. 'God,' declared the members of the City Council, 'gave him a character of great majesty.'

# JOHN KNOX AND THE REVIVAL IN SCOTLAND

SCOTLAND, four hundred years ago, was one of the most benighted countries in Europe. The towns were few, thinly populated, and wretchedly built; while the people were sunk in a degrading poverty, and in the grossest ignorance. The feudal system, which elsewhere, with the growth of the population, and the increase of trade, had broken down, was in Scotland still supreme at the beginning of the sixteenth century. That source of a nation's wealth and stability which we call the middle class did not then exist. The State was composed of three orders—the clergy, the nobility, and the people. The people existed merely as the vassals of the baron. He was their protector, and in return they tilled his land, fought his battles, and in all the other relations of life acknowledged themselves as his serfs.

In spiritual affairs a like condition prevailed. The people were the serfs of their ecclesiastical superiors, were sunk in the grossest superstitions, and in the most slavish obedience. Independence, as we know the term, had no real existence; the people were enslaved both in body and mind.

Three influences were at work, silently converging, and uniting to break up this condition, and, by destroying the old, clearing the way for reformation. The first of these was intellectual; the second, political; the third, religious.

I. The intellectual factor was the renaissance of

learning. For centuries the minds of men had been imprisoned, and held in servitude to the Church. Art, Science, and even Literature were subordinated to Theology. Freedom of thought, the rights of private judgment, liberty of investigation, and the opportunity of public criticism were all alike denied. Wherever an attempt was made to break the shackles it encountered an instant and implacable opposition; the hand of the ecclesiastic darted out to seize the victim, who was given the choice of recantation or the stake.

Slowly, as the world rolled out of those dark centuries, this bondage was broken. The mind of man cannot be permanently imprisoned, and the Middle Ages were but the slumbering winter-tide preparing for the festal joy and radiance of the spring. The birth of learning, its causes, and its influence in awakening a new hope, and preparing the way for a revived spiritual life, has already been traced, and that great wave which spread across the greater part of the continent of Europe sent a tiny ripple which broke against the shores of Britain, and which awoke a response even in the North. The connection between France and Scotland had long been close, and this was not without its compensations. Scottish noblemen fought in the French army, brought back with them into their rude homes something of polish and of courtesy, and the outward show, if not the inner refinements, of learning. The awakening of the intellect, though confined to the narrowest limits, was sufficient to inspire a certain number of youthful enthusiasts to leave their own shores, and, repairing to the Continent, to imbibe something of the new learning. When they returned they were not slow in infecting others with a like enthusiasm. This was one of the factors preparing the way, but there was a second and more important one.

## II. Political Conditions

For more than a century Scotland had been rent by internal dissension. On the one side were the powerful nobles, on the other side the king and the clergy. Each was fighting for supremacy. At the beginning of the sixteenth century victory seemed to rest with the nobility. Constant wars with England had depleted the country, and by weakening the central power, had added to the security of the nobles, who, aided by the physical structure of the country, shut themselves up in their fortresses, and bade defiance to all authority. On the death of James iv. in 1513, and during the minority of his son, the control of the State passed entirely into their hands. They held the king a prisoner, and the clergy, who were the natural allies of the crown, were powerless to help. In 1528, however, occurred an event which altered the whole situation, and which was destined to profoundly affect the history of Scotland. A conspiracy, organised by Cardinal Beaton, was set on foot, which aimed at the release of the king, and the subjugation of the nobles. The plot was successfully carried through, and the king, escaping, took refuge in Stirling Castle.

Once more the reins of government changed hands through this daring act. The Church was now supreme, and the nobles were ruthlessly persecuted and driven from the land. The struggle, however, was not over but broke out again and again with increased fury. On the one side was the Church, seeking to guard its authority and its riches; on the other side was the nobility, embittered by persecution, caring nothing for the Church, but thirsting for revenge, and looking with a greedy eye toward the Church's wealth. While between the two, the chief pawn in the game, sat the king, working for his own interests, and leaning naturally toward that side most likely to further them. With this in view, he increased the power of the clergy, nominated them for every important position under the crown, and by such acts so alienated and exasperated the nobles that their acceptance of Protestant principles, whether they believed in them or no, gave them their one hope of revenge.

### III. Religious Conditions

The corrupt state of the Church and clergy which we have found existing everywhere at the beginning of the sixteenth century found no exception in Scotland. Nowhere, perhaps, was the prevailing corruption more apparent. While the people were held down in a debasing poverty the clergy were everywhere bent on amassing wealth. Half of the wealth of the country was in their hands. Bishops and Abbots rivalled the nobles in the magnificence of their retinues, while they scandalously neglected their spiritual office. They never condescended to preach, and were too ignorant to have done so if they chose. The Bishop of Dunkeld, who 'thanked God that he knew neither the Old nor the New Testament,' was typical of his class. Benefices were openly bought and sold, and whole parishes were left without incumbents in order that the Bishop might enjoy their emoluments. Quentin Kennedy, the Catholic apologist, describes, with frankest candour, the system by which benefices were filled. 'And when they have gotten a benefice,' he says, 'if they have a brother or son who can neither sing nor say, nourished in vice all his days, he shall be immediately mounted on a mule, with a sidegown and a round bonnet, and then it is a question whether he or his mule know best to do his office.' The lives of the clergy were scandalously corrupt; many of them lived in open immorality, and the people perished through lack of knowledge. Such services as there were, were conducted in a dead language of which the people were entirely ignorant, and which many of the priests could not even correctly read. The country swarmed with ignorant and idle monks, who, both by menace and by force, robbed the poor of the very necessities of life, and, not content with this, forced themselves into the very chambers of the dying to extort bequests, disturbing their last moments by their rapacity. Prayer, as an act of communion of the soul with God, and as a means of consolation in times of distress, was practically unknown; to the people enslaved in superstition a paternoster acted like a spell; if it was repeated forward, it brought blessings from Heaven; if backward, it thwarted the designs of Hell. The turbulent state of the country, its poverty owing to the absence of manufactures and large industries, and its sanguinary and incessant wars, added enormously to the influence and to the numbers of the clergy. The timid sought the Church for its protection, the ambitious for its influence, the avaricious for its wealth. Exceptions, of course, there must have been, and were. Did not Thomas à Kempis live in encloistered retreat through all the corrupt period preceding the Reformation, directing the gaze of his soul exclusively on Christ, and living unspotted of the world? And there must have been in Scotland, too, as elsewhere, many who had not bowed the knee to Baal, and who, amid terrible temptations, kept the flame of spiritual love alight in their souls. But these were the exceptions; the light was dying out of the souls of men; darkness had covered the earth, and gross darkness the people. It was one of these crises in a nation's life when, if the race were not to sink back into a state worse than barbarism and lose all that the centuries had toiled for, some sudden and dramatic act was called for. The nation, like Israel of old, waited for the fulfilment of the prophecy, that when darkness covered the earth, and gross darkness the people, the Lord would arise, and His glory be seen, so that all those in darkness might come to the light, and to the brightness of His rising. And the great and comforting truth of history is that God is ever preparing new epiphanies ; that man cannot ' reel back into the beast,' and lose all that mankind has won ; that the powers of evil and corruption can flourish for a while, but a limit is put to their empire, and when that limit is reached the gathering waters are already heaped up, the avalanche is already preparing, and the dislodgment of a single stone is sufficient to set its mighty forces in movement. As in those movements we have already discussed, the hour had arrived, and with it the man.

## Early Days

John Knox was born at Gifford Gate in the town of Haddington in the year 1505. This little town, nestling in the heart of the richest agricultural district in Scotland, is of ancient fame. It became a royal burgh in the early part of the twelfth century, and in the ruthless wars of those days was several times burned to the ground. A bridge, which crosses the river Tyne, leads to a suburb known as the Nungate, and the place where Knox's house stood is marked by an oak tree surrounded by a wall and railing. This tree was planted by Thomas Carlyle, and across the river, only a stone's-throw away, in the beautiful Parish Church, is laid to rest Carlyle's wife, who claimed descent from the great Reformer. Nestling in a green valley, amid fields of rich cultivation, beautiful in situation the old town lies, once the scene of many bloody fights, but now steeped in peace, and sleepy with age.

Of Knox's parentage, of his early life and associates, little is known. Haddington possessed one of the few schools in Scotland which could offer to its scholars anything approaching what might be called a liberal education. In early annals this school is one of six mentioned as giving, in addition to the ordinary subjects of instruction, tuition in Latin, and, in rare instances, in Greek. To this school Knox was sent, and in Haddington he remained until at the age of seventeen he entered the University of Glasgow. How long he remained there is uncertain. His name appears among the Incorporati in the Annales of Glasgow college of the year 1522, but it is not found in those of subsequent years, or indeed in those of any other Scottish University. This leads to the supposition that he may have remained a student without matriculating. He made no claims to scholarship, though he was well acquainted with Latin, and in Geneva, at middle age, acquired proficiency in both Greek and Hebrew. Somewhere about the year 1530 he was ordained to the priesthood, though of his early life, until he embraced the reformed faith, little is known. He seems to have been occupied with tutorial rather than parochial duties, being mentioned as tutor in different houses in East Lothian.

Unlike the other Reformers, Knox had grown to middle age before he embraced the Protestant faith. With him it was not the rash exuberance of youth, with its love of change and adventure, which led him to attach himself to a new cause; it was the matured reflections of middle age, of a time when prudence takes the place of recklessness, and when the habits are so formed that change can only be effected with pain and difficulty. Doubtless for long his mind had been moving toward change, but he was forty years of age before he definitely detached himself from the existing Church. Beza declares that his change of opinions came largely through his study of the writings of Augustine, that early Father from whom all the Reformers drew inspiration, and from whom they gained their most distinctive tenets. But it was more the influence exerted upon him by George Wishart than anything else which gave to his mind the final *coup de grâce.* This learned and amiable youth, who, after a period of banishment, had returned to his native land, was one of the forerunners and first martyrs of Protestantism in Scotland. Having imbibed the reformed doctrines, he spent his time going from place to place instructing the people, and amongst other places visited East Lothian and met with Knox. Immediately Wishart's message found an echo in Knox's heart; a warm affection sprang up between the two men. Knox followed him everywhere, bearing before him, it is said, a huge double-edged sword, which he was prepared to use in defence of his friend. Wishart, however, was not destined to see the harvest of his labours. The emissaries of the wily Cardinal Beaton were dogging his footsteps. Being apprehended, he was put upon his trial, and being condemned, was burned at the stake. Knox was eager to accompany him, but the remonstrance of Wishart is well known. 'Nay,' said he, 'return to your bairns. One is sufficient for a sacrifice.' Wishart died with heroic fortitude, but he remained not long unavenged. On the 29th of May 1546 a body of men broke into the castle of St. Andrews, and dragging the Cardinal from his bed, put him to death. The assassination was partly political, for the cruel prelate had many enemies; but it was also a deed of vengeance by lawless men stung to madness through the death of one whom they regarded as a saint.

Knox's well-known sympathy with Wishart's views made him a marked man, and after being pursued from one place to another he at length reached the Castle of St. Andrews, where were gathered together the leaders of the reform movement, as also those who, in Pitscottie's quaint language, 'suspected themselves to be guilty of the said slaughter.'

## Knox's Call

The heroic character of Knox soon declared itself in the turbulent days which now ensued. In the sea-girt castle, filled with desperate outlaws, with ardent Reformers, and also with young lads who had followed Knox for the purpose of instruction, a man was wanted to cheer the garrison, and to publicly defend the stand many of them were making for freedom. They had listened to Knox as he instructed his pupils, and being struck with his intense earnestness, and with his knowledge of Scripture, they formed the resolution of appointing him as their minister. The call itself came with dramatic suddenness, and by Knox was totally unexpected. Sitting one day 'in the public preaching place,' listening to a discourse on the ministerial office, he was startled by the preacher turning and directing his address to him personally. He pointed out the needs of the times, the call for service, and Knox's own qualifications for the office; then turning to the congregation he asked them to ratify what he had said. This they solemnly did, with one voice calling Knox to exercise the office of minister in their midst. The effect upon Knox himself was overwhelming. He could not shake off the call and treat it lightly. He heard in it the voice of God, but his spirit, which knew no other fear, quailed under the weight of the responsibility. Bursting into tears he rushed from the place, and only after prolonged struggle did he accept the heavy task. Once accepted, however, there was for him no turning back; with his usual intrepidity and vehemence of character, he flung himself into the fight. His first sermon, preached in the Parish Church, drew a great crowd, amongst which were not only the chief men of the city, but also many monks and priests who watched over the perishing interests of their church. Knox's sermon, which exhibits even at that early date his vast powers of vituperation, caused an immense sensation. 'Some hew at the branches of Papacy,' men said, 'but this man strikes at the root.' Quickly, under Knox's ministrations, the reformed faith began to grow, the first visible signs of it being a Communion Service, after the reformed manner, presided over by Knox, and held in the Parish Church. At this service, the first of its kind held in Scotland, Knox dispensed the sacrament to over two hundred people. It was a small number, but it revealed better than anything else the change that was coming over Scotland.

The garrison at this time, which was practically in a stage of siege, was expecting help from England, when there appeared a new source of anxiety on the horizon in the shape of a French fleet. Knox at once prophesied disaster. 'Your corrupt life,' he told them, 'could not escape the judgment of God.' For a while the garrison held out, but the forces of the enemy, and the deadly precision of their artillery, proved too much for them. On the last day of July 1547 the garrison capitulated to the French Admiral, trusting in his promise that they should be taken to France, and allowed their liberty. But a promise to 'heretics' imposed no burden upon the conscience according to the French code of honour, and so, while the chief prisoners were cast into French dungeons, the rest, with Knox amongst them, were sent to the galleys.

For nineteen months Knox was chained to the oar, and his sufferings were so great that he never afterwards cared to recall them. His health was permanently damaged, and he contracted a painful disease which never afterwards left him without suffering. 'How long I continued prisoner,' he once said in a sermon at St. Andrews in 1569, 'what torments I sustained in the galleys, and what were the sobs of my heart, is now no time to recite.' During this terrible time his hope still survived, and his courage remained undaunted. On one occasion, 'lying betwixt Dundee and St. Andrews, the second time that the galleys returned to Scotland, the said John Knox being so extremely sick that few hoped for his life, Maister James Balfour willed him to look to the land, and asked if he knew it. Who answered, "Yes, I know it well; for I see the steeple of that place where God first in public opened my mouth to His glory; and I am fully persuaded, how weak soever I now appear, that I shall not depart this life till that my tongue shall glorify His godly name in the same place."'

Terrible as were his sufferings on board the galley, neither these, nor the threats of his captors, could quench his spirit. One day, it is related, a picture of the Virgin—'a painted brod' (picture)—was brought on deck, and the officers thrust it into Knox's hands, telling him to kiss it. Knox, 'looking advisedly round, took the image and flung it into the river, saying, "Let our Lady now save herself, she is light enough: let her learn to swim."' This 'merry fact' was dangerous jesting, and it was strange that Knox should have escaped with his life. 'After that,' he says, 'there was no Scottish man urged with that idolatry.'

Knox was not released until early in 1549, at the instigation, as it was supposed, of Edward VI. Scotland was then in so disturbed a state that nothing could be gained by his returning to it, and for the next ten years we find him submitting to exile. The first part of this time he spent in England, and as a minister of the English Church. The ecclesiastical affairs of England, at this time, were passing through a transition stage. Episcopal government was acknowledged, but the use of the Prayer Book was not obligatory, nor kneeling at the Communion. The Prayer Book has a note appended to the Communion Office, explaining that the attitude of kneeling is 'well meant for a signification of the benefits of Christ therein given . . . but therein no adoration is intended either unto the Sacramental bread and wine . . . or unto any Corporal presence of Christ's natural Flesh and Blood.' This is known as the 'Black Rubric,' and is from the hand of Knox.

First of all Knox was called to labour in Berwick, and early in 1551 in Newcastle, where it is said 'many Scots resorted to enjoy his fellowship.' In 1552 he was summoned to London as King's Chaplain, and there was one of the six who revised and sanctioned the 'Articles concerning an Uniformity of Religion' which became the basis of the 'Thirty-nine Articles' of the Church of England. The bishopric of Rochester, falling vacant, was offered to Knox, who declined it. A year later, when in exile on the Continent, he explained his reason for refusing all such appointments. 'What moved me to refuse, and that with displeasure of all men, those high promotions? Assuredly the foresight of troubles to come. How oft have I said that the time would not be long that England would give me bread?'

The troubles predicted by Knox were not long in arriving. Edward VI., long in feeble health, was removed to Greenwich in April 1553, and died there on the 6th of July. Immediately the country was plunged into confusion. Mary began her reign ostensibly with toleration, but it was not long before her real character was disclosed. Knox was reduced almost to beggary, and with others fled the country.

Arriving at Dieppe, Knox, after many wanderings, arrived at Geneva, and there came under the powerful personality of Calvin. Deeply conscious of his lack of scholarship, he hoped, in this city of freedom, to find opportunity for study, but he had not been long settled before he was called to minister to an English Church at Frankfort. Once more he returned to Geneva, where he was appointed to minister again to an English congregation, and here he remained for three years, until 1559.

Meanwhile the seeds of the Reformation were beginning to grow up in Scotland and to bring forth fruit. A great awakening was taking place amongst the people, who were beginning to shake off their lethargy, and to awake to a sense of their wrongs. The priesthood still hurled their anathemas at them, but they fell now on sceptical ears. 'They so lightlied the Mass,' the priests complained, 'that there was no longer a living to be made out of it.'

The Queen Regent at this time was Mary of Guise, an implacable enemy of the Reformers. A proclamation forbidding any reformed minister to preach or administer the Sacraments was issued, and it seemed as if the whole movement were on the point of collapse. There was only one man who could save the situation, and urgent messages were sent to Knox, then in Geneva, to return and assist the cause in his native land. Knox immediately complied, and on the 2nd of May 1559 he arrived in Edinburgh, and from there set out for Perth, the chosen meeting-place of the Reformers. Entering the Parish Church he preached an impassioned sermon to a huge congregation. His eloquence was so tempestuous that the whole congregation was roused to action. Before the night fell the churches were stormed, and every vestige of ‘ popery ’ destroyed.

News of these and similar events was conveyed to the Queen Regent at Stirling, and caused the greatest indignation. The Queen threatened to visit this contempt of her authority, and this violence done to her faith, with extreme penalties, and with her French troops she marched towards Perth. Ill would it have gone with the Protestants at this time had it not been for Knox. Danger, however, was the atmosphere which called forth his highest qualities, and instead of weakening before the perils confronting them he adopted the most imperious tone. Though the Protestant cause could number then but a few preachers, and in the ranks men of influence were sorely required, Knox bowed down to none. Writing to the nobles of Scotland at a time when smooth words were needed if safety were to be considered, he adopted instead a tone of menace. ‘Unless ye join yourselves with us,’ he declares, ‘ as of God ye are reputed traitors, so shall ye be excommunicated from our society. The glory of the victory, which God shall give to his Church, yea, even in the eyes of men, shall not appertain unto you.’ Such was the spirit of the times that, instead of alienating those to whom it was addressed, it brought over large numbers of waverers to the side of the Reformers. A new spirit was breathing over Scotland. Beneath all the political unrest, the clash of faction, and the bitterness of sect, a reviving breath of spiritual life was animating men's hearts. Serious men, and those inclined to better things, felt the glow of living conviction in the words of these new preachers; they spoke with that unmistakable accent of authority which so deeply impresses the human heart, and which is ever present in times of spiritual awakening. Even the Church fell to setting its house in order, and with furious energy sought to introduce reforms. But the people were too much exasperated to view these with favour. They grasped with sufficient clearness the message of the new preachers to know that they had been wronged, and the attempt at the last hour to set these wrongs right only inflamed them by its tacit acknowledgments.

The Protestant cause was thus gaining every day, and when Mary arrived before Perth its leaders were able to make terms with her. They agreed to disperse on condition that no one should suffer on account of the past, and that all questions of religion should be considered by the next Parliament.

Meanwhile, Knox was going from place to place carrying the fiery cross, preaching the new evangel, and calling his countrymen to free themselves from the bondage imposed upon them by the priesthood. At length he reached St. Andrews, whose towers he had seen when tossing with pain in the galleys, and where he longed again to lift up his voice. Archbishop Hamilton had entered the city the previous evening with a retinue of armed men, and forbade Knox to preach, warning him that if he did, 'twelve hackbuts would light upon his nose at once.' Vainly his friends entreated him not to make the attempt, but Knox refused to listen to them. Entering the pulpit of the Parish Church he proceeded to address the people. Neither Archbishop nor military appeared, and so overwhelming was Knox's appeal that the people rose *en masse*, and before the night fell had destroyed every vestige of the old faith. The violence with which this was done aroused neither misgivings nor regrets in the heart of Knox. 'Pull down the nests, and the rooks will fly away,' he believed. 'The long thirst of my wretched heart is now satisfied in abundance,' he writes . . . 'for now, forty days and more, hath my God used my tongue in my native country, to the manifestation of His glory. . . . The thirst of the poor people, as well as of the nobility here, is wondrous great, which putteth me in comfort, that Christ Jesus shall triumph for a space here, in the North, and in the extreme parts of the earth.'

Following their successes at St. Andrews, the Reformers next turned their eyes towards the Capital. As they entered, the Queen Regent retired to Dunbar with her troops. In Edinburgh, however, the Reformers found little left for them to do, as the burghers had already demolished the religious houses, leaving nothing but the walls standing.

The Protestant cause in Scotland was now taking definite shape, and the country was drifting into civil war. The Reformers were trusting to support from England, Mary of Guise and the Catholics to increased support from France. For long the result hung in the balance, but the appearance of an English fleet finally weighed the scales in favour of Knox and his followers. In the midst of these events the Queen Regent died, and the French allies, after agreeing to a treaty which conceded to the government the power to settle the ecclesiastical affairs of the country, embarked with what remained of their army for France.

In the August of the same year—1560—Parliament met in Edinburgh, and was found to be overwhelmingly Protestant. With almost incredible swiftness and unanimity it declared for the Protestant faith, abolished Roman Catholicism, and called for a form of Confession. This was drawn up and presented in four days, and was accepted almost without a dissentient voice. Bishops there were present, but they remained silent while every vestige of their old authority was being wrested from them. Several of the temporal lords, without combating the new doctrines, declared their adhesion to the old faith; but these numbered but three. 'The rest of the Lords,' wrote Randolph, 'with common consent, and as glad a will as ever I heard men speak, allowed the same.' The scene was profoundly affecting. Men were moved out of their habitual reticence to declare their profound gratitude to God; it was not political passions which thus moved them, but deep, spiritual earnestness. 'I am the oldest in this company,' said Lord Lindsay, 'but now that it hath pleased God to let me see this day, where so many nobles and others have allowed so worthy a work, I will say with Simeon, "Nunc Dimittis."'

Thus the old faith fell almost without striking a blow in its defence, a startling indication of how slight a hold it had obtained over the affections of the people, how unworthily it had maintained its high traditions, and used its power. On the 20th December of this same year the first General Assembly of the Church of Scotland was held, and the first chapter of the movement in Scotland was closed. Throughout it all one man soared high above all others. Through the stormy days it was Knox's voice that was heard, ever clamant and insistent, often strident, always intolerant, but ever dauntless. From the pulpit of St. Giles he thundered forth his appeals, his warnings, his threats even, and such was the force of his personality that he may be regarded at this time as being the real ruler of Scotland. His convictions were maintained at white heat ; his speech—rugged, impassioned, often when he assumed the rôle of the prophet, majestic—swept away the timid opposition of other men ; his sincerity, which none doubted, the transparent honesty of his motives, and his utter fearlessness of consequences, appealed even to his enemies ; while his outstanding ability, and his knowledge of affairs, made him an ally which no party in the state could afford to disdain.

The complete triumph of the reformed opinions, the acquiescence of the nation as a whole in them, as well as the tranquillity which everywhere abounded, seemed to promise times of peace and prosperity both for the nation and the Church, when there entered upon the pages of Scotland's stormy history one whose beauty and whose sufferings have strangely affected the human heart, and who, notwithstanding the crimes which stain her name, remains one of its most romantic and pathetic figures.

### Knox and Mary Queen of Scots

When James v. died of a broken heart after the battle of Solway Moss, he left behind him, as heir to the throne, a little daughter, afterwards to be known to fame as Mary Queen of Scots.

Being connected from her mother's side with the powerful Guise family, she was brought up in France, and as heir to the throne of Scotland, and next in succession to the throne of England, she became one of the chief pawns in the game of conquest then going on in Europe. When little more than a child she was married to the Dauphin of France, who died two years after, in 1560, the year which saw the triumph of the reformed opinions in Scotland.

Left thus early a widow, proud, ambitious, and

beautiful, left unprotected in the midst of cruel and ambitious men, herself the object of ambition because of her hopes, and the centre of attraction because of her beauty; called to govern a lawless people at a time of danger and of revolution, it is not to be wondered at that her way was beset with pitfalls, and that pity for her sufferings has blotted out the remembrance of her misdeeds.

During her sojourn in France she had not been kept ignorant of the history of affairs in her native land, and in determining to return to Scotland and assume the throne she had already determined her policy. As a devout Catholic she viewed with intense indignation the ecclesiastical changes which had taken place, and her intention from the first was to restore the old religion. She had heard of Knox, too, and vowed that she would either banish him from her kingdom or be banished herself. With these intentions fully established in her mind she set out for her native shores. On August 19, 1561, she landed at Leith. The day was chilly with fog, and Knox records that 'the very face of Heaven, the time of her arrival, did manifestly speak what comfort was brought into this country with her—to wit, sorrow, dolour, darkness, and all impiety.'

Mary had not been in her kingdom for a week before she was to taste something of the character of its people. On the first Sunday after her arrival she ordered Mass to be celebrated in the Abbey of Holyrood. Instantly the fiercest indignation was aroused, the worst fears of Knox were realised. Thundering daily from the pulpit of St. Giles, he declared 'that one Mass was more fearful to him than if ten thousand armed men were landed in any part of the realm of purpose to suppress the whole religion.' Mary, on her part, exercised, not without success, those gifts of attraction which she so supremely possessed. Even the most confirmed of the nobles who had embraced the new faith felt himself weakening in her presence; she seemed to possess 'some enchantment whereby men were bewitched.' Mary was not long in her realm, however, before she realised that her one obstacle was the preacher of St. Giles, and to silence him would be better than to win over an army. She determined, therefore, to confront him without delay, and summoned him to Holyrood. In the Council Chamber at Holyrood they met, and the meeting is historic. 'She was at the height of her glorious beauty; the fine, liberal outlines of her features were softened and rounded by youth and health, while strong vitality and a sense of power gave the sparkle and fascination that no painter could reproduce. She saw before her a man already old, below middle height, but broad and well made; a long black beard, already grizzled, shaded the lower part of his face, while deep-set grey eyes looked out keenly from under the narrow but prominent brow. Both were accustomed to read the characters of men quickly and keenly. In the beautiful girl opposite him Knox recognised the power of a practised diplomatist. . . . In the grave, worn preacher Mary found an unhesitating authority and a disregard alike of her womanly charms and her royal prerogative that for the moment almost disconcerted her.'

The encounter from Mary's side failed. Neither on this occasion, nor on any subsequent one, could she overawe him by her authority, or move him by her charms. Vainly she tried flattery, vainly power; Knox had suffered too deeply to become a gallant of the court. 'If there be not in her a proud mind, a crafty wit, and an indurate heart against God and His truth, my judgment faileth me.' However this judgment may be viewed there is no doubt that it saved Scotland from a grave political danger, and from its relapse back into the conditions from which it had emerged. Knox's attitude may have been uncompromising; he certainly had little of the spirit of compromise; but compromise on vital issues is betrayal, and in great crises is ruin. Bitter, implacable, intolerant, no doubt, he was but what the history of Scotland might have been had he been found at this time plastic, and open to corruption, it is not pleasant to imagine.

Mary's subsequent history, the crimes of her court, the mistakes of her government, the failure of her rule, and the pathos of her death, does not concern us here. Throughout all the trouble, the sin, and the terror of the times, Knox remained the same. These were years of anxiety and of strenuous toil; years when, but for Knox's intrepid character, the wheels might again and again have rolled backward, and the work of the Reformers have been undone.

At length, broken down with the labours of his stormy life, the great Reformer felt that death was drawing nigh. On the 9th of November 1572 Knox preached for the last time in St. Giles. So feeble was he that he had to be helped into the pulpit, but once there the old fire which had set Scotland in a glow once more broke out, the Cathedral rang with his trumpet notes, and so vehemently did he preach that 'he was like to rend the pulpit in pieces.' When the sermon was ended, however, it was seen that his strength was spent, and the end near.

His closing days were days of peace. The stormy spirit so long intent on public affairs withdrew itself into the inner chamber where peace abides, and where vision takes the place of sight. Once repeating the Lord's Prayer he was heard to stop, and to add with awe-struck whisper, 'Who can pronounce so holy words?' His friends gathered around him; all the great men of the kingdom visited him as he lay weak and helpless, and he bade them a kindly farewell. A little after noon on Monday, November 24th, he asked his wife to read to him part of the fifteenth chapter of 1 Corinthians, which he pronounced a 'comfortable chapter,' and later on, in the fourteenth chapter of John, 'where I cast my first anchor.' Being asked if he heard, he answered, 'I hear, and understand far better, I praise God.' Soon after the end came: he 'slept away at even, without any pain.' On the Wednesday following, amid the grief of the whole populace, he was laid to rest in the shadow of that old cathedral which had so often rung with his eloquence, and which had been the scene of his greatest efforts. From the greatest to the meanest in the land it was recognised that there had passed away a great man, a true lover of his country, and a faithful follower of Jesus Christ.

### Character of the Movement

The reform movement in Scotland has frequently been dismissed as a mere political upheaval, agitated by political intriguers, and consummated with only the minimum of religious feeling. This is to invert the facts. That political considerations entered in, contributing their own influence to the movement, is undoubted. It could not be otherwise. In every great spiritual movement which profoundly affects a nation's life political and social conditions are bound to enter. They are bound to enter because no part of a nation's life can be isolated from the whole; each part acts and reacts upon the others, and no part can be affected without the whole being stimulated or depressed. The Reformation in Scotland, just because it so profoundly challenged the whole existing order, produced an agitation which left no part of the nation's life untouched. It both affected the political conditions, and was affected by them; in some ways these promoted the Reformation, in others they retarded it; but in no sense did they create it. The dominant impulse was not political; the movement did not begin by a social or political revolution; it was not initiated by men who sought to change conditions in social or political life which had become intolerable; it was a religious movement set in motion by men who profoundly realised the corruption around them, and who, having received light to their own souls, were willing to lay down their lives to hand on that light to others. The 'reek which blew from the fire which burned Patrick Hamilton,' and which affected so many, did not arouse bitterness at existing political conditions; it aroused men who were weary of the empty seeking in empty cisterns for water which would quench their thirst, and who, with eager desire, turned to the new and found it. It is true that many nobles attached themselves to the new movement on unworthy grounds, that the 'sin of covetousness' had much to do with their decision; but this is true only of a part; it is not true of the greatest part, or of the best part. Even then all that can be said is that they took advantage of its existence; they did not bring it into life, nor did they maintain its life. Owing to the conditions then existing, the Reformation had to run alongside a political revolution, which largely it created, largely shaped; yet beneath this, as the supreme fact, was the new spiritual life which had been awakened. To neglect this is to fatally misinterpret the whole spirit of the times.

The movement in Scotland, however, has marked characteristics of its own.

First of all it was a popular movement 'broad based

upon the people's will.' It did not filter downwards from above, reaching first the well-to-do and intelligent parts of the community, and then slowly move the masses. On the contrary it began amongst the people. Nothing in our history is more remarkable than the change which came over the poorer classes when the first breath of the Reformation reached them. It seemed to call into instantaneous and active life elements of national character long slumbering; it seemed to call into being in a moment that intelligence, firmness, and independence so characteristic of the Scottish race. 'A poor barren country,' says Carlyle, 'full of continual broils, dissensions, massacrings; a people in the last stage of destitution. . . . It is a country as yet without a soul: nothing developed in it but what is rude, external, semi-animal. And now at the Reformation, the internal life is kindled, as it were, under the ribs of this outward material death. A cause, the noblest of causes, kindles itself, like a beacon set on high; high as Heaven, yet attainable from Earth; whereby the meanest man becomes not a citizen only, but a member of Christ's visible Church; a veritable Hero, if he prove a true man.'

Thus what the Reformation did in Scotland, was to call into being a nation; it awoke amongst the people a national consciousness. Before, they were serfs; suddenly, at the first breath of the Reformation, they became citizens. 'You would be astonished to see how men are changed here,' one writes to Lord Burleigh. 'There is little of that submission to those above them which there used to be. The poor think and act for themselves. They are growing strong, confident, independent.'

This new awakening startlingly revealed itself in the stormy days which followed. The nobles, who had adopted the Protestant faith for political reasons, found no difficulty in changing their faith when the same motives prompted a change of front. When, therefore, they turned to the people to carry their schemes into effect, they were astounded to find that their power was gone. They realised, to their amazement, that they could no longer use them as their tools for revenge and aggrandisement. A new order of things had arisen of which they had never dreamed. The old order of peasantry had silently passed away, leaving scarcely any trace of its existence behind it, and a new peasantry had arisen, whose independence, tenacity of purpose, and sincerity of conviction, were not to be surpassed by any other peasantry in the world. 'I know nothing finer in Scottish history,' says Froude, 'than the way in which the commons of the Lowlands took their places by the side of Knox in the great convulsions which followed. If all others forsook him, they at least would not forsake him while tongue remained to speak and hand remained to strike.'

We are here, then, at the resurrection of a nation. In no other country was the influence of the Reformation so immediate. In Scotland it seemed like a call to arms to men lying half asleep, yet expectant and eager for the call. When it came, they leaped into life.

The second characteristic was the birth of a living national Church.

Scenes of violent spiritual emotion, outbursts of intense joy, exhibitions of uncontrolled anguish for past transgression are not the predominant characteristics of the wave of spiritual revival which passed over Scotland through the middle of the sixteenth century; but he would sadly err who, from the absence of report of these things, would deny the depth of the movement. In no place in the world, perhaps, was the effect more deep, in none more lasting. The deplorable condition of the Church in Scotland before the Reformation we have seen, but the difference discernible amongst the Scottish peasantry, as compared with the peasantry of other nations, is, that while they were not less ignorant of spiritual things, they were much less superstitious regarding the Church, and much more contemptuous of the priesthood. In the 'Complaynt of Scotland' the peasant complains that the priest and the noble 'live by me, and I die by them.'

> 'Our parson here, he takes no other pyne (pain),
> But to receive his teind and spend it syne,
> Though they should want preaching seventeen year,
> Our parson will not want one sheaf of bear (barley).'

The threats of the Church fell on indifferent ears, and became a subject of laughter and mockery. Suddenly all this is changed. Religion becomes not only a factor, but the dominant factor of the nation's life. Already, in 1551, John ab Ulmis, a foreign divine visiting the Scottish Border, is struck with the religious character of the people. 'There appears to be great firmness and no little religion among the people of Scotland,' he says, 'but the chiefs of the nation resist and oppose truth in every possible way.' The movement seems to have spread at first largely of itself; no one could say of it, 'Lo here!' or 'Lo there!'—silently and unseen it did its work of regenerating and blessing. Even Knox, with all his intensity of character, is amazed when, returning from Geneva, he comes into contact with the deep spiritual life which has sprung up during his absence. 'If I had not seen it,' he says, 'with my own eyes, in my own country, I could not have believed it. . . . The fervency here doth far exceed all others I have seen. . . . Depart I cannot until such time as

God quench their thirst a little. . . . Their fervency doth so ravish me, that I cannot but accuse and condemn my slothful coldness. God grant them their heart's desire.' 'Night and day,' again he says, he found them, 'sobbing and groaning for the bread of life.' Teachers they had practically none, but meeting together in 'assemblies' they read the Scriptures, made confession of their sins, and united in earnest prayer. In the homes not only of the humble, but in the castles of the highest in the land these 'assemblies' were held, and over the lowlands of Scotland the breath of the Spirit of God seemed to pass, awakening a nation to newness of life. When Knox returned from Geneva, and traversed the lowlands, he found everywhere the fuel gathered, needing only a spark to set it ablaze.

The effect of the Reformation upon Scotland was thus to create a Church in which the poorest was made to recognise his responsibility as a member to maintain its purity, to promote its interests, and to share in its government; while the weekly expounding of Scripture became a great educational asset in the national life, giving to a people, naturally shrewd and intelligent, those intellectual and theological interests which they have never since lost.

But it did more than this. It brought religion to bear upon the common life; it made the awful verities of the Christian faith the supreme facts of existence. Its 'evangel,' as Knox loved to call it, was wholly Calvinistic—the awfulness of sin; the recoil of infinite holiness from the sinner; the 'comfort' of the elect; the doom of the reprobate; the sole efficacy of Christ's atoning sacrifice—these were the doctrines vehemently declared, and passionately accepted, which entered into the very fibre of the nation's life. Stern, illiberal, intolerant, though its theology was, it at least turned out strong men, men who, amid their daily toil, kept before them the awful fact that the Judge of all the earth did right, that His eyes were constantly upon them, and that at His stern Judgment-seat they all alike must stand and give their account. 'So far,' says Lecky, 'as one can look into that commonplace round of things which historians never tell us about, there has rarely been seen in this world a set of people who have thought more about right and wrong, and the judgment about them of the Upper Powers.'

A still more intimate picture of the religious life as it concerns the peasantry of Scotland is found in Burns's immortal poem 'The Cotter's Saturday Night.' Here, as nowhere else, we are made to realise how religion became bound up with the common life of the people, as we see this humble family kneel together in worship. This practice, which was begun at the instance of Knox, became one of the most beautiful characteristics of Scottish piety. 'Within their own homes,' he says, 'they were bishops and kings; and their wives, children, and families were their bishopric and charge.' So in his poem Burns introduces us to the humble cottage of the Cotter, to its simple joys and homefulness. Then, at the hour of rest, the father becomes the priest.

'The cheerfu' supper done, wi' serious face,
They, round the ingle, form a circle wide;
The sire turns o'er, wi' patriarchal grace,
The big ha'-Bible, ance his father's pride.
His bonnet reverently is laid aside,
His lyart haffets wearing thin and bare;
Those strains that once did sweet in Zion glide,
He wales a portion with judicious care,
And "Let us worship God!" he says, with solemn air.

. . . . . . .

Then kneeling down to Heaven's Eternal King,
The saint, the father, and the husband prays.

. . . . . . .

From scenes like these, old Scotia's grandeur springs,
That makes her lov'd at home, rever'd abroad:
Princes and lords are but the breath of kings,
"An honest man 's the noblest work of God."'

The third characteristic of the movement in Scotland was its awakening in the people the sense of individual freedom, and also the value it attached to education.

The first of these characteristics the awakening in Scotland shared with the awakening which took place elsewhere; but in Scotland it found a race of men, who, though long depressed by their masters, were by instinct freedom-loving, and by nature independent. The reform movement broke the stupor which so long had lain upon men's minds and energies, and the call to freedom, to liberty of conscience, to the rights of private judgment in the realm of religion, awoke the slumbering energies of the race, and created a new era of civil and religious liberty. It cannot be said, however, that these great benefits were gained without corresponding loss. Freedom is ever in danger of running into licence, and the effect of the Reformation was to rend western Christianity in half, and further to break up one of the halves into numberless and warring sects. Yet even this, no doubt, is better than slumbering uniformity; and though the Reformers very imperfectly learned the lesson of tolerance, it may still be admitted that the new-found sense of freedom was a gain of the most momentous character, and that, while its first effects produced outstanding evils, its ultimate effects were for the good of humanity and for the progress of the race.

This love of freedom which the Reformers awoke in the people's heart the Scottish Church has preserved.

No one will readily quote Buckle as an historian prejudiced in favour of the clergy—especially of the Scottish clergy—but even Buckle is roused to enthusiasm as he retails the struggles and sacrifices made by the Scottish clergy in the age succeeding Knox. 'Much,' he says, 'they did which excites our strongest aversion. But one thing they achieved which should make us honour their memory and repute them benefactors of mankind. At a most hazardous moment they kept alive the spirit of national liberty. What the nobles and the crown put in peril, that did the clergy save. By their care the dying spark was kindled into a blaze. When the light grew dim and flickered on the altar, their hands trimmed the lamp and fed the sacred flame. This is their real glory, and for this they may well repose. They were the guardians of Scottish freedom, and they stood to their post. Where danger was, they were foremost. By their sermons, by their conduct, both public and private, by the proceedings of their assemblies . . . they stirred up the minds of men, woke them from their lethargy, formed them to habits of discussion, and excited that inquisitive and democratic spirit which is the only effectual guarantee the people can ever possess against the tyranny of those who are set over them. This was the work of the Scottish clergy, and all hail to them that did it.'

This great quality, it may be admitted, the Church in Scotland has honourably preserved. It has identified itself with the people in a way, and to an extent, which has not been exceeded, if indeed equalled by any other Protestant Church.

The remaining characteristic of the movement, as it affects Scotland, is the value it attached to education. For this, Scotland is indebted to Knox, and nothing could be more enlightened or liberal than the scheme drawn out by him. In the *Book of Discipline* it is laid down that 'No father, of what state or condition ever he be, may use his children at his own fantasy, especially in their youth, but all must be compelled to bring up their children in learning and virtue,' so that they may live their lives in profit of the Church and Commonwealth. In remote parts 'the minister or "Reader" is to take care that the children learn their rudiments, and are instructed in the catechism. In towns, a schoolmaster, able to teach grammar and the Latin tongue, is to be attached to every Church; every large town is to have a college (a secondary school) where the Arts, at least Logic, Rhetoric, and the Tongues may be taught by approved masters, for whom honest stipends must be appointed.' All education is to lead up to, and be a preparation for, the University. There, after a liberal training in the Arts, Tongues, and Philosophy, each student must study the subjects in which he 'intends chiefly to travail for the profit of the Commonwealth.' This zeal for education the Scottish Church has honourably maintained. It insists upon a prolonged training of its own ministers both in arts and theology, who thus, even in the remotest parts, represent the value of education, and see to its efficiency. It is mainly owing to this fact that the village schools have reached so high a standard, and that for centuries the best education has been placed at the door of the humblest lad. The effect of this upon the national life has been incalculable. It has fitted the poorest for the highest walks in life; it has turned out a type of character at once strong and self-reliant; it has changed Scotland from a nation of outlaws to a nation that stands in the vanguard of progress. Whatever other countries lost through the Reformation it will be admitted by the most candid of observers that Scotland lost least, and that the middle of the sixteenth century saw the outburst of a new spiritual and national life, and the founding of a Church in keeping with the genius and character of the people. In Scotland, perhaps, more than in any other country, the spiritual movement of the sixteenth century reaped its finest and most lasting fruits.

### John Knox

Of the character of the great leader of the reform movement in Scotland various estimates have been formed according to the bias of the persons forming them.

First of all it is averred that John Knox was no saint, and certainly were he judged from the mediæval type of saint this would instantly be acknowledged. If saintliness of character belong exclusively to the contemplative life, if to attain to it the individual must hide himself in cloistered retreats, must deny himself the duties of life, and leave to others to fight its conflicts, then John Knox is the last man whose claims to such saintliness could be sustained. But if the religious life is not incompatible with the mingling in life's affairs, with a passionate attachment to one side in a great conflict, with the disposition to strike hard blows in defence of what is considered true, and with the willingness to suffer death itself rather than desist, then there is still hope for John Knox to be considered a deeply religious man, and for him to be recognised as a worthy leader in a great spiritual movement.

His chief offence in the eyes of those who judge him harshly is his intolerance, and intolerance is a peculiarly unattractive trait in character. In One only in history has perfect love of good, and perfect hatred of evil, been combined with perfect charity. Christ was able to say in the hour of conflict, when passions ran high and hearts were estranged: 'He that is not against us is on our part.' But this is a reach of lofty and noble tolerance of which the world possesses but one example, and one alone. Certainly not even his most fervent admirer could deny that Knox was the most uncompromising of opponents, and that his zeal often carried him far beyond the realm of what was true and just in conduct. Intolerance, however, is of two kinds. There is an intolerance which springs from a narrow mind and a cold heart, and the deeds born of it are without justice and without mercy; there is another intolerance, however, which has its source in a genuine hatred of evil, and with a passionate desire to see it overthrown and the good established. It is with this latter form of intolerance that Knox must be charged, and it is not impossible to say something in his defence. For there are times when to be tolerant is to commit the unpardonable sin; when men, if they have anything of God in them, must be intolerant; when the evils around them become such a menace that men lose their sense of proportion in their passionate desire to end them. No doubt, in the strife which follows, much suffers, which in itself is good. In the heat of the conflict those incensed by the battle do not pause to make fine distinctions, or delicately distinguish the varying character of their foes; all who are not on their side they regard as against them. Doubtless, also, this very intolerance of evil is carried too far, and strikes against that which is not evil; this is the inevitable mistake made by those who are passionately in earnest, but it does not condemn this form of intolerance as evil in itself; in itself it is a mark of heroism, it is the divine spirit in a man roused to heroic action. The work which Knox did would never have been done at all had it not been that in his inmost heart, burning at white heat, there was the intolerance of the intolerable. 'It seems to me hard measure,' says Carlyle, 'that this Scottish man, now after three hundred years, should have to plead like a culprit before the world; intrinsically for having been, in such a way as it was then possible to be, the bravest of all Scotsmen! had he been a poor Half-and-half, he could have crouched into the corner, like so many others; Scotland had not been delivered; and Knox had been without blame. He is the one Scotsman to whom of all others, his country and the world, owe a debt. He has to plead that Scotland would forgive him for having been worth to it any million "unblamable" Scotsmen that need no forgiveness! He bared his breast to the battle; had to row in galleys, wander forlorn in exile; in clouds and storms; was censured, shot at through the windows; had a right sore fighting life: if this world were his place of recompense, he had made but a bad venture of it. . . . But we have got above all those details of his battle, and living now in clearness on the fruits of his victory, we, for our own sake, ought to look through the rumours and controversies enveloping the man, into the man himself.'

When we look into the 'man himself' we see a nature of the most noble sincerity. No one has ever doubted this, or could ever doubt it. Right or wrong, Knox believed in the cause he advocated, believed in it in that way in which men willingly suffer death itself rather than relinquish the struggle. Nothing is nobler than this. When a man suffers as Knox did, when he lays his life open to daily peril, seeking for no earthly reward but the victory of the cause which to him is the cause of God, he may make a thousand mistakes, but his name will deserve to be enshrined on the pages of history, and there will be granted to him that noble immortality which attends only the great and the good.

To many the greatness of Knox is dimmed because of his interference in political strife. The political propagandist, it is asserted, took the place of the religious Reformer. A just recognition of the conditions then existing, however, will reveal the fact that the two were so inextricably mixed that it was impossible to be the one without the other. Not that it is meant that he was always wise, that ofttimes he would not have been better to have left public affairs alone when he rushed into them. Knox was not a perfect being. If, to be a religious reformer, it is necessary never to make a mistake, though daily plunged in the most exciting events, then Knox comes ridiculously far short. He was not always wise ; he made many mistakes ; he was intolerant and relentless often when he might wisely have given way ; but if a man is to be tried, not by the standard of perfection, but by the honesty of his intentions, and the unselfishness of his aims, then Knox's mistakes will swiftly be forgotten, while his services to his country and to truth are remembered. 'He had no mind to meddle with politics,' he said, 'further than it had religion mixed with it.' What he demanded from the State was this—'the liberty of our conscience, to serve our Lord God as we shall answer to Him.' In his austere figure, his flashing eye, his stern denunciations, and his solemn threats and warnings, he resembles, as Carlyle says, 'more than any of the moderns, an Old Hebrew Prophet. The same inflexibility, intolerance, rigid narrow-looking adherence to God's truth, stern rebuke in the name of God to all who forsake truth : an Old Hebrew Prophet in the guise of an Edinburgh Minister of the Sixteenth Century. We are to take him for that; not require him to be other.'

Knox was too much a Scotsman easily to lay open his inmost heart, or readily to betray the secrets of the soul, and, indeed, this spiritual reticence is a marked characteristic of the movement, as it is the marked characteristic of the Scottish people. To know Knox, it is necessary not only to sit in old St. Giles and hear the thunder of his voice, or watch him in Council, keen, unflinching, conscious of power, and not without a secret enjoyment of it; but we have to follow him to his home, see him throw off the cares of State, and become the loving husband, the gentle father, or the kindly friend. Much more have we to enter into his closet, when the door is shut, and when, in the silence, he opens his heart to God. Then the real nature of the man is disclosed, as for hours together he wrestles in prayer, agonising for his country, for Christ's cause, for the maintenance of purity in His Church. There he is no longer the stern uncompromising Calvinist, but the child, sobbing and pleading for forgiveness, acknowledging his deep unworthiness, his abject dependence upon God for daily help and guidance. Then the tears trickle down his furrowed cheeks, as the melted snows of spring trickle down the wrinkled face of the mountain, leaving behind a shining pathway which seems tremulous with pity and with love. It is in such moments, when the soul is laid bare before God, when the white rays are thrown into the hidden depths and its inmost secrets are disclosed, that the nature of man can be truly discerned. Knox before his fellows was intolerant, unbending, austere, often coarse even; but before God he was a broken-hearted penitent, seeking through tears and bitter self-reproaches the way to His Father's home, yet knowing full well that there was a place prepared for him, where, entering, he would find rest. 'Hast thou hope ?' they asked him as he lay dying. He was too weak to answer, but, lifting up his hand, he pointed upward, and in this hope he died, as by the strength of it he had lived.

The service which Knox rendered to his country in a time of revolution and of danger it would be difficult to overstate. At a time when all the powerful were grasping for power his voice was raised for righteousness, and that voice nothing earthly could silence. Of the part he had played he is himself nobly conscious. 'What I have been to my country, albeit this ungrateful age will not know, yet the ages to come will be compelled to bear witness to the truth.'

An interesting description of Knox, as he appeared to a young student, is given in the diary of James Melville, and refers to the year before Knox's death, when, for personal safety, he had to take refuge in St. Andrews. 'Of all the benefits I had that year,' he says, 'was the coming of that most notable prophet and apostle of our nation, Mr. John Knox, to St. Andrews. . . . Mr. Knox would sometimes come in and repose him in our college-yard, and call us scholars unto him, and bless us, and exhort us to know God and His work in our country, and stand by the good cause; to use our time well, and learn the good instructions, and follow the good example, of our masters. . . . He was very weak. I saw him every day of his doctrine go hulie and fear, with a furring of matriks about his neck, a staff in the one hand, and good godly Richard Ballantyne, his servant, holding up the other oxter, from the Abbey to the Parish Church, and by the said Richard and another servant lifted up to the pulpit, where he behoved to lean at his first entry; but or he had done with his sermon, he was so active and vigorous that he was like to ding that pulpit in blads and fly out of it.'

But the noblest testimony to his work and worth was given by one well able to estimate both. Standing in the churchyard of St. Giles beside his grave, in the presence of an enormous concourse of people who had followed the body to its last resting-place, the Earl of Moray, then Regent of Scotland, offered this testimony:

> 'Here lyeth a man who in his life never feared the face of man, who hath been often threatened with dagge and dagger, but yet hath ended his days in peace and honour.'

# WESLEY AND THE EVANGELICAL REVIVAL

THE religious awakening under Wesley is one of the most important events in modern religious history. In the influence it exerted, and the dynamic changes which it introduced, it is not outdistanced by any of the great movements already considered. As an epoch in English history it is, says Lecky, 'of greater importance than all the splendid victories on sea or land won by Pitt.' When, on March 9, 1791, John Wesley was carried to his grave by six poor men, as he himself had arranged, he left behind him 'a good library of books, a well-worn clergyman's gown, and a much-abused reputation,' but also an England moved to the very depths, and a Church thrilled through and through with an awakened spiritual life.

Owing to the nearness of the events, the painstaking care with which Wesley kept his journal, and the amazing frankness with which he relates every incident in his long life, we are enabled to test the generalisations and conclusions already reached in relation to such movements, by the accurate information which this affords. Here, on a magnified scale, because of the nearer view, we are enabled to see those laws in operation which call such movements into being, and which enter in to expand or modify them in their subsequent history. A consideration of the conditions of the times will reveal, as in other movements, its necessity in history as a revolt against prevailing corruption, as an expression of the expanding nature of man, of his unconquerable spiritual instincts, of how the changing needs of each new epoch are met and supplied out of inexhaustible stores of divine grace. It will show from the human side that, however far humanity may wander, it cannot rest in the far country; that in the darkest hour home-sickness overtakes it; that with a fresh-begotten hope it arises and says, 'I will go to my Father, and say, "I have sinned!"' From the divine side it will declare Love's instant response to humanity's cry, that by such awakenings God revives His Church, and that by slow and successive movements He is leading all things onwards to their perfection. Such movements, therefore, through their very obedience to law, come as a buttress to faith; they give heart of grace to those who lament the spiritual deadness of their times, and they awaken in the believer a lofty confidence in God, a noble trust in man's destiny, and a radiant optimism as he surveys the future of the world.

## England in the Eighteenth Century

The progress of civilisation, it has already been pointed out, is not characterised by a steady upward march, but by an undulating movement in which times of great progress are followed by times of lassitude and seeming disintegration. Awakened by some fresh ideal, humanity braces itself to heroic effort, snaps every chain which hinders its progress, and reaches upward to greater heights than ever before attained. Then, wearied by its exertions, it falls back, becomes sceptical and listless, until, through some fresh awakening, it is once more aroused to renew the conflict, and to attain to some loftier peak.

In this undulating, though upward movement, the

eighteenth century represents a depression. It is a century of exhaustion, of a listless faith, of low ideals—a miniature dark age in the history of modern civilisation.

The causes of this are not far to seek. England had been passing through a prolonged period of unrest. The separation from Rome, which elsewhere had been attended by a great wave of religious enthusiasm, had in England been effected without such enthusiasm, at the will of its monarch, and from motives far from religious. The reform spirit, therefore, found no popular outlet; with victory wholly assured to neither party, an incessant intrigue was carried on, and the nation kept in a state of constant apprehension.

After the death of Charles I., with the Puritans in power, the national character was forced out of its natural groove by false austerities and by a rigid discipline, while the conflicts of parties within the State in no way declined either in number or in bitterness.

With the return of the Monarchy a new adjustment of ecclesiastical parties took place, but with an increase rather than a diminution of bitterness. Episcopalians, depressed during the Puritan régime, now reasserted their authority, and a series of laws was passed against Nonconformists which embittered public life and which led to the grossest wrongs.

At length, wearied by the incessant strife, and by the bitterness of the controversialists, half indignant, half contemptuous, men turned from the war of creeds, and from orthodox and dogmatic Christianity, to inquire whether there might not be found some doctrine, held in common by all, which would act as a new basis for faith.

Meanwhile men's thoughts had already been turning

with interest to the natural world, and to that new realm opened up for human investigation through the discoveries of Newton. With the rise of scientific methods, and the increased importance given to the reason through the growth of the scientific spirit, a sceptical spirit grew up inimical to the prevailing belief.

Out of these two forces of revolt Deism was evolved, which was an attempt to rationalise Christianity, to state it in a formula which all could accept, and by stripping it of what was regarded as its superstitious element, to make the natural rather than the supernatural the basis of belief. The authority which the Catholic found in the Church, and the Protestant in the Bible, was to be discarded in favour of the new authority of the Reason.

The effect of Deism upon the life of England was of the most desolating character. The tolerance which it engendered was not that of conviction, but of indifference; the liberty it claimed was not to do right, but to do wrong; its boasted freedom degenerated into licence; while religion, emptied of its spiritual contents, became a mere code of ethics, utterly incapable of stemming the tide of ungodliness or of inspiring men to live a holy life.

Soon the blighting influence of scepticism began to chill the national life, with a consequent depression of its vigour, and an increase of wretchedness and of crime. Gibbon, who entered Magdalene College in 1752, describes in his *Autobiography* the low spiritual condition of the universities of this time; their indolence and immorality, as well as the general indifference to religion. Even worse was the state of society. 'In the higher circles of Society,' said Montesquieu, on his visit to England, 'every one laughs if one talks of religion.' Of the effect of this unbelief upon the moral life, the following quotation from Green's *Short History of the English People* will suffice: 'Of the prominent statesmen of the time the greater part were unbelievers in any form of Christianity, and were distinguished for the grossness and immorality of their lives. Drunkenness and foul talk were thought no discredit to Walpole. A later Prime Minister, the Duke of Grafton, was in the habit of appearing with his mistress at the play. Purity and fidelity to the marriage vow were sneered out of fashion, and Lord Chesterfield in his letters to his son, instructs him in the art of seduction as part of a polite education.'

Nor was the Church unaffected by the evil spirit of the times. Hardly ever was the spiritual life within the Church at a lower ebb. The clergy, who were mostly Jacobites, were estranged from their Bishops, who were mostly Whigs. All 'enthusiasm' in the pulpit was condemned; sermons were either harmless moral essays, or were shallow apologies for the Christian faith. It was the time when, as Johnson cynically observes, 'the Apostles were tried regularly once a week on charge of committing forgery.' Gradually this chilling frost spread until the spiritual life became numbed and dead. 'The English clergy of the day,' says one observer, 'are the most remiss of their labours in private, and the least severe in their lives.' The system of 'pluralities' still further reduced their status. Many of the clergy, while enjoying their revenues, never resided or even saw their benefices. Green quotes a Welsh bishop who boasted that he had never seen his diocese but once, and that he habitually resided at the lakes of Westmorland. The consequence was a lowering of the social status of the clergy, and with this a growing contempt for their office. Men of low standing and of inadequate scholarship were admitted, who performed their functions with coarse indifference and with a main eye upon the fee. 'Those who have read some few books,' says Bishop Burnet, 'yet never seem to have read the Scriptures.' Church services declined, Church buildings fell into disrepair, and worship became more and more neglected. 'It has somehow come to be taken for granted,' says Bishop Butler, in the Introduction to his *Analogy*, 'that Christianity is not so much a subject for inquiry, but that it is now at length discovered to be fictitious. . . . Men treat it as if in the present age this were an agreed point amongst all people of discernment, and nothing remained but to set it up as a principal subject of mirth and ridicule.' Nothing, perhaps, shows the prevailing tone better than Swift's *Project for the Advancement of Religion*, where, while admitting that hardly one in a hundred of the upper classes appears to act by any principle of religion, he lays down as the best means to renew it, not a new breath of life from God, but the making church attendance 'the necessary step to favour and preferment.' To revive religion it was necessary, he declared, to make it 'the turn and fashion of the age.'

Meanwhile, the lowering of the moral tone of the nation's life produced, as it always does, a baneful effect upon the lives of the poor, the weak, and the defenceless. With the weakening of the religious life of a nation or an individual, there is a rapid growth of indifference toward those whose weakness or defencelessness make them an easy prey to the cruel, or objects of pity to the just. Consequently at this time there was an outbreak of cruel legislation, of indifference to life, and of callousness towards weakness and suffering. 'At the other end of the social scale,' says Green, 'lay the masses of the poor. They were ignorant and brutal to a degree which it is hard to conceive; for the increase of population which followed the growth of towns, and the development of commerce, had been met by no effort for their religious or educational improvement. Not a new parish had been created. Schools there were none, save the Grammar Schools of Edward and Elizabeth, and some newly established circulating schools in Wales for religious education. The rural peasantry, who were fast being reduced to pauperism by the abuse of the poor laws, were left without much moral or religious training of any sort.' 'We saw but one Bible in the Parish of Cheddar,' says Hannah More at a far later period, 'and that was used to prop a flower-pot.'

Within the towns things were worse. There was no effective police, and in great outbreaks the mob of London or Birmingham burnt houses, flung open prisons, and sacked and pillaged at their will. The criminal classes gathered boldness and numbers in the face of ruthless laws which only testified to the terror of society, laws which made it a capital crime to cut down a cherry-tree, and which strung up twenty young thieves of a morning in front of Newgate; while the introduction of gin gave a new impetus to drunkenness. In the streets of London at one time gin-shops invited every passer-by to 'get drunk for a penny, or dead drunk for twopence.'

The moral ruin of the times can be seen in the politics of Walpole, in the writings of Smollett, but most of all in the art of Hogarth, who set himself faithfully to depict a society around him which, as it has been said, seemed as though 'all the menageries of the passions had been unchained.'

Evil as were the times, religion was not extinct in the nation's life. Carlyle's cynical phrase regarding the eighteenth century, 'Soul extinct; stomach well alive,' was happily only partly true. The Puritan spirit, though hidden, was not dead; there were godly and devout men both in the established and nonconforming Churches, men who deplored the prevailing scepticism, and who faithfully proclaimed the message of salvation. Amongst these were Doddridge, Watts, Wilson, the author of the *Sacra Privata,* but most of all, William Law. This great writer, who more than any other prepared the way for better things, was a tutor for a while in the house of Gibbon's father, and had the future historian as his pupil. Of him even Gibbon, 'who snapped a creed with a solemn sneer,' had to acknowledge that 'he believed all he professed, and practised all he enjoined'; and also that 'if he finds a spark of piety in his reader's mind, he will soon kindle it into a flame.'

Slowly the national conscience, so long dormant, began to wake up. Men began to sicken at the prevailing ungodliness; a sense of nausea and unrest began to show itself, along with a craving for better things. In the night of sin, amid its passions and debaucheries, men had forgotten God; but when the night was past, and the raw morning began to break, they awoke to a sense of their misery, to a shame of their evil courses, to a shuddering consciousness of how far they had been led astray, and to a bitter self-loathing and disgust. Yet more was needed. To bring fresh hope and joy to an age worn out and surfeited with sin, a revival was needed. Men longed for a breath of God to blow upon the land, to sweep away its miasmas and heavy poisoned atmosphere, and bring back to it the joyous sunshine of God's presence and the gladness and freshness of a living faith. Once more human nature was declaring that the way of transgressors is hard, that sin has no final empire over the human heart, that for the soul of man there is no rest except it rest in God. Gradually the longing for better things grew in the hearts of the best men and women of the age, and the cry once more went up to God full of passionate entreaty, the cry for forgiveness, for renewal, for a fresh awakening to the blessedness of the spiritual life. The cry was heard. The hour and the man were come. Into the life of England of that century, to dominate it and inspire it, there enters the prim, alert figure of John Wesley, Anglican, Methodist, Revivalist, and Man of God.

### Early Days

Wesley came of good stock. His great-grandfather on his father's side was one of the clergymen turned out of his rectory by the Act of Uniformity in 1662; his grandfather suffered under the infamous Five Mile Act, and was frequently imprisoned. Notwithstanding this, Wesley's father entered the Church, conforming to its tenets, and after a struggling career was settled at Epworth. Samuel Wesley stands out as a distinct character in his way. Short, sharp-featured, irascible in temper, unpractical in affairs, full of mettle and determination, he forces a half-humorous, half-exasperated admiration. His stipend was small—for long only fifty pounds per annum; he was constantly in debt, constantly at variance with his parishioners—who, on one occasion, tried to burn his house down—and with his neighbouring clergy, and left his more practical wife to tend to his affairs, and to struggle to make ends meet.

Wesley's mother, the daughter of a dissenting clergyman, was a remarkable woman, and her influence upon her son was maintained to the last day of her life. Equal to her husband in scholarship, she was far superior to him in sagacity and in natural shrewdness of mind. Herself the twenty-fifth child of her parents, she was married at nineteen, and bore her husband nineteen children in twenty-one years, of whom John Wesley was the fifteenth. Bringing up her family upon a wage which a modern mechanic would despise, she not only with infinite labour provided for their material wants, but found time to give each some religious instruction during the day, and actually set rigidly apart the middle hour of each day for 'devotion and quiet.' The struggle for existence in Epworth Parsonage was too keen, however, the fight for the daily necessities of life too constant, to make it a sanctuary of domestic peace and comfort. Mrs. Wesley was a Spartan mother in the environment of the eighteenth century; she was deeply devout, with a piety which was full of heroic self-sacrifice, but which lacked that serenity which is devotion's finest flower. Nevertheless she was a great woman in her way, one of the great mothers of great men.

John Wesley was born on June 17, 1703. Amongst the members of that family, so strangely characterised by misfortune and by genius, he was distinguished in early days by his 'docility,' and by a gravity beyond his years. An incident which occurred when he was six years old deeply impressed him, and left an indelible impression upon his memory. This was the burning of the rectory in the dead of night, in which he almost perished, and from which he was only rescued as the roof collapsed. The weird scene, the swift devouring flames, the awful terror, and the seeming miraculous escape when escape seemed impossible, took possession of his imagination and coloured his whole religious life. His escape was to him the direct act of God. Forty years after, on the anniversary of the event, he described to a huge congregation gathered at a watch-night service the thrilling incidents of that night.

Ever after, his favourite metaphor, appearing even in his epitaph written by his own hand, was, 'a brand plucked from the burning.'

In these early days his intense belief in the reality of apparitions and of witchcraft, as well as his love of the marvellous, seem to have been developed by the weird knockings of 'Old Jeffery,' the famous ghost of the Epworth household. These strange noises have never been explained, but they did much to fill the youthful Wesley with that sense of the supernatural and that vein of superstition never absent from his character.

At the age of ten Wesley was admitted to Charterhouse School through the influence of the Duke of Buckingham. Up to this time he had lived a singular life. 'I believe,' he says, 'till I was about ten years old I had not sinned away that washing of the Holy Ghost which was given me in baptism.' This is the High Churchman speaking, but another evidence that he was grave beyond his years comes from the fact that when he was only eight years of age his father deemed him fit to partake of the Communion.

Little is known of his Charterhouse days. He adopted his father's advice to 'run three times round the garden each morning before breakfast,' and that with the scantiness of his fare seems to have laid the foundations of his wonderful physical health. 'From ten to fourteen,' he says, 'I had little but bread to eat, and not great plenty at that. I believe this was so far from hurting me, that it laid the foundation of lasting health.' His entrance into the larger world, however, dimmed the purity of his early vision. He refers to himself as having at this time lived without any real sense of religion, though still maintaining the forms of it.

In 1720 he gained a scholarship at Christ Church,

Oxford, of the value of forty pounds per annum, an amount almost sufficient to keep him in those days. Something of the condition of Oxford at this time has already been described. As an educational institution it was at a low ebb, the insincerity of the age had attacked even its tutors and professors. Gibbon says of his own tutor that 'he remembered that he had a salary to receive, and forgot that he had a duty to perform.' It was the age of slackness, when 'enthusiasm' was the unpardonable sin, when idleness and its attendant vices were dominant to a degree difficult now to realise. That Wesley escaped, pursuing his studies successfully in an atmosphere so tainted, is an indication of his strength of character, and that aloofness which marked his nature at this time. In 1724 he took his bachelor's degree, and the year after, at the age of twenty-two, he was appointed to a fellowship.

Before him now there arose for decision the all-important choice of a life career. 'When I was about twenty-two,' he says, 'my father pressed me to enter into Holy Orders. I began to alter the whole form of my conversation, and to set in earnest to enter upon a new life.' Intellectual difficulties naturally confronted him, as well as questions of personal fitness. He began to search for help in devotional literature, and found it in the writings of Thomas à Kempis, of Jeremy Taylor, but most of all in the writings of William Law. Looking back long afterwards to this stage of his career, and especially to the grounds upon which he ventured to assure himself of his fitness for the office he took up, Wesley shakes his head, and condemns the ground of his assurance. Nevertheless, no one can follow his meditations at this time without seeing the gradual deepening of his spiritual nature. His conscience awoke, and his whole being, responding to the deep call of religion, gave promise of a noble manhood and of a nature exalted and full of spiritual aspirations.

## Wesley as High Churchman

When Wesley decided to take orders, after having graduated at Oxford in 1724, and became his father's curate, he conceived religion as 'a tireless industry in pious acts, an intense zeal in the charge of external duties, a form of piety to be nourished by an incessant use of all external means of grace.' For two years he remained at Epworth, and although he was endowed with remarkable gifts, with scholarship, with fluency, with marvellous power of commanding and of moving men, he failed. 'I preached much,' he says, 'but saw no fruit of my labour.' The reason he himself supplies: 'Indeed it could not be that I should, for I neither laid the foundation of repentance, nor of believing the gospel, taking it for granted that all to whom I preached were believers, and that many of them needed no repentance.'

At the end of two years Wesley was recalled to Oxford, where his brother Charles was then in residence. Charles Wesley, hardly less famous than his brother, appears as a character of singular sweetness and attractiveness. He became the poet of the movement, and his hymns have enriched the world. In Oxford, also, when John Wesley returned to it, there was a youth named Whitfield, the son of an innkeeper at Gloucester, destined to share with Wesley himself the leadership of the new movement, and to be known as well to fame as perhaps the greatest preacher England has ever possessed. These two, along with several other devout young men, had formed a society for the culture of the spiritual life. Their piety was of an ascetic type; they laid great stress upon keeping fasts, upon frequent communions, upon self-denial, and upon visiting the poor, the sick, and the criminals.

When John Wesley returned to Oxford, he not only joined this new society, he became its head and leading spirit. Something of that intense, dominating personality, which afterwards revealed him to be a born leader of men, was now appearing. He added to the austerities already practised others of a more rigid character. The little society met every evening, they severely examined themselves as to the day's conduct, they tried their consciences by a set of rules drawn up by John Wesley of a character which would have almost put Loyola out of countenance, and in addition to all this they were High Churchmen of the extremest type. Wesley thought of founding a society on a stricter basis; he laid the greatest stress upon the observances of fasts and festivals of the ancient Church,—he could not, as a matter of conscience, partake of the wine at Communion unless it were mixed with water. He began to rise at four o'clock in the morning, to live on twenty-eight pounds per annum, giving the rest away in charity, and carried his austerities so far that he broke down in health.

Meanwhile the existence of the society became known to the members of the University, and immediately became the subject of ridicule and contempt. Various sobriquets were coined by the wits in residence to express their amusement. The society was called 'The Holy Club,' its members 'Biblemoths,' till at length one name stuck, and became finally adopted. Seeing the ordered character of their lives, some unknown coined the name of 'Methodists.' So the name first appears; little did its inventor realise how much that name was to mean in the after-life of England.

Wesley's father was now old, and was fast breaking up. He was eager to see his son John installed in the rectory at Epworth before he died, but Wesley himself was disinclined, and he passed away without seeing his desire fulfilled. It appears that after his death formal application was made on John Wesley's behalf, but the application proved unsuccessful, and the living was presented to one who never visited it. The old father, who had become strangely softened in his latter days, passed away on April 25, 1735. In a letter to the eldest brother, Samuel, also a clergyman, but who never entered the movement, Charles describes his father's last days. 'He often,' he says, 'laid his hand upon my head and said, "Be steady. The Christian faith will surely revive in this kingdom. You shall see it, though I shall not."' To John he said: 'The inward witness, son; the inward witness! That is the strongest proof of Christianity.' Of this 'inward witness' Wesley, as he himself declares, knew nothing. But he was to know, and the knowledge was to sweep like fire into his heart, and through him into the hearts of tens of thousands of others.

At this time a certain General Oglethorpe, the founder of a colony in Georgia, was in London, in quest of a clergyman who would conduct services amongst the new settlers and the Indians. The post was offered to Wesley, and after some hesitation he accepted. Oxford was beginning to lose its hold on him, austerities and self-mortifications had been tried and found wanting, his spiritual nature was still unsatisfied. On October 13, 1735, he and his brother Charles set out for their new destination, and it is curious to analyse his motives as explained by himself. 'My chief motive,' he says, 'is the hope of saving my own soul. I hope to learn the true sense of the Gospel of Christ by preaching it to the heathen. . . . I cannot hope to attain the same degree of holiness here which I may there.' This is a strange document, and shows how utterly the system of penance had failed to bring peace to either mind or heart. Wesley spent nearly two and a half years in Georgia in the double experiment of finding a complete satisfaction for his own spiritual nature and in striving to reveal it to others. The result in both cases was a complete failure. In his work in Georgia his asceticism, his rigid High Churchism, and his continual magnifying of trifles into great errors of faith and practice made him so unpopular that he had to quit the country, leaving a record of failure and exasperation behind him. As to his spiritual state at this time let his *Journal* declare. 'I went to America to convert the Indians; but, O! who shall convert me? . . . It is now two years and almost four months since I left my native country in order to teach the Georgian Indians the nature of Christianity; but what have I learned myself in the meantime? Why, what I the least of all expected; that I, who went to America to convert others, was never myself converted to God.' These words are overstrained, and long afterwards Wesley himself added the criticism, 'I am not sure of this,' when his *Journal* was reprinted; but the paragraph shows the mental and spiritual unrest which he was in. All his mortifications, his rigid abstinences, his severe persistence in the treadmill of Church observance, had broken down. He was wretched in heart, and utterly dissatisfied. For ten years he had fought against sin, he had striven to obey the commandments, he had struggled to keep the minutiae of the law, but peace he had not gained, or assurance of salvation. Mysticism had failed, Ritualism had failed, the Law, though he strove never so hard to keep it, had failed. He was a

Christian, but without the assurance of one, without its rich joys and abiding peace. This was the darkest hour of Wesley's life. But the darkest hour precedes the dawn, and for Wesley, too, the dawn was at hand.

### Wesley's 'Conversion'

On the ship which carried Charles and himself to Georgia, Wesley came into contact with a little band of Moravian missionaries. Their simple faith, the undismayed calm with which they conducted themselves during a violent storm, awoke first curiosity, and as he grew to know them better, a deepened admiration.

On his return to London from America he sought out the Moravian settlement, and on Tuesday, February 7, 'a day long to be remembered,' he met Peter Böhler, a man who had come under the influence of Count Zinzendorf, and who was then giving addresses in London to small companies of men and women. The influence of Böhler upon Wesley was immediate and profound. Writing to Count Zinzendorf, Böhler describes John Wesley as 'a man of good principles, who knew he did not properly believe in the Saviour, and was willing to be taught.' Days of intense strain followed, in which Wesley sought to test this new interpretation of belief. 'Böhler amazed me more and more,' he says, 'in the account he gave of fruits of faith, the love, holiness, and happiness that he affirmed to attend it.' On March 4 he tells us that he spent a day with Peter Böhler, 'by whom, in the hands of the great God, I was clearly convinced of unbelief; of the want of that faith whereby alone we are saved.'

To Charles Wesley, though not yet to John, the hour of deliverance had come, and that in the most striking manner. Lying ill in bed, he was attended by a woman of a deeply devout character, and to her there came an intense conviction that she ought to speak some words of comfort to him. Long she struggled against it, but at length, overpowered, she entered his room, and with an intense voice said: 'In the name of Jesus of Nazareth, arise! Thou shalt be healed of all thy infirmities.' Wesley was, according to his own confession, composing himself to sleep. Suddenly the words, breaking in upon the silence around him, fell upon his ears with startling effect. 'They struck me to the heart,' he says. 'I never heard words uttered with like solemnity. I sighed within myself, and said, "Oh that Christ would thus speak to me!"' Suddenly the light dawned, his whole being seemed to be caught in a transport. From the lips of a woman without education, and driven by a mysterious and uncontrollable impulse, the message of deliverance came.

Not less dramatically came the light to John Wesley. Convinced of his need, he was for days, he tells us, seeking for peace and assurance, following the path along which Böhler was directing him, by (1) 'absolutely renouncing all dependence, in whole or in part, upon my own works of righteousness, on which I had really grounded my hope of salvation, though I knew it not, from my youth up; (2) by adding to the constant use of all the other means of grace continued prayer for this very thing:—justifying, saving faith; a fuller reliance on the blood of Christ shed for me; a trust in Him as my sole justification, sanctification, and redemption.'

Notwithstanding all his zeal and earnestness, however, there still lay upon his soul 'a strange indifference, dullness, and coldness, and a constant sense of failure.' At length there dawned for him that great and ever memorable day, the 24th of May 1738. It was full to him, from earliest morning, of whisperings and prophecies. When he opened his Bible at five o'clock in the morning his eyes were caught by these great words: 'There are given unto us exceeding great and precious promises that we should be partakers of the divine nature.' A little later, as he left the room, he opened his Bible again, and there came a mighty rush of hope to his heart as he read this sentence:—'Thou art not far from the Kingdom of God.' Throughout the day he was kept in a constant state of agitation; everything around him seemed to be vocal, heralding some coming event. What followed had best be read in his own words. 'In the evening,' he says, 'I went very unwillingly to the Society in Aldersgate Street, where one was reading Luther's preface to the Epistle to the Romans. About a quarter before nine, while he was describing the change wrought by God in the heart through faith in Christ, I felt my heart strangely warmed. I felt I did trust Christ, Christ alone, for salvation; and an assurance was given me that He had taken away my sins, even mine, and saved me from the law of sin and death. I began to pray with all my might for those who had in a more especial manner despitefully used me and persecuted me. I then testified openly to all there what I now first felt in my heart.'

So at last, after long struggle, the light had come.

Even this hour, however, was not without its doubts. 'It was not long,' he goes on to say, 'before the enemy suggested, "This cannot be faith; for where is thy joy?" Then was I taught that peace and victory over sin are essential to faith in the Captain of our salvation; but that, as to the transports of joy that usually attend the beginning of it, especially in those who have mourned deeply, God sometimes giveth, sometimes withholdeth, them according to the counsels of His own will.'

The first act of Wesley and his friends was to hasten to carry the glad tidings to Charles, then ill in bed. 'Towards ten,' says Charles, 'my brother was brought in triumph by a troop of our friends, and declared, "I believe." We sang a hymn with great joy, and parted in prayer.' The hymn, it is supposed, was that composed by Charles in the hour of his conversion; the first hymn, therefore, of the new movement, full of the joy of salvation:

> 'Where shall my wondering soul begin?
> How shall I all to Heaven aspire?
> A slave redeemed from death and sin,
> A brand plucked from eternal fire.
> How shall I equal triumphs raise,
> Or sing my great Deliverer's praise?'

## Beginning of the Movement

All the elements of awakening seem now to have appeared. The ebb-tide of unbelief had reached its furthest limits, a weariness and satiety had fallen upon the nation as a whole; a strong craving for a deeper spiritual life was appearing in the best sections of society; there was a revolt in literature already appearing, and a deepening seriousness especially in those books which were of a religious character. Masses of the people, long neglected by the Church, were awakening also to a sense of their rights and of their needs. Bound down by cruel and intolerable laws, left uneducated and uncared for, they presented a growing menace to the state, unless their wrongs were righted, and unless the hand that awoke and led them were one that sought their highest good. From many different directions, thus, the streams were uniting at one definite point, the gathered-up waters were fretting and chafing behind their barricades, groping for some way of escape. What the times demanded was a messenger of God, a man with burning spiritual convictions, who could interpret to his own day and generation its own spiritual needs, and lead the thirsty back to the eternal source of living waters. And with the hour, the Man had arrived. Through long and desolate paths he had wended his way, through dark days of depression and misconception he had at last passed into the blazing light. Through the thunders as of old the Voice had cried, 'Whom shall I send, and who will go for Me ?' And in answer came the voice of one man, weak, but dauntless, and prepared for high endeavour, 'Here am I; send me!' What follows is the history of one of the most remarkable movements in the spiritual history of England.

The Wesleys, having now a gospel to preach, made no delay in preaching it. The effect was instantaneous and amazing. Vast spiritual energies seemed to be suddenly let loose; the congregations, which sat before uninterested and unmoved, were now shaken into surprised and often indignant attention. Two results followed. A great interest, especially manifested amongst the common people, began to awaken; the churches were crowded whenever Wesley, his brother, or Whitfield—for he also had come into 'the light'—preached. But with this awakening interest amongst the people there accompanied it an awakened distrust amongst the clergy. The burning earnestness of these men was in part an appeal, in part an accusation. The great majority rejected the appeal and resented the accusation. This was that 'enthusiasm' which they so carefully protected themselves against, and with which they were again being threatened. The Bishop of London found the whole thing 'irregular'—that terror of the conventional ecclesiastic; the clergy were shocked by the eager crowds; one by one the churches closed their doors against them. Wesley's *Journal* at this time is full of such entries: 'Preached in the evening to such congregations as I never saw before at St. Clement's, in the Strand; as this is the first time of my preaching here, I suppose it will be the last.'

Meanwhile small societies of earnest men were being gathered together, the fire was passing from heart to heart, and with the increase the glow was deepened. The early days were not without those manifestations which frequently attend the beginnings of such movements, and which, indeed, attended the beginnings of Christianity itself. 'On the first night of 1739,' says Wesley, 'Mr. Hall, Kinchin, Ingham, Whitfield, and my brother Charles were present at our love-feast, with about sixty of our brethren. About three in the morning, as we were continuing instant in prayer, the power of God came mightily amongst us, insomuch that many cried out with exceeding joy, and many fell on the ground. As soon as we were recovered a little from that awe and amazement at the presence of His majesty, we broke out with one voice, "We praise Thee, O God; we acknowledge Thee to be the Lord!"'

Across the valley of dry bones the first breath of reviving life was now beginning to blow, the stillness of death was being broken, the shaking had begun which was to bring these dried bones together, and make them stand up, clothed with life, an exceeding great multitude.

## Open-Air Preaching

In the opening stages of the great revival it was Whitfield, more than John Wesley, who was the daring innovator and dominating personality. Preaching in

Bermondsey Church, the crowd was so great that it overflowed into the churchyard, which also became packed. The spectacle of this crowd, he declared, 'put me first upon thinking of preaching without-doors.' He mentioned his idea to some friends, who thought him mad. Such an 'irregularity' was not to be dreamed of; it shocked even advanced minds; it was a lowering of the status of the clergy to the point of insult and degradation.

With Whitfield such considerations had singularly little weight. His nature was too intense, his spiritual passion too deep, to be deflected by questions of propriety when he heard the Voice within. 'Oh that I could fly from pole to pole,' he cried, 'preaching the everlasting Gospel!' Finding himself in Bristol, in February (1739), with the doors of the churches all closed against him, what was he to do? Tens of thousands around him in that city were as ignorant of the Gospel as the Indians of Georgia whom Wesley, and afterwards Whitfield himself, went out to convert. So with gown and bands, on a rising knoll outside the city, he took his stand, and there, to a congregation of two hundred strong, the listeners too much amazed readily to understand even what the thing meant, Whitfield preached his first open-air sermon, and inaugurated a movement which was to have the most portentous results in the immediate future. For the start once made was followed by scenes which no one even remotely imagined possible. The congregations, which began at two hundred, swelled day by day, until vast multitudes assembled numbering close upon twenty thousand people. The impressiveness of these gatherings Whitfield himself has described: 'The open firmament above me, the prospect of the adjacent fields, with the sight of thousands and thousands, some in coaches, some on horseback, and some in the trees, and at times all affected and drenched in tears together, to which sometimes was added the solemnity of the approaching evening, was almost too much for and quite overcame me. Blessed are the eyes which see the things we see.'

Six weeks later John Wesley stood at Whitfield's side. The call which he had received to come and help him in the work Wesley had received almost as a call to suffer execution. Wesley was a High Churchman, he had been born and brought up in an atmosphere which would have regarded such action with the utmost detestation; he himself had all a High Churchman's punctiliousness and love of order; it was bred in the bone, and belonged to the very fibre of his nature, and it was all present in him as he took his stand at Whitfield's side on the grassy knoll, with the free air blowing around them, and with the heavens for a panoply. The event constitutes one of the great historic scenes of the eighteenth century. It was the momentous prelude to a great spiritual drama. For there, on that slight elevation, stood two of the century's greatest and most gifted men. On the one hand Whitfield, tall, graceful in figure and fair in face, the matchless orator, the impassioned preacher, the noble and gentle friend. And at his side John Wesley, small, active, with prim figure, piercing restless eyes, the scholar's brow; torn by conflicting emotions as he looks at the crowd below, now drawn, and now violently repelled. At last in the silence there rings out Whitfield's marvellous voice, carrying every gentlest inflection to the outskirts of the great crowd, who stand spell-bound, now inspired by terror as he pictures with startling images the awfulness of sin, now shaken by sobs as he declares the infinite sufferings and mercy of Christ, until, with loud cries, they sink upon their knees, carried away by a torrent of emotion.

With amazed eyes and disturbed heart Wesley looked down upon this strange scene. Let him tell the issue in his own words: 'I submitted to be more vile and, standing on a little grassy mound, preached on the following day to a great crowd from the words, "The Spirit of the Lord is upon me, because He hath anointed me to preach the Gospel to the poor."' A few days later the following entry appears in his *Journal*: 'Yesterday I began to play the madman in Gloucester by preaching on a table in Thornbury Street.'

So the appeal of the heart prevailed. Before those upturned faces, black with human toil, save where the tears of contrition had washed them white; before the infinite appeal of their ignorance, their spiritual hunger, their shepherdless and lonely lives, all the prejudices of this zealous High Churchman sank into nothingness. He saw them 'beaten down, and scattered abroad as shepherdless sheep,' even as his Master saw the common folk of His day, and, like his Master, he had compassion upon them. Much of the High Churchman remained in him to the last day of his life, for who can get rid of the child in us? but of the call itself Wesley became ever more clearly convinced. 'I look upon the whole world as my parish,' are his noble words. 'In whatever part of it I am, I judge it meet, right, and my bounden duty to declare unto all that are willing to hear, the glad tidings of salvation.' In this step he was soon followed by his brother, the reward to both being the embittered persecution of their brethren of the clergy, who would rather not see men saved at all than saved outside the ordinary 'channels of grace.'

### Expansion

The movement had now at its head three superlatively gifted men, each capable in his own way of moving by their speech great masses of men. Of the three, Charles Wesley was the most emotional and the most appealing. Tears flowed down his cheeks as he spoke, and he awoke a like emotion in his hearers; but his power was on a lower scale than that of the other two. Whitfield was pre-eminently the orator of the movement, and as such is perhaps the greatest preacher the English pulpit has possessed. His printed sermons give little indication of their tremendous power. Asked once for permission to print a sermon which had created a profound impression upon his hearers, he answered, 'I have no objection, if you will print the lightning, thunder, and rainbow with it.' It was the lightning, thunder, and rainbow which gave to the spoken words their spell, and held vast audiences in breathless stillness. A scene described by Dr. James Hamilton shows his wonderful dramatic power. Lord Chesterfield was listening to him as in the course of his sermon he described the sinner as a blind beggar led by a dog. The dog leaving him he was forced to grope his way, guided only by a staff. 'Unconsciously he wanders to the edge of a precipice; his staff drops from his hand down the abyss, too far to send back an echo; he reaches forward cautiously to recover it; for a moment he poises on vacancy, and—"Good God!" shouted Chesterfield, as he sprang from his seat to avert the catastrophe, "he is gone!"' Whitfield was a Calvinist, and for a while doctrinal differences threatened to disturb, and even to check, the revival. These, however, were forgotten in the larger demands of the work, and the friendship between Whitfield and Wesley remained unbroken to the close.

John Wesley lacked the superlative oratorical gifts of Whitfield, but he was a more dominating personality, and he outlived him by twenty-one years. From that hour when he determined to make himself 'vile' by preaching to the crowds in the open air outside Bristol, to the day of his death, the movement had one, and only one, leader. He brought to this work an iron frame, an inflexible will, a genius for organisation, and an ambition as selfless as it was exalted. Nor even as a preacher was he outshone by Whitfield in the effects he produced upon his hearers, though he was far outshone in the splendours of speech. 'What was the secret of Wesley's power as a preacher?' asks Fitchett. 'In many respects it might be imagined that he was the last man to sway an eighteenth-century crowd. He was a gentleman by birth and habit, a scholar by training, a man of fine and almost fastidious taste, with an Englishman's uneasy dislike of emotion, and a High Churchman's hatred of irregularity. He had little imagination, and no descriptive power. He told no anecdotes, as a rule, and certainly fired off no jests. What fitness had he to talk to peasants, to miners, to the rabble of the city, to the slow-thinking farmer drawn from the plough-tail? Yet he stood up, a little, trim, symmetrical figure; his smooth black hair exactly parted; his complexion clear and pure as that of a girl; his hazel eyes flashing like points of steel. And beneath his words the crowd was melted and subdued until it resembled a routed army shaken with fear and broken with emotion; men and women not seldom falling to the ground in a passion of distress. . . . There was something in his discourse—a note in his voice, a flash in his eye—that thrilled the crowd with awe, awe that not seldom deepened into dread. The mood of the speaker was one of perfect calmness. But it was the calm of power, of certainty, of an authority which ran back into the spiritual world.'

When Wesley broke through his prejudices and began his open-air preaching he was thirty-six years of age. The record of what follows is perhaps unique in history. For fifty years, in summer and winter, in sunshine and in rain, Wesley continued his work, visiting almost every town and hamlet in England, never resting, never wearying, with the cares of all the movement upon his shoulders, yet declaring the same message with the same freshness, the same certainty, and the same power over his hearers as before. In those fifty-one years he was said to have travelled 250,000 miles, in days when there were no railroads, and when the roads themselves were dangerous ; and to have preached 42,400 sermons, or an average of more than two per day for every day in these fifty-one years. Nor were the sermons themselves of ordinary length, sometimes lasting for two hours, and addressed to crowds reaching even to 30,000 people. As a mere feat of physical endurance this is perhaps without a record. He relates, for instance, that in one day he rode a distance of more than ninety miles, and at the end was 'little more tired than when he rose in the morning.' No hardship of storm or weather deterred him, his engagements were made in advance, and on he went through snow or sleet or rain, encountering a thousand obstacles, yet scarcely ever acknowledging defeat. Often when he had entered some quiet spot, after some exhausting journey, the temptation to rest presented itself to him in alluring forms. Here are some characteristic entries :

*March* 17, 1752.—'At the Foundry. How pleasing it would be to flesh and blood to remain at this little quiet place, where we have at length weathered the storm! Nay, I am not to consult my own ease, but the advancing the kingdom of God.'

*August* 27, 1775.—'I went to Miss Bosanquet's, and prepared for the Conference. How willingly could I spend the residue of a busy life in this delightful retirement! But

"Man was not born in shades to lie!"

Up and be doing. Labour on, till

"Death sings a requiem to the parting soul."'

When he was eighty-six he wrote:

*September* 11, 1788.—'I went over to Kingswood; sweet recess! where everything is now just as I wish. But

"Let us work now; we shall rest by and by."'

'Let us work now!' and this, after fifty years of such labour as no other man of that, or indeed of any other, generation in England ever attempted in the cause of Christ! Here, indeed, was a passion for service which might rank with that of the Apostles.

Like the Apostles, too, his way was beset by cruel persecutions. He was scorned by the clergy in many places as if he were a malefactor, and the mob, ever eager in that cruel age to inflict pain, had only to hear of his presence for them to unite in attacking him. Here is a characteristic entry: 'I made haste to Goston's Green, near Birmingham, where I had appointed to preach at six. But it was dangerous for any who stood to hear, for the stones and dirt were flying from every side, almost without intermission, for nearly an hour. However, very few persons went away. I afterwards met the Society, and exhorted them, in spite of men and devils, to continue in the grace of God.'

Wesley's method of beginning work in a place where he had not before entered is well illustrated in the following description :

'At seven I walked down to Sandhill, the poorest and most contemptible part of the town of Newcastle, and, standing at the end of the street with John Taylor, began to sing the Hundredth Psalm. Three or four people came out to see what was the matter ; who soon increased to four or five hundred. I suppose there might be twelve or fifteen hundred before I had done preaching ; to whom I applied these solemn words : "He was wounded for our transgressions." Observing these people, when I had done, to stand gaping and staring upon me with the most profound astonishment, I told them : "If you desire to know who I am, my name is John Wesley. At five in the evening, with God's help, I design to preach here again." At five, the hill on which I designed to preach was covered from top to bottom. I never saw so large a number gathered together, either in Moorfields or in Kennington Common. I knew it was not possible for the half to hear, though my voice was then strong and clear ; and so I stood so as to have them all in view, as they were ranged on the side of the hill. The Word of God which I set before them was : "I will heal their backslidings ; I will love them freely." After preaching, the poor people were ready to tread me under foot, out of pure love and kindness. It was some time before I could get out of the press. I then went back another way I came ; but several people were got to our inn before me ; by whom I was vehemently importuned to stay with them, at least a few days ; or at least one day more. But I could not consent, having given my word to be at Birstal, with God's help, on Tuesday night.'

Through this informal and itinerant ministry of Wesley

and Whitfield, a profound change began to appear in the religious life of England. The stupor, which had so long dulled its activities, now began to disappear; the Church was forced to wake up and take sides, the clergy were roused either to the energy of opposition or of acceptance; while wherever the preachers passed they left behind them crowds of men and women whom their ministry had lifted up into a new religious life. What was to be done with these? This was the problem which beset Wesley from the first, and his solution of it we have now to consider.

### Organisation

Wesley, to the last day of his life, regarded himself as a loyal member of the Church of England. His one desire, he declared, was to quicken its spiritual life. The idea of forming a denomination outside of it was repugnant to his mind. All his life long he struggled to maintain this pathetic fallacy, and he died maintaining it. The history of the movement, however, illustrates how in every crisis circumstances were too many for him; how he was driven by the remorseless logic of facts to do the very thing he desired not to do.

When at the sound of the new evangel men and women turned with fresh longings after the spiritual life, they found the doors of the Church closed against them. Nothing, perhaps, is more deeply regretted by the Anglican Church of to-day than the treatment meted out to Wesley and his followers by the bishops and Anglican clergy of the eighteenth century. By their hostility a movement was driven into exile, and ultimately into opposition, which, had it been wisely regarded, would have poured its rich blessings into the existing organisations, and made the Anglican Church the true Church of the people. Yet our previous studies have prepared us for just such a contingency. To all such movements the organised Church adopts usually an attitude of suspicion or hostility. The reason of this is, that all human organisations lose sooner or later their primitive enthusiasms, pass through the stage of persecution to that of respectability, then, becoming ease-loving and somnolent, learn to regard with suspicion and dislike all that would interfere with their habits, and so slowly perish. The Church would share the fate of all such societies, since she shares their other experiences, were it not that she is being constantly rejuvenated by infusions of new spiritual life, of the very kind we are now considering. But the process of rejuvenation is not welcomed by those who have grown lax and sluggish in the old; the power of kindling enthusiasms in them is gone, but the bitterness with which they oppose its awakening in others remains. Hence the awakening is frequently attended by the establishment of a new organisation outside the Church, since it has to encounter the opposition of those who are within.

Driven by just such a set of circumstances, Wesley had, at the very outset, to form some sort of organisation to preserve his work, and unite those impressed by his message.

At first he united with the Moravians, who had a 'Society' in Fetter Lane, but in 1739 he found the disunion amongst the members so great that he broke away from them and formed another Society, which met at the Foundry. This was a dilapidated building in Windmill Street, near Finsbury Square, used once for the casting of cannon. Upon this site Wesley erected a 'preaching-house,' and in the same building the Society met from time to time for prayer and mutual encouragement. As Wesley's influence spread, these societies spread with it; wherever his message met with acceptance, groups of converts united themselves together, and so swiftly did the movement spread that it became necessary to draw up a set of rules for guidance. These 'Societies' were defined as 'a company of men having the form and seeking the power of godliness, united in order to pray together, to receive the word of exhortation, and to watch over one another in love, that they may help each other to work out their salvation.'

The next step in the organisation of the new movement came with the founding of the Class Meetings. As the numbers grew, perplexities grew with them; differences of temperament led to differences of view; some grew lax, others broke out into dangerous excesses, and the absence of discipline began to be seriously felt. This growing need sorely burdened the heart of Wesley, and he pondered long and anxiously how to solve it. The solution he himself explains:

'At length, while we were thinking of quite another thing, we struck upon a method for which we have had cause to bless God ever since. I was talking with several of the Society in Bristol concerning the means of paying the debts there, when one stood up and said, "Let every member of the Society give a penny a week till all are paid." Another answered, "But many of these are poor, and cannot afford it." "Then," said he, "put eleven of the poorest with me; and if they can give anything, well, I will call on them weekly; and if they can give nothing, I will give for them as well as myself. And each of you call on eleven of your neighbours weekly; receive what they can give, and make up what is wanting." It was done. In a while, some of these informed me, they found such and such a one did not live as he ought. It struck me immediately—This is the thing, the very thing we have wanted so long. I called together all the Leaders of the Classes (so we used to term them and their companies), and desired them that each would make a particular inquiry into the behaviour of those whom he saw weekly. They did so. Many disorderly walkers were detected. Some turned from their evil ways. Some were put away from us. Many saw it with fear, and rejoiced unto God with reverence.' Later on this was modified, as it was found impossible for the class leader to visit regularly each week at the homes of the members, so a meeting was arranged instead each week. 'It can scarce be conceived,' says Wesley, 'what advantages have been reaped from this prudential regulation.' Such was the origin of the 'Class Meeting,' so important an item in Methodism, and out of it naturally grew what came to be known as the 'Conference,' being a gathering at stated times of the responsible leaders of the various districts.

In the rapid growth of the movement Wesley was confronted with the imperative need of providing preachers. He had first of all to overcome an inveterate prejudice in his own mind against lay-preaching. 'To touch this point,' he says, 'was to touch the apple of my eye.' It soon appeared, however, that there were men in his Societies who had superlative preaching gifts, and from the folly of refusing the exercise of such he was saved by the common-sense advice of his mother. Step by step he was thus being driven, though ever outwardly protesting, to the organisation of a religious society outside the Anglican Church. There were, it is true, a certain minority of clergymen within the Church favourable to the movement, but the number was small and without influence; the bishops and the great body of the clergy were so opposed, that inclusion within the Church would have meant the relinquishing of the principles, and a consequent destruction of the spiritual vitality, of the whole movement. In 1745 Wesley declared that he and his coadjutors would make any sacrifice which their consciences would permit in order to placate the clergy, and keep the movement within the borders of the Anglican Church; but they would not give up their doctrine of an inward and present salvation by faith alone; they would not stop preaching in private houses or in the open air; nor would they dissolve their Societies or prohibit lay-preaching. These, however, were the very grounds of offence. The freedom from ecclesiastical conventions and formalism which they had gained they were asked to relinquish, and bare their necks again to the intolerable yoke from which, with great exultation, they had escaped.

It was not to be expected that such terms could be accepted, and however much it may be regretted, it was not desirable that they should. The new movement had to cut out new grooves for itself, and to have forced it into the old would in all probability have chilled its ardour and imperilled its life.

With the formation of the Societies and the admission of lay-preachers the movement was now taking definite shape, but it still lacked the constitution of a Church. Its members were without the Sacraments and without an ordained ministry. Wesley held on these matters extreme High Church views. 'We dare not,' he said, 'administer Baptism or the Lord's Supper without a commission from a bishop in the apostolic succession.' For valid ordination, he believed, a like episcopal commission was necessary. Upon these points, however, his views underwent a change. Reading a book on the Primitive Church, by Lord King, he came to the conclusion that apostolic succession was a mere figment, that he was a 'scriptural episcopos as much as any man in England.' Some years later he read Stillingfleet's *Irenicon,* which proved to his mind that no system of Church government was laid down either by Christ or by His Apostles, and that ordination was valid when performed by a presbyter. When, then, ordination was refused by the Bishop of London, he himself ordained preachers by the laying on of hands, with power to administer the Sacraments.

Thus the last chain was forged: the movement had now become a Church.

### Closing Years

The revival of evangelical faith and fervour under Wesley stirred such deep emotions, and set free such mighty energies, that it is not to be expected that it could run its course without dangers. Even in the best movements unexpected elements arise which threaten evil, and which often mar, if they do not arrest, its progress. Wesley was not without his troubles, without years spent in anxiety, without his ardent controversies in which he had to fight almost single-handed. It is not remarkable that he had this to do, but it is remarkable that the controversies were so few, that the movement was hardly even retarded by them, and that so many of the dangers which arose were circumvented by the genius of Wesley himself.

Early in its history the movement was threatened by a theological difference between its leaders. Whitfield was a Calvinist, Wesley an Arminian. The differences at one time became accentuated, but they were overcome through the graciousness of both, and although the differences remained, bitterness was averted.

Dangers and divisions also sprang up within the movement through the extravagances of its members, through jealousies and unworthy ambitions. These are common to all movements, but they were never permitted by Wesley to assume serious dimensions. His hold over the movement was so profound, his wisdom so certain, his sincerity so obvious, his zeal so untiring, that divisions, which otherwise might have assumed dangerous proportions, were healed, or ejections were made, without harming the essential unity of the body.

As the revival spread, and with it the Societies and their various organisations, the responsibilities of Wesley increased. Up and down the land, never resting, moved this wonderful figure, bearing ten thousand cares and responsibilities, opening chapels, examining preachers, founding societies, administering discipline, conducting services, writing commentaries, building schools, founding orphanages, and keeping up a vast correspondence. One by one those who began the movement with him dropped from his side. Whitfield died in 1770; Charles Wesley, for long retired from active participation in the work, died in 1788. John Wesley outlived them all. He was eighty-six before his indomitable spirit would acknowledge signs of weakness. In 1789, for the first time, this admission appears in his *Journal*: 'I now find I am growing old.' In the following year the admission deepens: 'I am now an old man, decayed from head to foot. My eyes are dim, my right hand shakes much.' With his old fire, however, he adds: 'I can preach and write still.'

An account of Wesley a few months before his death is given by Henry Crabbe Robinson in his diary: 'He stood in a wide pulpit, and on each side of him stood a minister, and the two held him up, having their hands under his armpits. His feeble voice was hardly audible, but his reverend countenance, especially his long white locks, formed a picture never to be forgotten. There was a vast crowd of lovers and friends. It was for the most part a pantomime, but the pantomime went to the heart. Of the kind I never saw anything comparable to it in after life.'

Gradually the weakness increased. His last sermon was preached in a magistrate's room at Leatherhead on Wednesday, February 23, 1791, from the text, 'Seek ye the Lord while He may be found.' His last letter was a noble protest against the slave trade. He met death with that magnificent fortitude which characterised his life, greeting it with a cheer, and sending back from its dim gates the exulting message: 'The best of all is, God is with us.' So he passed away on the 2nd of March 1791, worn out by his incessant labours, but undefeated in faith, and nobly tranquil in presence of death.

### Character of the Movement

Each revival of religion, while possessing things common to all, possesses also its own characteristics and individuality. A striking feature of this revival is that of simplicity of aim. In those movements which sprang up at the Reformation, for instance, the demand for individual freedom joined hands with the demand for a deepened spiritual life, the politician united with the Reformer, and while the influence upon the religious life was deep, it was not always unmixed. The spiritual aim was often lost sight of in the political passion. The movement we are considering, however, had no such mixed motives, it was undivided in its aims and in its enthusiasms.

Nor even was the movement characterised by an aggressive crusade or even condemnation of the existing Church, by any opposition to its doctrines, or by the unfolding of some new discovery in the realm of theology. Wesley, instead of arousing opposition to the Church, avowed to the last day of his life his affection for it, and his desire that his followers should not, if possible, separate themselves from it. The doctrines which he preached, he declared, were the old doctrines of the Anglican Church, which had been allowed through neglect to become ossified, but which, rediscovered and restated, had sprung forth with radiant blossoming into a glorious and all-conquering life.

The Wesleyan revival, then, offered no protest against any existing Church, against its doctrines, practice, or liturgy ; it sought only to pour into the empty channels and dried cisterns of the Anglican Church a revived spiritual life.

In the simplicity, the intense spirituality, and the non-contentious character of its aims the movement under Wesley bears closest resemblance to that under Francis of Assisi. Both sought the revival of religion within the Church, but while Rome was astute, as she ever is, in finding a place for the Franciscans within her fold, the Anglican Church showed a lamentable folly in not finding room for the Wesleyans in hers. This mistake has cost her dear, but it has enriched the world with a Church which far outweighs, both in numbers and in influence, the Church from which it sprang.

The essential spirituality of the movement Wesley maintained to the last. Although he lived in stirring times, when great wars and great political changes were taking place, he never allowed these things to deflect him from his main purpose of preaching salvation and winning souls for Christ. Amid all the ferment of war, of changes of dynasty, of social and political movements, Wesley moves up and down the country, knowing the people as no other man of his generation, and yet of all this his *Journal* takes no notice. He was engaged on the King's business, which required haste; his mind was preoccupied with the profound concerns of the Kingdom of God; he had received his commission from his King, and his mind was straitened until it was accomplished.

This preoccupation in things concerning the salvation of the individual, and detachment from the secular affairs of life, so characteristic of its founder, have been characteristic of the Church which bears his name. The remarkable growth of the Wesleyan Church has sprung from the importance which it has attached to the saving of the individual, and to the concentration of all its energy to that great end.

Like Francis of Assisi, Wesley reinstated the preacher. The Wesleyan revival was a revival of preaching. In the Churches of that time sermons were delivered, but preaching in the true sense of the word hardly existed. Moral essays, innocent homilies, soulless platitudes, with a text attached to them, were droned out Sunday after Sunday from the various pulpits of the land, but preaching—the living message pouring from the living heart, appealing, warning, convicting—all that form of it was practically unknown. When, then, Whitfield and Wesley stood up; when their voices, thrilling with emotion, fell upon startled ears, men awoke, their hearts awoke, they realised their hunger and despair, they felt the first throbbings of a new and divine life stirring within them.

Wesley realised also the profound truth that it is not the duty of the Church to wait within the Church until the people come to it, but that it is the duty of the

Church to go to the people. When on that day at Bristol, standing at Whitfield's side, he looked down upon that vast sea of upturned faces—the unpitied progeny of the streets, the lapsed and neglected masses of the people whom no one loved or cared for—the call came to him to separate himself from all the habits and conventional beliefs in which he had been trained, and discarding all ecclesiastical forms, deal directly with human needs. The struggle which followed was intense, as we have seen, for Wesley had been trained from his infancy to regard ecclesiastical forms and order with a veneration bordering upon awe. But stronger than all these inherited prejudices was the recognition in him of the divine will, and the power of absolute submission possessed only by the greatest natures. In the presence of that mute but infinitely pathetic appeal which came to him from the upturned faces of that awe-struck crowd, his prejudices withered within him; pity and love awoke in his heart, and made him willing to suffer all things if only he could win them for Christ.

Thus was begun that informal ministry which kept him all his life long wandering from place to place, preaching in the streets, by the roadside, anywhere, indeed, and at any time, if only he could get men to listen. And slowly the people began to awake to the fact that some strange thing was happening in their midst. This informal ministry began to stir into life the dormant spiritual forces of the nation. At first it aroused curiosity in all, then in many bitterness and persecution, but in others a strange joy. To the poor, at last, was the Gospel being preached; to the outcasts and the abandoned once again was the glad offer of salvation made, and into the open doors of that gracious kingdom where the penitent and the needy are made welcome, they began to stream—first by ones and twos, next by hundreds, at last by thousands, until the whole land was filled with the song of the redeemed.

This informal ministry, the Church which bears Wesley's name has attempted to maintain. The recognition of the lay-preacher, of the unordained ministry of the word, the use which the Wesleyan Church makes of men gifted with preaching power, has doubtless added enormously to that Church's influence, especially in rural parts where, owing to scarcity of population, there could be no sanctioned charge. What England owes to those little chapels scattered everywhere over the land it would be difficult to say. Their simple worship appeals to simple minds; they have maintained the traditions of their great founder, and have kept the light of faith burning in many places where otherwise it would have died. As an asset in the nation's life the influence for good exerted by the lay-preacher and his informal ministry can hardly be overestimated.

While Wesley's contention—that he preached nothing that was not found in Anglican doctrine—was true in substance, the message which he did proclaim had all the elements of a new discovery. Robbed of all theological terms, this message in effect was the need and the possibility of salvation for all, and the assurance to all that salvation had been given. This message, rung out with the intense conviction of Wesley and Whitfield, came to that generation with all the force of a fresh revelation.

What the best belief of his age was, we may learn from Wesley's own early beliefs. He was taught, he tells us, to believe that his sins were washed away in baptism, and that salvation was only possible by his keeping throughout his life the commandments of God. On the subject of assurance he was taught that 'an absolute certainty that God has forgiven us we can never know until we reach Heaven.' 'I had some confused notion,' he says, 'about the forgiveness of sins, but then I took it for granted that the time of this must either be the hour of death or the day of judgment.' To win salvation, therefore, by merit, Wesley bent all his energies, with the end that he utterly failed to gain peace of mind, and no less utterly failed to convey any peace of mind to those to whom he preached. Having realised the victory which comes to the soul through a living, trusting faith in God, Wesley went forth with his heart on fire. He called on men everywhere to repent, to seek salvation from daily sin, and by a life of trustful faith possess the blessed certainty of forgiveness and of being united to God.

Each revival derives its power from the rediscovery of some forgotten Biblical truth, and coming with all the power of a rediscovery it awakens in the heart a joyful recognition of its power, and a fresh blessing in its acceptance. The doctrine itself is frequently overstated and lifted out of contact with other truths, but the joy of its discovery overrides all limitations which come through a wrong sense of proportion; it bursts upon the world with the invigorating power of the spring, and brings radiant happiness to tens of thousands of lives. This is what happened through the rediscovery of those evangelical doctrines already stated. They awoke in men's hearts a radiant joy; they transfigured tens of thousands of lives. Men who were criminals before, who lived the most brutal lives, who were drunkards and law-breakers, coming under the spell of the new preaching, were changed. A miracle of grace was wrought in them. Not many rich, not many mighty, were called, but the revival swept in upon the multitudes of the people; upon the toilers of the workshop and the mine ; into the crowded tenements of the labourers and the poor.

Like all such movements, too, when once begun it seemed to awaken incalculable and mysterious forces, and move to laws beyond all human prescience. From England it spread to Scotland, to Ireland, and to America ; it seemed to be borne along by unseen hands ; it broke out in the most unlikely places. So potent, so mysterious was its presence felt, that many were known, even while mocking it, to fall to the ground in terror of conviction. Strangest place of all, it broke out in the army fighting in Flanders under the Duke of Cumberland. There, at night, in the open bivouac, when the battle was over, might have been heard amid the groans of the dying the prayers of the revivalists and the sound of Charles Wesley's hymns.

While the direct result of the revival under Wesley was to create a Church, the indirect result was to quicken into newness of life other existing Churches. Especially did it stir the conscience of that which he had left. Lecky declares that the evangelical revival 'gradually changed the whole spirit of the English Church.' It kindled the spirit of devotion ; it made the old hunting parson, with his indolent neglect, and often contempt for his duties, an impossibility ; it reformed the manners, and altered the tone of the preaching of the clergy, and it restored Christianity to its rightful place in the national life.

In addition, it gave an immense impetus to work amongst children, especially in the Sunday school, and it threw a new ardour into work in foreign lands. The London Missionary Society, the Church Missionary Society, the British and Foreign Bible Society, the Religious Tract Society, these, and many other like organisations, owed their origin or received their chief impulse from the evangelical movement. So swiftly did the movement spread that, according to Lecky, 'by the close of the century the Evangelical party was incontestibly the most numerous and the most active party in the Church.'

The growth of the Church which bears Wesley's name has been no less wonderful. In 1791, when Wesley died, there were 300 preachers, and 76,000 members connected with the different societies. Now it has been recently estimated that the different Methodist organisations throughout the world number 49,000 ministers, with no less than 30,000,000 adherents. Greater than numbers, however, is the spirit which animates it. 'Its noblest result,' says Green, 'is the steady attempt which has never ceased from that day to this to remedy the guilt, the ignorance, the physical suffering, the social degradation of the profligate and the poor.'

## John Wesley

In the Picture Gallery of those whom God has chosen to revive His Church we have now to place John Wesley. In that select society of the great and the good who have been called to this noblest service which man can render to his fellows, he is not unworthy of a place. Differing greatly from those whose portraits we have already examined, he is not overshadowed by any in the faithfulness with which he performed his great task, or in the depth of his devotion to the cause of his Lord and Master. If he lacked the sweetness of St. Francis, the 'terribilita' of Savonarola, the massive grandeur of Luther, the penetrative subtlety of Calvin, the tempestuous force of Knox, he had qualities all his own which made him no less attractive to his followers and no less efficient as a leader.

Much as we know of those others our knowledge of Wesley is more exact and intimate. All his life long Wesley was in the habit of keeping a journal, in which he entered day by day his inmost thoughts and feelings, his daily experiences and his reflections on them, the places he visited and the men he met. All these intimate and secret things are written down with a simplicity and guilelessness which leave nothing of his nature hidden ; we can see him to-day almost as clearly as when on horseback he trudged along the heavy roads, with pencil and note-book in hand, or with head bent over a book. For although, perhaps, the busiest man in England of his day, Wesley found time not only to keep up a huge correspondence, but found time also to read many, and to write many books. His writings reveal a clear and penetrative intellect ; according to Southey he possessed the 'most influential mind of the eighteenth century.' Of his literary style he writes with his usual directness : 'I dare no more write in a fine style than wear a fine coat. A man with one foot in the grave must waste no time on ornament.' Without attempting to reach a finished style, Wesley none the less is one of the masters of English prose. 'He shows remarkable literary power,' says Leslie Stephen. 'His writings are means to a direct practical end. . . . It would be difficult to find any letters more direct, forcible, and pithy in expression. He goes straight to the mark without one superfluous flourish.'

Great as were his intellectual gifts, however, it is not because of these, in which he was equalled and outdistanced by others of his generation, that his call to veneration consists. The supreme greatness of his character lay in his subordination of every personal ambition to the will of God. He had, as Matthew Arnold finely says, 'a genius for godliness.' From his childhood the hand of God seemed to be upon him, and to a nature already impressionable and seriously inclined there came that experience of rescue from the flames of his father's house, which ever afterwards gave to the words 'a brand plucked from the burning' an awful meaning in relation to God's personal dealings with him.

Throughout youth and early manhood this same intense earnestness of spirit characterised his daily life. Since salvation, as he thought, was to be gained by keeping God's commandments, he set himself to the task with more than Puritan severity. Restless and unsatisfied he still cried out for God, for a deeper spiritual experience; his every ambition was spiritual. When the light came it shone on a nature singularly pure and selfless. There was no violent eruption, only the deep satisfaction of something eagerly and painfully sought for, and at last found.

Amid all his arduous labours, his innumerable engagements, his coming and going, Wesley lived a hidden life of intimacy with God. On the first page of his diary there was always written the following sentences: 'I resolve, *Deo juvante,* (1) To devote an hour morning and evening to private prayer, no pretence or excuse whatever. (2) To converse with God, no lightness, no *εὐτραπελία.*

This genius for godliness showed itself not only in his private devotions; it showed itself in all his public utterances. As an orator, as we have seen, he was inferior to Whitfield; but in the effect of his preaching he had no superior. His influence upon his hearers is thus described:

'As soon as he got upon the stand he stroked back his hair

and turned his face towards where I stood, and, I thought, fixed his eyes upon me. His countenance fixed such an awful dread upon me, before I heard him speak, that it made my heart beat like the pendulum of a clock; and when he did speak, I thought his whole discourse was aimed at me. When he had done, I said, "This man can tell the secrets of my heart; he hath not left me there; for he hath showed me the remedy, even the blood of Jesus." I thought he spoke to no one but me, and I durst not look up, for I thought all the people were looking at me. But before Mr. Wesley concluded his sermon, he cried out, "Let the wicked forsake his way, and the unrighteous man his thoughts; and let him return to the Lord, and He will have mercy upon him; and to our God, for He will abundantly pardon." I said, "If that be true, I will turn to God to-day."'

It was this power to convict, to see into men's souls, to reveal to them what they were, to reveal at the same time the entreating Christ, which made Wesley's journeys a triumphal march to tens of thousands of depressed and degraded men and women.

In the pursuance of his work, too, there was the most absolute self-abnegation. Bodily ease, bodily comforts, rest from the endless strain of responsibility, he knew not. He rose at four every morning, winter and summer; he sought no relaxation, nor is there to be found a single sentence of complaint about the hardships of his calling. His conversation revealed a rare lightness and gaiety of heart; he was ever cheerful, never knew, he says, lowness of spirits; 'Ten thousand cares are no more weight to my mind,' he declares, 'than ten thousand hairs on my head.'

Along with this cheerfulness there was an absolute clearness of the one thing he was called to do. No one ever put off less time in doing it than John Wesley. Although he travelled through all the most beautiful parts of England, no word of it enters his *Journal.* Once, when he was tempted to linger on the way to admire a beautiful piece of landscape, he forced himself on. 'I believe there is an eternity, I must arise and go hence,' he cried. On, on, ever on, year in, year out, in rain or wind, in sunshine or snow, it mattered not. Ever with indomitable courage, with earnestness never varying, he toiled, consumed by the thought of the shortness of time, of the great work to be done, of the need of haste in doing it. On he marched, preaching, pleading, warning, guiding, until the end came—and the reward—'Servant, well done!'

Along with this genius for godliness Wesley possessed a wonderfully sane mind. His judgment of men, his skill in using them, his power to employ them to the best advantage, and of attaching them to himself in loyal submission to his authority, amounted likewise to genius, and saved the movement from the most serious dangers. Macaulay says that Wesley 'had a genius for government not inferior to that of Richelieu,' and Buckle calls him 'the first of ecclesiastical statesmen.' Certainly his power over his followers was remarkable, and the genius of his organisation is still seen in the Church which he founded. It was owing to this marvellous organisation which Wesley left behind him that the movement remained unshaken even when bereft of his presence and guidance. In this respect the Wesleyan revival is almost unique. In no other such movement, perhaps, were the spiritual interests so wisely safeguarded, or was the recoil less pronounced.

It cannot be claimed for Wesley that he showed a like skill in his judgments of women. Wesley's love stories are strange reading, and his own comments upon them both piquant and ludicrous. To the consternation of his friends he married late in life a widow who proved to him a sad thorn in the flesh. Consumed by inordinate jealousy, she allowed him no peace, and it must be said on her behalf that Wesley must have proved a trying husband. He had no domestic interests, he was never at home, and his guilelessness and approachableness gave abundant exercise for the insane jealousy of his wife. Wesley, however, was too busy a man to be deeply affected by domestic discomforts. He passed through the troubled waters with wonderful composure, and with that singular detachment which was his characteristic when dealing with life's vexations.

And now the end is come, and we bid farewell to those great men in whose company we have been dwelling for a little while. And as we recall them one by one, as we remind ourselves of their faithfulness to God, of the vast services they have rendered humanity, and also of their sufferings, their sacrifices, and their unflinching courage and devotion, it cannot be without devout thankfulness for their lives and for all they were able to effect. Nor can we doubt that the future has in store other such men, who, in the providence of God, and in the fulness of the times, will lead their day and generation to a revived spiritual life, to an intenser faith, and to larger and clearer knowledge of the power of God's saving grace.

# LESSONS FOR TODAY

The publishers have reprinted this volume because they know that it has a vital message for evangelicals today, especially ministers and lay leaders. Here and there certain items may have only passing interest, as facts of history. But in the main these laws still operate. The example of the six leaders ought to prove timely in a day when we have been trying all sorts of methods, without first sitting down to get our bearings. In many such ways the volume from Burns suggests a practical philosophy for today.

## A Practical Philosophy

During the half century and more since Burns wrote this volume, conditions on the surface of life have vastly changed, and often not for the better, religiously. But God has not changed. Neither has His will concerning the need for revival among those who profess to be His children; and for evangelism among the unsaved and the unchurched. All of these ideals and principles have to do with Missions at home and overseas. Here we shall think about the laws and leaders only as they concern revival and evangelism, mainly in the local church under the guidance of a worthy pastor.

1. *A Longing for Revival.* During the past fifty years and more the saints of God have kept yearning and praying for widespread revival. However long this time of awakening may yet be deferred, it is at least fifty years closer to our day than when Burns wrote. There can be no reason for waiting much longer before

we can have a revival in almost any local church. Here the pastor and the people have everything under their control, subject only to the will of God. He will not fail to send a local revival as soon as we fulfill the conditions that He has laid down in the Book (Isa. 55:10-11 *et al.*), and exemplified in church history.

2. *A Revival Through Evangelism.* In apostolic times, and in those of John Wesley, spiritual awakening and quickening came to many of God's professed children when they became concerned about the unsaved and the unchurched, especially in the home community. Inasfar as we can judge, this is still the surest way to bring about a revival. Often we say that before we can reach out to win the unsaved we must first have a renewal of grace among our church members and officers, including the pastor. Surely no congregation can ever go too far in seeking the betterment of those whose names appear on the rolls of the home church.

But experience shows that the majority of our efforts toward revival without evangelism prove disappointing. If any minister no longer young will look back over his pastoral experiences he will find that officers and people, like their minister, have come closest to God when they have been most actively praying and working for the salvation of their relatives, friends, and neighbors. At such a time of ingathering, as in city crusades under Billy Graham, many church members find that they themselves still need a personal experience of redeeming grace.

When a pastor and his people become tremendously concerned about the spiritual welfare of the local community, God has a way of taking first-class care of their souls. Whenever a Christian begins to engage actively in "individual work for the individual," the worker soon feels the need of wisdom and strength that come through Bible reading in the spirit of prayer. In times of spiritual depression the minister often wishes that the home people would show what an old catechism means by "the diligent use of the outward and ordinary means of grace." But in a harvest time of ingathering a pastor can thank God for the reflex influence on the spiritual lives of the soul-winners. What a blessed way to bring about a local revival!

However, one step ought always to precede any endeavor to bring about a local revival through community evangelism. Before any congregation can hope to excel in soul-winning, the officers and members must first be at peace with each other. Not only must they believe in the forgiveness of sins, however deadly; they must also practice the forgiveness of wrongs, however serious. Insofar as I have been able to judge from my own pastoral experience, and from wide observation, the lack of Christlike forgiveness among the officers and the members of many a local church stands out as the chief obstacle to any worthy movement for revival through evangelism. Sometimes the minister himself needs to forgive other officers, as he himself wishes to be forgiven of God. In other words, revival through evangelism costs!

When the officers and members of a local church live and worship together as a united family of God's redeemed children, they can make ready for a movement of active soul-winning. The best way to prepare is to start winning souls. Learn to do better by doing well! If there were space for facts and figures, I could tell in detail about an experience of the sort, where the Lord once opened the windows of heaven and poured out showers of mercy on a congregation and a community dear to my heart. Without any imported leadership, and without any unusual methods that called for the expenditure of money, the officers and members did their utmost to present the claims of the Lord Jesus to every unsaved or unchurched man, woman, or older child in the community. As a consequence we witnessed a glorious ingathering. We also felt sure that the Lord had refreshed and strengthened our own souls, and that through evangelism He had wondrously revived all the worship, the teaching, and the work of the local church. How simple all of this seems, and how sublime!

3. *The Basis in the Scriptures.* In revival and evangelism everything ought to begin, continue, and come to fruition according to the ideals and the teachings of God's Written Word. This line of thought applies to the prayers, the preaching, the personal work, and everything else, including the music. Not only should all of this lead to salvation and uplift, personally; it should all help to prepare unbelievers and backsliders for taking an active part in the worship, the teaching, and the work of the home church, which bases its activities solidly on the Book. For many such reasons the home pastor ought seriously to consider the wisdom of serving as the leader in this revival through evangelism.

At least indirectly, the volume by James Burns shows how to engage in all these holy endeavors on a basis completely Biblical. In view of prevailing uncertainty about all these matters, someone learned in the Scriptures and in things practical ought to write a book about the Scriptural teachings on revival through evangelism. Scholars have prepared worthy volumes about the Scriptural basis of Theology, Ethics, Public Worship, Preaching, Missions, and other subjects of perennial concern. Why has no one ever set forth what the Old Testament tells and shows about "the varieties of religious experience" in days of declension and revival? Also, about what the New Testament teaches and embodies about Christian outreach for lost souls, one by one, both in the home community and far beyond? As John Wesley used to say, while busily engaged in helping to transform many a community in

England, "The world is my parish." As a motto he could have taken the words of a later philosopher, "The world and the individual." How Biblical, and how sublime!

4. *The Light of Church History.* There is a worthy saying that no person understands any vital subject unless he knows its history. With both revival and evangelism the history begins in Old Testament and New Testament times. It also continues throughout the succeeding centuries. The volume from Burns has proved more lasting and helpful than many others because it followed a sound historical method in a most fascinating form, that of Christian biography. But we still need a work that would survey the progress and the decline of revival and evangelism throughout all the "Christian" centuries. Concerning certain periods, such as the Great Awakening in New England, we already have competent books. But about the subject as a whole, as it appears in church history, there is nothing that compares with works on the history of Missions, preaching, and other like endeavors.

Once I started out to trace historically the rise and progress of revival and evangelism. After a study of the Old Testament and the New I turned to a field with which I was not so familiar. In lieu of a scholarly work about the progress and the decline of revival and evangelism throughout church history, I used as a guide the seven volumes by Kenneth S. Latourette, *A History of the Expansion of Christianity* (1937-45). In that best work of its kind I found a wealth of material indirectly relating to revival and evangelism, but comparatively little (See IV, 191-95) directly on my subject. I wished then, as I wish now, that someone would write as much and as well about the history of revival and evangelism as Latourette has written about the history of the kindred movement, World Missions.

In six chapters, largely biographical, Burns has

shown the fascination and the value of historical study in the hands of one who believes in revival and evangelism. If we had more books of the sort we might avoid many of the pitfalls that have beset the pathway of soul-winners in every era. For example, here in America we could learn how the movement in and about 1858, and the later one under Dwight L. Moody, held free from the excesses of the Great Awakening in New England and of the later revival in Kentucky. Also, how the city-wide crusades of Billy Graham have avoided commercialism, sensationalism, and other unfortunate features of the campaigns under the gifted leadership of Billy Sunday. In all matters relating to revival and evangelism, thank God for the searchlight of history, starting with the Bible!

5. *The Reliance on Christian Doctrine.* Burns everywhere makes clear that each of his six exemplars made large use of Bible doctrine. From one man to another, because of varying temperaments and times, the stress would shift from justification by faith to the sovereignty of God, and afterward to the saving experience of redeeming grace. With Savonarola (d. 1498), and often with Knox (d. 1572), as with Chrysostom (d. 407) long before, the emphasis fell on Christian ethics, which in turn grew out of Christian doctrine. Especially with the sons of Susanna Wesley in the eighteenth century, the singing, the praying, and the preaching nearly all had to do with saving truths about the Lord Jesus Christ.

Here in the States the work of revival and evangelism has often lacked a firm basis in the Scriptures, and a large use of Christian doctrine. Too often we have thought of revivalistic music in terms of emotion divorced from doctrinal truth, and of accompanying prayers as the heated expression of emotions not in keeping with God's revelation of truth. Among the six men whom Burns studies, it would be hard to find one who did not appeal for a response in the light of truth that came from God. In fact, some persons who never have read the letters of John Calvin may wonder whether or not he ever had any strong emotions to express. About his right to a place of honor in the book at hand, opinions may differ. (I myself have no such questions.) But every student of church history knows that without relying on Christian doctrine any movement for revival and evangelism must proceed with peril.

6. *The Influence on Public Morals.* The volume by Burns stresses what other books ignore: the inevitable connection between Bible doctrine and Christian duty. With Savonarola the appeal for moral amendment was direct and moving. With him, as with Chrysostom, ethical preaching led to a martyr's death. Even so, as Emerson says, " 'Tis man's perdition to be safe when for the truth he ought to die." With most of the other exemplars in this volume, the stress fell on doctrine more than on duty. But no student of church history can ignore or minimize the moral betterment that followed the work of Luther in middle Europe, of Calvin in Geneva, of Knox in Scotland, which he largely recreated, and of Wesley in England. As a rule, then as now, moral betterment came as a by-product of revival and evangelism, both of them Biblical and doctrinal.

Today the less conservative critics of Billy Graham insist that he ought to widen and diversify his evangelistic appeal, so as to make it strongly ethical. They would have him repeatedly set forth the Christian solution of vast world problems, especially those relating to race and to war. Even if he could do all of that to their satisfaction, where would he find a precedent and a warrant in the history of revival and evangelism? Much the same criticism would apply to the leadership in worship and preaching of countless ministers who term themselves evangelical. If Graham's critics ever notice us they insist that our Gospel and our prayers are too simple, and that our soul-winning sermons are too thin. They seem to forget that in dealing with the Ethiopian eunuch Philip did not discuss the race problem in Ethiopia, and that in counseling with the Philippian jailer Paul did not discuss the need of reforms in the management of such a dungeon.

On the other hand, as we have seen, reform ought always to follow conversion. (So it did with the jailer, Acts 16:33.) From this ethical point of view we conservatives appraise and approve revival and evangelism in Holy Scripture and later in church history. On this very same basis we decry much of our past American revivalism. "By their fruits" in the way of transformed lives and communities we ought to judge any movement of the sort. For a generation or two we have watched men and churches that have made the boasted broader appeal, often all-inclusive. We have yet to see any case where this sort of diffused promotion has resulted in the kind of moral betterment that the critics demand after the crusades of Billy Graham. Surely we who accept the doctrines of Holy Writ must never rest content with revival or evangelism that does not issue in transformed lives and communities. Christian ethics must come through revival and evangelism as in the day of Wesley or of Paul!

### An Effective Leader

In my book, *Pastoral Leadership* (1949), I strove to make clear what I here take for granted. In the Bible and throughout church history God has worked, spiritually, through chosen leaders. Usually He has committed each enterprise to one leader, such as John Wesley or Dwight L. Moody. This leader in turn has enlisted associates, such as George Whitefield or Ira D. Sankey. But all the while everyone concerned has looked to Wesley or to Moody as the responsible leader, subject only to God.

1. *The Call for a Strong Leader.* Under God the work of revival and evangelism in the local church depends largely on the size and caliber of the pastor. The same holds true in broader fields, but they do not directly concern many of us. As a rule the men who have excelled as ministers of spiritual, soul-winning churches have not been blessed with genius. But every one of them has had ability to size up the situation in a new field; to lead in devising ways and means of evangelizing the community; to enlist the co-operation of lay officers and many other people; to delegate all that they can do, and to accord hearty credit for all good deeds. With such a pastor as leader almost any congregation of people who love each other can engage effectively in community evangelism, and even have a continuous local revival.

2. *The Role of the Local Minister.* At first glance the role of the evangelistic pastor may seem to call for a vast deal of exacting work other than in preaching and pastoral care. Really it need not be so. In the leadership of public worship, especially in prayer; in preaching and teaching on the Lord's Day, as well as in the mid-week service, and in various kinds of pastoral care, a resourceful minister can promote and foster among officers and other members a desire to engage in soul-winning. Among the soul-winning congregations that I have admired most, the ministers have excelled in the pulpit and in pastoral work. For these very reasons, and because the people love him as a man, such a pastor can inspire his people to engage actively in soul-winning.

3. *The Ideal of a Soul-Winning Church.* Under such a minister the officers and the other lay folk soon begin to think of the home church as a soul-winning agency. From the cradle roll up through the home de-

partment every part of the Church School aims to discover and enlist for Christ the unsaved and the unchurched folk of the community. So does every group of elected officers, such as trustees, deacons, and elders; and every society that elects its own leaders, as among the women and the young people. Even among boy and girl scouts the leaders in such a church have at heart the spiritual welfare of lads and lasses who will become leaders of the home church tomorrow. In short, whatever is not related to the winning of souls need have no place in the program of a local church, or of its minister.

In my book, *Evangelism in the Home Church* (1942), I dealt with these matters at more length. In preparing to write it I learned much from an inspirational book by Frederick E. Taylor, a Baptist pastor at Indianapolis, *The Evangelistic Congregation* (1927). For twenty-one years he served as ministerial leader of a congregation that seldom had special meetings, because it relied on the enthusiastic use of regular services for worship, and on the continuous soul-winning activities of all the boards, societies, and other groups in the congregational life and work. Evidently that minister and his lay leaders had lived with the New Testament long enough to learn what their local church was for. Evidently, also, the spiritual lives of the workers responded to their God-given regime of depending on the Bible in the spirit of prayer, and on the exercise of all their powers for the winning of souls.

Unfortunately, available cases of the sort nearly always relate to large congregations. One reason may be that in a community where unsaved and unchurched people abound, a small soul-winning church normally continues to grow in numbers, as in grace. But another element enters into the picture. Personally, I have known many more churches with limited numbers than I have among those that seem to me large. With exceptions here and there, I have not found these smaller congregations alive with evangelistic fervor. Believing as I do that beyond five hundred members the difficulty of leadership may quadruple whenever the numbers double, still I must report that where the difficulties seem least such activities do not appear to abound. On the other hand, there may be obstacles of which an outsider can not know; for example, that old Satanic custom of unwillingness to forgive. For some reason, lack of forgiveness flourishes most in small churches, where everybody knows everybody else. God forgive us all for being so human!

4. *The Enlistment of Personal Workers.* The pastor of a soul-winning church sets others an example by engaging in personal work. Without calling special attention to his activities, he soon becomes known locally as a person who feels much concern about the salvation of every person he meets, if unsaved, unchurched, or unstable. Among God's noblest lay folk such a pastoral example tends to become contagious. More than a few of them long to engage in something more important than casually shaking hands with strangers in church. I well remember how as a young minister I began to see beneath the surface of a strong layman's religion. At a mid-week service I had opened up a passage in the Acts, perhaps about the winning of the eunuch from Ethiopia (8:26-40). Among the questions and remarks came this from a leading elder, intensely loyal to the home church and to me: "Pastor, you ministers keep exhorting us to do personal work. Sometimes you scold us mildly for not doing it. You seem not to know that we want to enjoy that sort of thing, but we do not know how to start." Like most pastors, I never had tried to answer the "preacher's forgotten question, How?" Instead of trying to teach a lesson that I had not prepared, I asked him a question: "Elder D - - -, if I give you in private the name of a certain man will you see

him this week and report to me privately next Wednesday after the meeting?" "Yes, indeed, and I'll keep on seeing men, one by one, as long as I keep getting their names."

Beginning with that elder the minister enlisted other workers, both men and women, one by one. There was no public appeal, and there was no publicity, or "society of soul-winners." Theoretically, as in Korea, every member of the home church ought to become a soul-winner. Practically, not every saved person has the needful tact, resourcefulness, and persistence. Even in time the number of enlisted soul-winners never became large. But among them the minister could always find the right person to interview anyone whom the pastor had discovered to be in need of Christ and a church home. On the other hand, these workers discovered such needy persons and reported any case that required expert attention and counsel. Whatever the procedure, the minister of a soul-winning church needs to enlist a dozen or a score of special personal workers.

5. *The Plans for Christian Nurture.* A minister of this kind may need a negative caution. In his zeal for winning the lost and other displaced persons, he may fail to show equal concern about the nurture of new believers and of children not yet old enough to unite with the church. Unfortunately, a church and its pastor may become known as excelling in evangelism or in Christian nurture. In nine cases out of ten the regular church activities have to do with nurture, supplemented with occasional sporadic attempts at evangelism. In more than one church that I have known the reverse held true. But in the ideal congregation the two ways of serving the Lord — evangelism and nurture — seem as inseparable as the heat and the light of the sun!

Under the kindly supervision of the home church and its pastor, the nurture of a child begins when he is born, if not before. All through his early years, home and church work and pray together so that by the age of twelve, or thereabouts, he discovers in Christ his Saviour and accepts Him as Lord. Among boys and girls who have profited from loving nurture the local church finds many of her most promising members. After other persons become converted as adults, never having known the nurture of a Christian home and church, they too need the loving and expert oversight of a minister who is as good a pastor as though he were not an evangelist, and as good an evangelist as though he were not a pastor. After he has served long enough to excel in his calling, he finds that the two activities never conflict with each other. Why not? Because they both come from God. For example, study the life and teachings of Paul about soul-winning and soul-culture.

### A Simple Program

At the risk of overlapping let us now look at such a program of evangelism in a hypothetical congregation not large or wealthy. As for details, they differ widely according to the nature of the community, the personality of the minister, the character of the lay workers, and other factors difficult to classify. For many such reasons nobody at a distance can draw up any sort of local blueprint.

1. *The Simplicity of Evangelism.* In the New Testament everything of the kind went forward according to a definite plan, which was always simple. According to A. B. Bruce, a student of the New Testament, our Lord had a plan for His "synagogue ministry." Many scholars have pointed out in the extension work of the Apostle Paul a more or less definite plan of a different sort, but still quite simple. And so throughout church history the congregations that have done the best work in evangelism have employed methods far from com-

plicated and costly. Among the leaders whom Burns studied, not a one seems to have relied largely on organization and machinery.

Conditions of a different kind obtain in what we call "professional evangelism." Personally I believe in the sort of teamwork that Billy Graham employs in a citywide crusade. In former days American "big business for God" may have led to extreme stress on men, money, and machinery, rather than prayer, preaching, and personal work. In other words, it tended toward "working up a man-made movement" more or less like the Tower of Babel, not looking for a God-given movement like that on the Day of Pentecost. But from all such American revivalism Graham seems to have kept largely aloof. If so, thank God!

All the while the work of evangelism still centers in the local church and its minister. Even in a city like San Francisco, after Graham holds meetings blessed of God, he leaves the work of soul-winning and later culture exactly where he found it, in the local church and in Christian homes. Instead of trying to become another Billy Graham, "a poor imitation of the real thing," striving to pattern after Graham's organization, the local pastor and his lay advisers may resolve to depend on ways and means so simple that to an outside observer they seem absurd. That is the way men of the world have always looked at "the simplicity and the purity that is toward Christ" (II Cor. 11:3c, A.S.V.).

2. *The Importance of Public Worship.* In any program for congregational soul-winning, however simple, a pastor stresses the public worship of God. He knows that many adult conversions will come through personal work in homes. Even so, the music and the prayers of the sanctuary go far to create and foster the sort of spiritual atmosphere in which soul-winning becomes the normal activity of believers in Christ. Without

letting the sermon dominate everything else, the pastor can plan every hour of worship so that it will lead up to the desired effect, whether evangelistic or pastoral. Therefore he may thank God if the local program on every Lord's Day calls for two hours of worship, not identical, so as to meet heart needs of two different sorts. If so, he may find the best opportunity for soul-winning at what we call "the eleven o'clock service."

In other decades some pastors did these things differently. For the morning hour the minister would prepare as carefully as for a church wedding. The morning service was nearly always for the saints, so called. But at the second service, sometimes almost forty-second in quality, the cheap hymns, the unprepared prayers, and the emotional appeals abounding in timeworn anecdotes — all combined to make people think that the pastor did not care much about evangelism, or he would work harder in preparation. If a minister really believes in soul-winning as much as he believes in soul-culture, he will soon find that it is as difficult to make ready for an evangelistic service as for one that we term "pastoral." In the pulpit work of Charles H. Spurgeon, or of Phillips Brooks, if we may judge from published sermons, approximately half of the time the aim was evangelistic; the other half, pastoral. In other words, at one hour they ministered largely to seekers; at another time, more directly to finders. What an obvious way to secure the variety often lacking in public worship!

3. *The Primacy of the Spoken Word.* In the history of revival and evangelism, preaching has always taken a foremost place. "It pleased God through the folly of what we preach to save those who believe" (I Cor. 1:21b). Elsewhere I have dealt with such pulpit work, ideally, as Biblical and doctrinal, practical and hard to prepare. It need never prove hard to assemble a senti-

mental talk devoid of Scriptural content and intelligent discussion. But to prepare sermon after sermon of the kind that seekers after God need today requires both ability and toil. The difficulty is due in part to the need for simplicity. How can a person trained in technical theology talk about God to people who know little about Him and often care less? How can one answer the unspoken questions of persons who are groping after God, and failing to find Him near?

Once again, a soul-winning sermon calls for simplicity — simplicity of purpose, simplicity in the choice of a text, simplicity in the plan of the discourse, simplicity in the selection of the materials, simplicity in the literary form, and simplicity in the resulting appeal for decision. Examples of such simplicity for Christ's sake appear in published sermons by Dwight L. Moody. When he spoke about the Lord Jesus, a boy of ten or twelve could understand every word, and a man of mature years could learn from the message how to escape from sin and find the peace of God. If anyone feels that all of this can come without hard work, let him try to prepare a sermon in answer to the question, "What must I do to be saved?" (Acts 16:30).

4. *The Dependence on United Prayer*. The Bible and later history show that all such endeavors blessed of God have been possible through dependence on prayer. Really it is God Himself on whom we must rely, and on His promises. But popularly we may speak about depending on united prayer. Ever since the Day of Pentecost the blessing of God on soul-winning has come in response to the united prayers of His children. In the lack of such prayer lies the chief weakness of many congregations now, and the prime cause of their failure to witness local revival through evangelism. So if any minister wishes the home church to become evangelistic through and through, he should lead to

united prayer for the salvation of the lost and the helpless.

5. *The Oversight of Personal Workers.* In congregational evangelism the effectiveness of all the work, under God, depends on intensive cultivation of the local field. Through various organizations and activities, mainly through the Church School, the pastor and other active soul-winners discover persons whose names should appear on the "opportunity list." Such a list ought to mean that every unsaved man or woman for whom the Lord holds this church responsible becomes the loving object of intercessory prayer, and that he soon receives a tactful call from a man or woman who loves the Lord. Except where husband and wife call on husband and wife, I always preferred to let one man deal with another (Jn. 1:35-51; Acts 8:28-40), and one woman call on another woman.

Such a quiet, intensive movement does not call for complicated machinery. As for the pastor's time, he can do much of his work through regular hours of worship and pastoral instruction. Otherwise it does not require much time or effort to single out the right person to visit a certain man or woman who needs to know and love the Lord. Neither does it take much time, as a rule, to confer later with the caller and receive his report. But even when an occasional case does require much expenditure of time, how could one invest it more profitably than by doing what our Lord once did with Nicodemus, or the woman at Jacob's well? For such use of time any pastor and his lay associates can find abundance of warrant in the New Testament and in the later history of soul-winning churches.

6. *The Necessity of Conservation.* Every congregation that engages in evangelism needs a program of Soul Conservation. However we explain the facts, doctrinally, a large proportion of our new members do not in later years bring forth the expected fruits of right-

eousness. It may be that some of them have never been born again, and that they have been received on profession of a faith that they never experienced. Again it may be that many of them have not received from pastor and lay friends the kind of tender and skillful nurture that keeps a new-born soul well and strong, so that it will grow in every Christian grace. For many such reasons Paul and Peter, John and James, seem to have been as much concerned about the careful nurture of new converts as about the winning of still others for Christ.

Conservation of souls would call for much care in the admission of members new to the church. This in turn would mean keeping the requirements for church membership in line with New Testament ideals, which are not easy and pleasant. Also, it would call for teaching would-be members, so that when admitted every one of them would know clearly what the new relationship calls for in the way of time, substance, and heart love. The program would likewise include some sort of follow-up, so that no new convert would ever seem like a child left loose on a highway filled with heavy traffic.

Under these two headings — evangelism and conservation — it would be possible to sum up the large proportion of what the Lord expects from a local church and its pastor. If in these two ways, as well as in World Missions, the home congregation continues to seek first the Kingdom of God, the Lord has promised to provide the means necessary to do His will, through the local church, which is ever dear to His heart. If such a program requires all the time and the strength, the ability and the resourcefulness of a pastor with many gifts and graces, that is exactly what it means to be a minister of Christ and His Church.

### A Modest Forecast

The volume from James Burns has suggested all

these Lessons for Today. Every one of them has to do with carrying out his ideals under our changed and changing conditions. As for hopes about the speedy coming of widespread revival through evangelism, I am not so sanguine now as Burns was before World War I. But I share with him in the feeling, now intensified, that our old world — sin-cursed, war-blasted, sorrow-stricken, and fear-filled — sorely needs a visible demonstration of super-atomic power that comes from God, who alone can answer by fire. (In I Kings 18:16-39 read a thrilling account of an oldtime revival.)

If somehow a widespread movement of revival through evangelism has already begun, we all ought to thank our God and ask Him to forgive our lack of faith, due to the blindness of our souls. If any such movement Godward begins around the next bend in the roadway that we call history, we who abide in the flesh will have every reason to rejoice. Meanwhile we should continue to believe in "the God of hope," from whom cometh every such aspiration; and to rejoice in His perseverance (Isa. 40:28-31; Phil. 1:6), knowing that in His good time and way He will bring about revival through evangelism. Hence we can keep on singing beloved old hymns of assurance and triumph; for example,

> The morning light is breaking, the darkness disappears;
> The sons of earth are waking to penitential tears;
> Each breeze that sweeps the ocean brings tidings from afar
> Of nations in commotion, prepared for Zion's war.

1. *The Prospect in the Local Church.* There need be no hesitation about predicting the coming of revival through evangelism in a local church. Under the right kind of pastoral leadership, among Christian people who love each other in the Lord, such a movement will come whenever they fulfill the prior conditions. About matters of the sort the Heavenly Father is not so me-

ticulously exacting as we sometimes suppose. He wishes every congregation to worship, live, and work amid the conditions that lead to soul-winning and Christian nurture such as we have considered throughout this chapter. So let us conclude that in due time any congregation can have a blessed awakening and quickening, but only if the officers and the people long for such a consummation, and if in faith and hope they are willing to pay the cost in the way of piety, prayer, and personal work, under the leadership of a pastor who knows how to pray, preach, and plan for the coming of revival through evangelism.

2. *The Opportunity for Evangelicals.* Humbly, gratefully, and without fault-finding, let us awake to the fact that conditions today give evangelicals an unparalleled opportunity for congregational evangelism. By evangelicals I mean those who accept the beliefs and the ideals of the six leaders chosen by Burns to set forth New Testament teachings and standards about what I have been calling revival through evangelism. The Lord only knows — surely I do not — how many churches, ministers, and laymen can qualify in His sight as evangelicals. Here again, I feel sure that He is not so exacting as we sometimes suppose. The larger the number and variety of the forces that He can use in bringing revival through evangelism, the more ought we to thank our God. In other words, I feel that we should be broad-minded, inasfar as Christ is so, and no farther.

One fact ought to be clear. In order to have any such movement within a church, certain conditions seem to be necessary. The pastor and the leaders ought strongly to believe in the necessity of such a local movement. They ought to desire it more than anything else within their whole horizon. Then they ought to do everything in their power to transform their dreams into the reality that outsiders can see, so that they will know the meaning of revival through evangelism. Meanwhile, if any pastor or local church has not yet caught this vision, let us not throw any sticks and stones, not to speak of slime. Let us also take for granted that our critics among the clergy and the local churches are sincere. In our American past we have given them abundant reason for finding fault with outmoded ways of promoting a work that has come from God.

Let us think about a case. In the local community a young clergyman has become the minister of a congregation that has never taken part in such movements as we now have in view. Like them, he may have been exposed to the crudest, crassest kind of revivalism. He may think that all evangelicals today believe in such a travesty of New Testament teachings. If so, what should an older evangelical pastor or layman do to help the young brother? Two things!

First, in time and in importance, pray for him, in private. Thus a seasoned veteran once prayed for a new recruit who did not yet understand the ways of God in the lives of men: "O Lord, I pray thee, open his eyes that he may see" (cf. II Kings 6:17a). When the Lord does open the young man's eyes may he behold in a nearby evangelical church and its pastor the present-day meaning of revival through evangelism. That meaning has to do with fire from the Spirit of God.

Second, by way of showing faith through works, give the young minister a copy of this book, by James Burns, *Revivals, Their Laws and Leaders.*